A BRIEF HISTORY OF VIOLENCE IN MEXICO

A BOOK IN THE SERIES

LATIN AMERICA IN TRANSLATION / EN TRADUCCIÓN / EM TRADUÇÃO

This book was sponsored by the Consortium in Latin American and
Caribbean Studies at the University of North Carolina
at Chapel Hill and Duke University.

A BRIEF HISTORY OF VIOLENCE IN MEXICO

PABLO PICCATO

Translated by Quentin Pope

THE UNIVERSITY OF NORTH CAROLINA PRESS

CHAPEL HILL

Translation of the books in the series Latin America in Translation /
en Traducción / em Tradução, a collaboration between the Consortium
in Latin American and Caribbean Studies at the University of North Carolina
at Chapel Hill and Duke University and the university presses of the
University of North Carolina and Duke, is supported by a grant
from the Andrew W. Mellon Foundation.

A complete list of books published in Latin America
in Translation / en Traducción / em Tradução is available at
https://uncpress.org/series/latin-america-translation.

Set in Calluna and Gotham by codeMantra
Manufactured in the United States of America

Originally published in Spanish by El Colegio de México.

Cover art: *De cierto* by Mario Núñez, 2023. Oil on
canvas, 170 by 200 cm. Used by permission.

Library of Congress Cataloging-in-Publication Data
Names: Piccato, Pablo author | Pope, Quentin translator
Title: A brief history of violence in Mexico / Pablo
Piccato ; translated by Quentin Pope.
Other titles: Historia mínima de la violencia en México. English |
Latin America in translation/en traducción/em tradução
Description: Chapel Hill : The University of North Carolina Press, [2025] |
Series: Latin America in translation/en traducción/em tradução |
Includes bibliographical references and index.
Identifiers: LCCN 2025022980 | ISBN 9781469689937 cloth alk. paper | ISBN
9781469689944 pbk alk. paper | ISBN 9781469689951 epub | ISBN 9781469689968 pdf
Subjects: LCSH: Violence—Mexico—History | Violence—Social aspects—Mexico |
Social conflict—Mexico—History | BISAC: HISTORY / Latin America / Mexico |
SOCIAL SCIENCE / Ethnic Studies / Caribbean & Latin American Studies
Classification: LCC HN120.Z9 V557513 2025 | DDC 303.60972—dc23/eng/20250812
LC record available at https://lccn.loc.gov/2025022980

This book will be made open access within three years of publication thanks to
Path to Open, a program developed in partnership between JSTOR, the American
Council of Learned Societies (ACLS), the University of Michigan Press, and the
University of North Carolina Press to bring about equitable access and impact for the
entire scholarly community, including authors, researchers, libraries, and university
presses around the world. Learn more at https://about.jstor.org/path-to-open/.

For product safety concerns under the European Union's General Product
Safety Regulation (EU GPSR), please contact gpsr@mare-nostrum.co.uk
or write to the University of North Carolina Press and Mare Nostrum
Group B.V., Mauritskade 21D, 1091 GC Amsterdam, The Netherlands.

para Xóchitl

CONTENTS

ILLUSTRATIONS

PREFACE TO THE
ENGLISH-LANGUAGE EDITION

THE ORIGINAL SPANISH EDITION of this book proposed history as an antidote to the overabundance of images and opinions on violence in Mexico. This translation can serve a slightly different purpose. I continue to believe that history is the best way to avoid drowning in the flood of dubious information about violence in Mexico, but the nature of the information that reaches audiences in the United States and other countries is particularly skewed by politicians exploiting anti-immigrant sentiments and promising hardline policies. As I write this introduction, this discourse is becoming increasingly violent, and the danger of moving from the symbolic to the material is looming. This translation offers a counterpoint to this distorted rhetoric.

The English-language edition mirrors the original text published in 2022 with only a few additions and updates. There certainly have been and will continue to be developments to this history, so readers will have to make connections to the present themselves. In the United States, for example, an awareness of the long history of US violence in Mexico—the 1846 war between the two countries, incursions or invasions in 1906 (against the Cananea strike), 1914 (the occupation of Veracruz), 1916 (the punitive expedition against Pancho Villa), and multiple other less visible actions involving government agencies and private actors—may be helpful to understand the resonances of contemporary claims about Mexican violence in right-wing political discourse.

The relationship between Mexico and the United States has shaped violence south of the border in other ways, both formal and informal, including advice and support for counterinsurgency operations, sponsorship of the "war on drugs," and the unlimited supply of weapons used by criminal organizations. US law enforcement agencies have operated in Mexico with varying degrees of negligence, perhaps reaching their apex in the 2006 Fast and Furious operation, which you can read about in chapter 6. In the minds of some politicians and parts of the US public, Mexico continues to be a laboratory. Justified by stereotypes of Mexican society and politics, it is viewed as a place for the experimentation of violent procedures designed to respond to panicked diagnoses of the public health problem of drug addiction. Although the history of US violence in Mexico remains relevant, the history of violence in the chapters that follow is fundamentally the product of Mexican actors and ideologies.

Every reading changes a book. Mexican readers have improved the text by questioning this history from the complexity of their perspective; I can only hope the same improvement will take place with this English-language edition. It does not seem overly wishful to imagine that your reading will, once again, make history a way of redressing the injustices of the past, as an unexpected protest against the poisonous effects of forgetting in the present.

ACKNOWLEDGMENTS

THIS BOOK WOULD NOT HAVE BEEN POSSIBLE without the encouragement of Erika Pani. I am also indebted to Pablo Yankelevich, two anonymous readers, and El Colegio de México's Publications Department. Several colleagues generously read and commented on different chapters: Gema Kloppe-Santamaría, Leonardo López Luján, Thomas Rath, Ariel Rodríguez Kuri, Benjamin Smith, and Susana Vargas Cervantes. The detailed comments and corrections by Alex Aviña and Adela Cedillo were essential to improving chapter 5. Romain Le Cour Grandmaison helped improve my understanding of the panorama discussed in chapter 6. Federico Finchelstein and Paul Gillingham read the entire manuscript and gave me their observations. I am also grateful for the comments received on preliminary versions at Columbia University, Oxford University, the Universidad de Guadalajara, the University of Texas at Austin, and El Colegio de Michoacán: from Alan Knight, Carlos Pérez Ricart, Eduardo Posada Carbó (Oxford and London); Sarah Beckhart, Fabiola Enríquez, Andrei Guadarrama, Sara Hidalgo, Mariana Katz, Paul Katz, Daniel Kressel, Rosa Mantilla, Xóchitl Medina, Nara Milanich, Jay Pan, Caterina Pizzigoni, Alfonso Salgado, Elizabeth Schwall (New York or virtually), Martha Chávez Torres, Isabel Juárez Becerra (Mexico), and Jonathan Brown and Matthew Butler (Austin). The research assistance I received from Marco Balestri and, in particular, from Rosa Mantilla and Jay Pan, was invaluable. I am grateful to Quentin Pope for his careful reading and translation. My thanks to everyone mentioned above and my family for their generosity and friendship during a year that was difficult for everyone.

ABBREVIATIONS

ACG   Asociación Cívica Guerrerense
(Guerrero Civic Association)

DFS   Dirección Federal de Seguridad
(Federal Security Agency)

FER   Frente de Estudiantil Revolucionario
(Revolutionary Student Front)

FLN   Fuerzas de Liberación Nacional
(National Liberation Forces)

LC23S/La Liga   Liga Comunista 23 de Septiembre
(September 23 Communist League)

LNDLR   Liga Nacional de la Defensa
de la Libertad Religiosa
(National League for the Defense
of Religious Liberty)

MAR   Movimiento de Acción Revolucionaria
(Revolutionary Action Movement)

MP   Ministerio Público
Public Prosecutor's Office)

PJF   Policía Judicial Federal
(Federal Judicial Police)

PRI   Partido Revolucionario Institucional
(Institutional Revolutionary Party)

A BRIEF HISTORY OF VIOLENCE IN MEXICO

INTRODUCTION

———

THIS SHORT BOOK attempts to offer a clear and historical analysis of violence. Mexicans today are besieged by images, fears, and pain related to attacks, homicides, and other forms of physical or psychological aggression. This blurs the very concept of "violence" so that it can mean many things at once, although it is always assumed that everyone has experienced it firsthand. Violence appears to be everywhere, from the simplest everyday interactions (getting in and out of a subway train) to abstract theories of political power (the foundations of the state or the causes of the Revolution). The lack of clarity in our conversations about violence makes it tempting to suggest the phenomenon is ahistorical. Many people consider that violence in Mexico has never been worse and simultaneously that the country has always been violent. The universal objection to violence makes it seem undeserving of a history. It is much easier to regard violence as the product of erratic psychological impulses or corrupt political power than as a form of interpersonal relationship that has long-lasting effects but changes over time.

Recognizing the urgency of the present forces us to distance ourselves from it. That is why the following pages are written in the past tense, even if the phenomena they describe still seem familiar. If we put aside for a moment our indignation at the current situation in Mexico, we may be able to define more accurately what we are talking about when we discuss violence. This historical clarity reveals the different forms that violence takes in our experience, allowing us to distinguish its specific causes and effects and eventually to consider the possibility that, just as violence has changed in our past, we may not have to live under its yoke in the future.

Violence is a social phenomenon. It occurs only in interactions between humans, or between humans and other animals. People determine violence. Whether premeditated or impulsive, it always erupts in situations where nonviolent exchanges prevail or end up prevailing. A Hobbesian permanent state of war does not exist. Violence always has a moral dimension because both perpetrators and victims understand it as a choice that can be deemed right or wrong. It is an act that cannot be explained in isolation from other social relations: to varying extents, violence is one of the links in the chain that unites and separates people by class, gender, or any other distinction. In labor relations, for example, violence has varied according to time and place. Whereas slavery relied primarily on the direct use of force, the lashes of the master's whip, and restrictions on movement, contemporary capitalism theoretically works through a voluntary agreement in which an employer agrees to exchange money for a worker's time and effort. Violence can erupt when that agreement has to be negotiated and when workers attempt to do so collectively: strikes and repression by employers have defined the history of the world of work more frequently than slave rebellions, despite the use of brute force in the day-to-day relations between employers and workers being less frequent than that meted out to subjugated slaves. Whether political or criminal, military or civilian, this moral dimension is not intrinsic but derives from the opinion of those who justify or condemn it.

Violence is a material phenomenon. It causes the (total or partial) destruction of the victim's body and possessions. As a material act, its effectiveness depends essentially on the tools it uses. The twentieth century saw revolutionary technological development and also the deadliest wars the world has ever known. From the atomic bomb to the bullets shot by firing squads, technology multiplied humanity's destructive capacity. Pulling the trigger has very different consequences depending on whether the weapon is a .22-caliber pistol or a .50-caliber rifle. The effect of small-caliber projectiles with a hard casing, which can ricochet inside a body before exiting, is quite unlike an expanding bullet that enters at high velocity and explodes soft tissue. The availability of medical care and antibiotics radically affects the lethality of almost any projectile.

The material nature of violence does not preclude discussion of its symbolic and psychological effects. They always go together: just as an insult is intended to humiliate, its implicit reference is a possible act of violence; injuries not only affect the direct victim but also spread fear among witnesses. Considering violence as a symbolic act highlights the need to understand it as a social relationship. When people are injured, insulted, or threatened, they establish short- and long-term connections. Riot police's batons or tear gas will make protesters retreat, but beyond such immediate and instrumental goals, violence is also about communication. As Rita Segato writes, "It is unusual for crime to use the violence strictly necessary to achieve its objective. It always includes one further gesture . . . that goes beyond its rational purpose." In the case of political violence, this communicative function is even more important, but the same basic mechanism also exists in the intimacy of gender violence or in the anonymity of the mugger on the street.

For Hannah Arendt, the long-term effects of violence are almost impossible to predict. It may be rational to use violence in the moment: riot police may succeed in dispersing protesters from the street, but over time their actions may strengthen protests and weaken the government from which they take orders. Repression can undermine a regime's popular support as much as it can silence its critics. But to think it is possible to predict the future would be irrational. This was the lesson of the October 2, 1968, massacre for those aware of its magnitude at the time. Many thought it more expedient to accept temporarily the authoritarianism of the Partido Revolucionario Institucional (Institutional Revolutionary Party, PRI) and seek gradual reforms "from within," despite this meaning the perpetuation of a regime that did not fully embrace democracy. Others rejected such an approach. The images that circulated of the events at Tlatelolco and the accounts of those who managed to escape or survive after being arrested had significant ramifications in later years. Some concluded that armed struggle was the only way to force the regime to accept opposition or to do something for Mexicans who had not benefited from the country's economic "miracle." Like Frantz Fanon, they argued that a regime based on violence would only understand the language of violence. However, armed insurgents in Mexico would not replicate the success of their counterparts in Algeria, where Fanon had written his work. But this was unknowable at the time to people in Mexico who were eager to emulate the strategy that led to the Cuban Revolution's victory in 1959. They believed that violence, discipline, and tactics—in the mold of Che Guevara and Fidel Castro—could make up for their material disadvantages and bring about long-term political and social change.

Arendt's observation applies here too. Whereas Castro established an extraordinarily long-lasting socialist regime, albeit one based on a different

3

type of repressive violence, state forces defeated Mexico's guerrilla groups in the 1960s and 1970s. They captured, tortured, disappeared, or killed a still-unknown number of victims. Did their sacrifice bring democracy? The PRI did not become a dictatorship and, as other historians have argued, the guerrillas forced the regime to open the door to electoral reforms that ended in its loss of the presidency thirty-two years later. The massive student protest broken up on October 2 forced Luis Echeverría's government to open up spaces for criticism and to broaden access to higher education, eventually forming new generations that would go on to consolidate a more democratic state. Many others argue, with similarly persuasive evidence, that the counterinsurgency repression of Gustavo Díaz Ordaz, Echeverría, and their successors, created a security apparatus defined by impunity, brutality, and corruption. Some years later, the same system played a role in the growth of organized crime and other kinds of violence. It is impossible to be sure whether just one of these interpretations of violence in the 1960s and its aftermath is correct. But we can say that the government security forces who fired on the Plaza de las Tres Culturas (Three Cultures Plaza) from the Chihuahua housing block and the soldiers who arrested the students and took them to Campo Militar 1, just as those who gave the orders, could not know their actions' consequences in later years.

This uncertainty about violence is one premise of this book. Instead of suggesting a hypothesis about its cumulative effects, or proposing the existence of omniscient, all-powerful forces behind repression or crime, this brief history will describe the various forms taken by violence—or rather violent practices, in the plural—in Mexico's history over the past century. And rather than describing how violence created contemporary Mexico, the text explores how different types of violence erupted during this period in the country, without positing a causal relationship between each kind but rather the contingency of their underlying factors.

This does not mean that violence was merely a symptom of a breakdown in society. On the contrary, as we will see, each manifestation of violence responded to a largely coherent and independent system of values. As in any human relationship, it had a moral dimension. Multiple social actors could use violence simultaneously and argue that they were doing so legitimately. Not all of these normative systems were (or claimed to be) licit, but they all included a justification for violence. Therefore, the history of violence is also a history of the changing explanations given to justify it. The chronological order of the chapters is designed to provide a thread for these uses and justifications over the past century.

A national perspective on this subject does not mean that Mexico's history is essentially or particularly violent. The notion that Mexicans are a "race" indifferent to death creates a stereotypical, false image that ascribes shared characteristics to an invented collective group. Violence is a relationship between people; it has no intrinsic existence. The same could be said of a nation. Therefore, this book will examine the kinds of violence that dominated the Mexican experience for a century, without suggesting that it was a single force that changed its nature over time, or that one type of violence (for example, the violent acts of revolutionaries 100 years ago) necessarily led to another (such as religious violence). The final chapter, which also serves as a conclusion, posits a common perspective that can help us to face up to the present, although without proposing one overarching causal explanation. In other words, people can decide whether or not to use violence, and when they do, they are not obeying some reflexive or ancestral impulse as a result of having been born in Mexico or elsewhere. War, agrarian disputes, crime, domestic or sexual abuse, state repression, and political insurrection were a significant part of Mexico's overall history during the past hundred years. But when we look at these forms of violence in detail (or in as much detail as this brief history allows) we are reading only a tiny fraction of Mexican history. As the sociologist Norbert Elías wrote, it is as important to understand why and how human societies descend into wars or tend to resolve their conflicts through duels as it is to comprehend why, most of the time, they do not. This is truer than ever for contemporary Mexico. Therefore, we must be clear from the outset that this text, despite its many examples of pain and cruelty, is only a dark and distorted mirror of a broader reality in which Mexicans have successfully multiplied, coexisted, and continued in a peaceful struggle for a fairer country.

CHAPTER ONE

REVOLUTIONARY VIOLENCE

———

HISTORIES of the Mexican Revolution written since the start of Francisco Madero's 1910 uprising have explained it as a consequence of the relentless violence underpinning Porfirio Díaz's regime. Since 1876, the dictator had consolidated his authority, enabling him to amass economic power and place control of society in the hands of the few, and making elections a worthless exercise for most citizens. Entire communities were stripped of their land. Indigenous Mexicans and convicts were dispatched to the plantations in the south under slave-like conditions. In the cities, the regime harassed journalists and political opponents in many different—and not always legal—ways. Therefore, even the most mistrustful of the upsurge of popular unrest triggered by Díaz's last reelection could not deny the dictatorship's role in spawning what they now saw as "thuggish" mobs roaming the countryside and cities, laying waste to everything civilized in their path after three decades of "peace." Mariano Azuela's 1915 novel *Los de abajo* (The underdogs) for example, paints an unforgettable portrait of a popular uprising that was both chaotic and deeply rooted in society. In one scene, the troops under the command of Demetrio Macías charge a position on higher ground where the federal troops' machine guns have left a meadow "thick with corpses." But the revolutionary fighters swiftly attack the soldiers, bayoneting them, lassoing the machine guns "like a bull herd throwing a steer." Afterward the slope "was literally covered with dead, their clothes clotted with grime and blood. A host of ragged women, vultures of prey, ranged over the tepid bodies of the dead, stripping one man bare, despoiling another." For another character, a revolutionary officer, the image showed "the psychology of our race, condensed into two words: Robbery! Murder!"

But the same violence that educated onlookers perceived as wanton destruction had begun as a move to restore rule of law. Therefore, the original violence of the dictatorship explains why the campesinos of Morelos decided to dust off the weapons that had belonged to their forefathers and dated back to the Reform Wars and the French Intervention. They used these old rifles to defend a system threatened by the dictator's modernization program. Emiliano Zapata's rural followers thought that the uprising against Díaz would help them recover and defend land that rightfully belonged to them but that the hacendados had usurped through pseudo-legal means and coercion. As John Womack notes, the hacendados and their estate managers' response to any resistance was "local, unofficial, and brutal—a proper beating, maybe murder." The government could also lawfully arrest people who tried to prevent these landgrabs and send them to an almost certain death on the southern plantations. For these campesinos from the state of Morelos, and for many other communities that took up arms in the months following Madero's rebellion in response to the publication of Madero's Plan of San Luis Potosí on October 5, 1910, the Revolution had a predominantly local meaning, and was anything but chaotic. Its leaders prepared for repression. Before exchanging gunfire and trading machete blows with the *defensas rurales* (a police corps operating in rural areas), *guardias blancas* (armed security guards hired by the haciendas), and regular soldiers deployed by the wealthy to take away their land, the insurgents attacked military posts or police stations and hacienda buildings to seize weapons but without engaging in formal battle. This increased their combat readiness, so they did not have to wait for Madero's coalition forces from the north to coordinate a nationwide offensive.

It is unhelpful to create a stereotype based on this rebel uprising, which took its most iconic form in Morelos. The call for agrarian reform was important everywhere people rose up alongside Madero, including in the north. From the outset, the revolutionaries used many methods that were not always effective. Lacking weapons, the early rebels were forced to attack small outposts, firing at government forces until their ammunition ran out and then retreating into the hills. The rebels sometimes tried to counter the federal troops' artillery with sticks of dynamite stolen from mines, but they generally scattered to escape the shelling. On both sides, brand-name or improvised firearms often malfunctioned and injured the person using them. But what they lacked in numbers and firepower, the rebels (like those fighting with Macías) made up for in speed, knowledge of the terrain, and fearlessness.

Despite this asymmetry, in different parts of the country the Maderista rebellion sparked a wide range of uprisings. In many places, people grabbed this opportunity to settle old scores created by political bosses' harassment of ranch owners. Rather than fighting to defend collective access to land and water, these belligerents sought the freedom to prosper and exercise the political influence to which they felt entitled as independent citizens. For this middle-class rural group, agrarian demands were not a top priority. In the town of Pisaflores, in the state of Hidalgo, both Madero's supporters and his adversaries were landowners. In these rural rebellions, political disagreements and personal feuds were a combustible mixture. One rancher from Zacatecas described by Azuela explained his decision to take up arms as the result of an incident one day in the market, when the locals were enjoying "a bit of a drink" and singing, until the police began bothering them too much:

> But by God! You've got guts, you've got red blood in your veins, and you've got a soul too, see? So you lose your temper, you stand up to them and tell them to go to the Devil! Now if they understand you, everything's all right; they leave you alone and that's all there is to it; but sometimes they try to talk you down and hit you—well, you know how it is, a fellow's quick-tempered and he'll be damned if he'll stand for someone ordering him around and telling him what's what. So before you know it, you've got your knife out or your gun leveled, and then off you go for a wild run in the sierra, until they've forgotten the corpse, see?

Similar stories were key to the rapid rise through the ranks and leadership of revolutionary leaders such as Pancho Villa, known to his men for his skill with weapons and bravery.

Sometimes, as in the case of the Santos family in San Luis Potosí, the initial decision to take up arms against the authorities involved the father, children, relatives, neighbors, and farmhands. The impact of such revolutionary cells depended on their leaders' opportunism, connections, and tactical skills. Their rifles and pistols could be more effective than the knives, carbines, and shotguns (without much ammunition) available to peasant rebels. Some availed themselves of Winchester 94s, federal army–issued Mausers, high-caliber pistols (Smith and Wesson .32s) and expanding bullets that destroyed bone, muscle tissue, and internal organs. Some revolutionary units also acquired grenades and cannons. As Jorge Aguilar Mora points out, the Revolution magnified the impact of new firearms technologies that transformed the effects of fighting and made them more visible: gunpowder was now smokeless and tripled the range of steel bullets that could be fired more rapidly by automatic rifles. This increased their effectiveness from more than half a kilometer, without giving away the shooter's location. Revolutionary groups in rural areas employed various types of attack in which they voiced their motives. Shouting "¡Viva Madero!" or "¡Muera el mal gobierno!" they launched surprise attacks on federal troop detachments, haciendas, and enemy homes. After the attacks, they executed officers, policemen, or soldiers, or else recruited them as "volunteers" to join the rebels. Enemies could be defined by a history of class oppression but essentially by their hostility to the leader and his followers. The leader's satisfaction might come with the revenge for wrongs that predated the Revolution.

These early revolutionary groups also shared a belief in Madero's democratic cause. Madero is a paradoxical figure in the history of revolutionary violence. His temperament made him uncomfortable with the use of force. As the son of a wealthy family from the state of Coahuila, he had enjoyed all the advantages of Porfirian modernization; he had a close relationship with the political elite of *científicos* (influential officials and writers surrounding Díaz); he was able to study in the United States; and he rubbed shoulders with a cosmopolitan elite. Madero argued that clean and transparent elections were the best way to ensure a peaceful transition after Díaz's inevitable departure. When the regime obstructed his candidacy to set up yet another Díaz reelection, Madero decided that he had no choice but to call on the people to take up arms, although this was based on the assumption that the rebellion would continue the urban democratic mobilization that was integral to his electoral campaign. The goal was to minimize the armed struggle in the interest of the democratic transition. However, a gulf existed between what Madero envisioned for the rebellion, and the ideas of rebels who gradually began to follow him. The initial moments after the start of the uprising that had been called for November 20, 1910, contrasted with the popular movement that led to the dictator's fall some months later. A few days before November 20, the fighting that had broken out in the city of Puebla bore little resemblance to the later rebellion. Police surrounded the Aquiles Serdán household, aware of the plans afoot for a revolt. Serdán and several other Maderistas were killed in a gunfight. The lesson was clear:

the insurgency would fail in urban areas with a strong government presence and where rebels lacked the support of the working class. Madero crossed the border into Mexico from the United States, where he had been coordinating the uprising, to find no one—neither supporters nor adversaries—awaiting him. The rebellion began haltingly in various parts of the country, until rebel forces in the north converged on Ciudad Juárez in April 1911, where they handed the federal army its first major defeat, leading to Díaz's resignation.

It was clear from the outset that the government would not offer the rebels any truce or legal guarantees. In the case of the Serdán brothers and other rebels, the police were willing to use methods that had become commonplace in campaigns against rural bandits since the nineteenth century. These included the *ley fuga*, a term that refers to the extrajudicial executions of prisoners on the pretext that they were trying to escape. The term is ironic and has equivalents in other countries. In the context of 1910, it specifically meant that the summary execution of prisoners had a certain legitimacy, despite contravening penal codes and the rules of war. Whoever took up arms could not expect the enemy to show any mercy. The revolutionaries, for their part, could therefore justify cruel treatment of army officers and often of *pelones*—a nickname for soldiers that alluded to their close-cropped hair. In his memoirs, Gonzalo N. Santos, of the Santos family of San Luis Potosí and who later became a cacique in the state, recorded various examples of the rebel violence. After fighting Gen. Victoriano Huerta's men in the Huasteca region, he saw a "damned Huertista" had been wounded, the same man who had "murdered a hundred poor Huastecan Indians in cold blood at the start of the Revolution." He shot him down "and without dismounting, I used my Winchester 94 to put an expanding bullet to blow his brains out." He later told his comrades that "it wasn't to put him out of his misery. I killed him in a fit of revolutionary passion."

The civil war began tentatively with skirmishes in rural and mountainous areas; the gunfights revealed both sides were cautious. Casualties were few. Rebels attacked haciendas or local government buildings and then retreated before government troops arrived. They harassed federal detachments and then fled; they could advance nimbly across difficult terrain while slowing the enemy's movements by destroying railroad tracks, telegraph and telephone networks, and bridges. This drew regular troops into places where they could be ambushed and encircled; rebels usually positioned themselves on higher ground, giving them a strategic advantage in firefights and a ready escape route if necessary. Many enemy soldiers were killed when such traps went to plan, and their weapons and ammunition fell into the hands of the revolutionaries. Madero's efforts and financial support, combined with his followers' skill at crossing the border undetected, gave revolutionary fighters in the north better and more numerous weapons. In some cases, they were able to use the federal army's artillery and machine guns themselves. But the rebels' superior mobility and capacity to surprise larger contingents of fighters proved to be their most effective resources. This was the key to the capture of Ciudad Juárez by revolutionaries under the command of Pascual Orozco and Pancho Villa, who launched their attack and entered the city without waiting for Madero's orders.

At that triumphant moment, it became apparent that the victors had different ideas about what was considered legitimate punishment for the defeated enemy. Whereas Madero considered that federal troops had only to surrender and tried to negotiate a period of transition, Orozco and Villa wanted to execute the commanders and disarm their troops; both specifically called for the punishment of a federal commander who had executed revolutionary fighters with bayonets (the revolutionaries avoided this practice when they captured federal troops). Madero refused and signed agreements with Díaz's representatives, slowing down the Revolution's momentum. The disagreement was not only about the resentment felt toward federal officers; it also represented two contrasting ideas about what violence meant in the struggle against the former regime and its heirs.

This contradiction was left unresolved at that time, and many contemporaries believe that Madero's half-heartedness spawned the second, far-bloodier phase of the Revolution. Porfirio Díaz allegedly pronounced that Madero had "unleashed the tiger" and could no longer control it. Díaz had certainly succeeded in keeping the tiger hungry and angry. Other members of the elite feared anarchy, with Miguel Hidalgo's chaotic uprising in 1810 lingering in the collective memory. Martín Luis Guzmán coined the phrase "la fiesta de las balas," an apt description for the gun-happy revolutionary years. To define the Revolution for its frenzied violence, however, would be problematic. The deadly ferocity of the fighting changed as the different groups saw their cause as one of avenging or punishing the enemy for its actions, beyond Madero's democratic goals. Battlefield tactics evolved, escalating the destruction for combatants and civilians alike. The leaders of the anti-reelectionist forces tried to maintain the discipline necessary to prevent looting and to respect foreigners, and to avoid executing prisoners by firing squad or with the use of expanding bullets. They issued receipts in exchange for expropriated haciendas or mines. But such controls gradually diminished, as did those that protected civilian lives. The Revolution claimed the most victims when the struggle became a full-blown civil war, a clash between highly organized and well-equipped armies seeking control over the entire country.

To equate the Mexican population to a wild and unpredictable "tiger," according to "the psychology of our race," overlooks an aspect of this history that became evident for contemporaries after Madero's victory: the Revolution's most violent phase began with the "pacification" that followed, and then expanded with the infighting among the different revolutionary factions. Under the interim administration of Francisco León de la Barra and with Madero already president, the federal army, its allies, and other supporters of the Díaz regime began to disarm the rebel troops, citing the Treaty of Ciudad Juárez, to call for the return of land seized during the popular mobilization and to punish the insurgents who seemed most dangerous. For inhabitants of the state of Morelos, this marked the start of a particularly aggressive campaign for the rest of the decade, causing many deaths and turning people's lives upside down in Zapatista territories. Locals remembered the burning of entire villages as being the work of indistinct enemies: Maderistas, federal troops, or, later, Carrancistas. In the north, Orozco rose up in 1912 against Madero, his former commander in Ciudad Juárez whom he now saw as his potential adversary. He was defeated by federal troops, who were not so easily surprised on this occasion. The government forces now had the support of revolutionary fighters who had become defensas rurales in some northern states. The army's renewed intransigence was evident in the executions of Orozco's men and in the suicide of Gen. José González Salas, who suffered the dishonor of being defeated by the Orozquistas at the Battle of Rellano. Salas was replaced by Gen. Victoriano Huerta, a veteran of Porfirio Díaz's campaigns against Indigenous groups and a notoriously unscrupulous officer already known for his effective methods. A few months after Orozco's defeat, Huerta led a coup against Madero and executed him and his vice president, José María Pino Suárez, by applying the ley fuga in front of Mexico City's penitentiary. This took place in February 1913, during the ten days known as the Decena Trágica, which marked a turning point in the history of the Revolution. Political violence became increasingly militarized and widespread. Two aspects of the new forms of violence deserve closer analysis: one relates to moral issues and the other to civilian experiences.

The first, of course, was the betrayal of Madero. In theory, Huerta should have defended him against a rebellion initiated by Bernardo Reyes and other military officers. The surprise increased with the brutal treatment of men close to the deposed president, such as his brother Gustavo A. Madero, who was tortured and executed in the barracks of the Ciudadela by the supporters of Félix Díaz (nephew of the former president). For Pancho Villa—in prison at that time because Huerta had accused him of stealing horses, but who had escaped just in time—the double-crossing of Madero confirmed what he had already thought in Ciudad Juárez in May 1911: treacherous federal forces had to be eliminated for the Revolution to succeed. Avenging the death of the apostle and martyr of democracy, Madero, became an article of faith shared by the revolutionary leaders who then took up arms once again. The campaign bore no resemblance to the pronouncements of 1910, when violence was kept in check to ensure the success of negotiations. This new stage resembled an all-out war, like those being waged elsewhere in the world. But whereas in those conflagrations nationalism dehumanized the enemy to seek its total defeat, in Mexico's conflict the enemy was defined through a mix of moral indignation and racism. Many saw Huerta's treachery as the revenge for Madero's own betrayal of the initial band of revolutionaries after the Treaty of Ciudad Juárez. Gen. Juvencio Robles's campaign against the Zapatistas was supported by images printed in the press after 1910 that depicted Mexico's Indigenous inhabitants as barely human savages and bandits. The racist ideology underlying the federal army's violence in Morelos could well be classified as genocide today. But racism also existed within the ranks of the revolutionaries. Targets included Chinese immigrants, as described below, and Indigenous groups in northeastern Mexico who fought with some of the factions. The uprising against Huerta also differed from the 1910 movement in terms of military strategy and tactics. The collaboration of "irregular" former revolutionaries with federal troops against the Orozquistas in 1912 allowed the transfer of knowledge that was especially useful to the 1913 revolutionaries, such as the use of artillery and infantry.

The second reason why the Decena Trágica was a significant moment in the history of the Revolution was that it gave the urban population a direct and widespread experience of civil war. The coup against Madero was coordinated with a military rebellion in the Ciudadela barracks, orchestrated by Félix Díaz. Huerta along with other, supposedly loyal officials who had secretly decided to support the rebels, pretended to fight them for several days. They fired cannons, but deliberately misaiming them, hitting buildings occupied by civilians or exchanging gunfire on the capital's streets without advancing on enemy positions. Shells punched holes in the walls of the Belem prison, next door to the Ciudadela, allowing hundreds of prisoners to escape. As a result, Félix Díaz was unharmed, while many civilians who had nothing to do with the uprising were killed. One civilian recalled how anyone just leaning out to watch the fighting from a distance risked having "their brains blown out by an expanding bullet." The victims' bodies were piled up on the streets; some were burned on the spot because no one dared to recover them for a dignified burial. Others were carted to cemeteries or fields on the suburban fields of Balbuena to be cremated or buried in mass graves. This was the first time that modern and destructive weapons designed for conventional warfare had been widely used against civilians in urban combat. The chaos was a necessary consequence of the civil war and simultaneously justified more deadly fighting.

A popular visual motif appeared in photographs from Mexico: corpses, civilians sprawled dead on the capital's streets, federal troops lying half-buried on the battlefields, and rebels being executed by firing squad, crumpled against walls. These images, published by the press and even sold as postcards in the United States, shaped the collective memory of a particularly harsh period in the lives of Mexicans. For the generation that survived the Revolution and following years, memories of the suffering caused by the civil war could not be separated from those brutal and indelible images. Nellie Campobello's 1931 novel *Cartucho* describes in detail the corpses from the perspective of a child uninterested in politics; perhaps for this reason, her account is more representative of the civilian experience than the professional histories of the period.

In Mexico City, the Decena Trágica was the first chapter of a history marked by several difficult years of shortages, high prices, epidemics, and even hunger—problems that only began to abate toward the end of the decade. In the rest of the country, displacement exacerbated these scourges. Families of the combatants, generally children and women, were forced to flee hunger and enemy attacks, moving from one place to another to find food and safety, like refugees without shelter in their own country. Starvation was a real possibility, a slower but no less terrible and unexpected death than one delivered by a bullet. The fighters themselves suffered hunger: in Campobello's account, the Carrancista soldiers were notoriously disheveled and malnourished. The armies found food as they moved from place to place, whether in the kitchens of civilians or on farms, which were often abandoned.

Even in Mexico City, the showcase of Porfirian progress, people were driven to scavenge for food. Looting was commonplace and affected more than grocery stores. Organized food riots, often led by women, could express outrage at hunger but also appeal to the xenophobia directed at Spanish or Chinese immigrant storekeepers. These conditions aggravated the deadly influenza pandemic that struck Mexico in 1918. For many, medical care and medication for "the shivers" was simply inaccessible. Compounding the problem of disease and poverty, residents in the capital and other large and small towns also had to endure the outrages caused by the armies marching in and out of their cities, leaving in their wake monetary inflation as a result of the changes in the bills that each faction forced the civilians to accept. Citizens associated theft, abuse of authority, and a widespread sense of fear of crime with uniformed soldiers whose lawlessness went unpunished.

The Gray Automobile Gang came to symbolize the type of crime that exploited the chaos and received protection from the authorities. This gang's members wore military uniforms and probably had connections to revolutionary bosses, although the crimes attributed to them may have been carried out by various groups. Under the pretext of searching for weapons, the gang looted wealthy households. It was also accused of kidnapping and rape. The movie *El automóvil gris* (The gray car) (dir. Enrique Rosas, 1919) was a highly realistic portrayal, including footage of the real-life execution of the gang members, and dramatizing—rather graphically—the murder of a child and a rape. This realism was for propaganda purposes, however. The film was produced with the support of the Constitutionalist general Pablo González, who was widely believed to have protected the gang, and it was screened in 1919 during González's bid to succeed Venustiano Carranza as president. In any case, the movie became another element in the collective memory of those chaotic years when impunity and firearms were rife in the semideserted capital. What remains of the city's court and police records from those years paints a picture of gendarmes trying unsuccessfully to limit the abuses of the most heavily armed and numerous revolutionary troops, bent on looting and going on drunken rampages.

For those active in the revolutionary struggle, the Decena Trágica and civilian suffering offered another lesson: the war had to be taken to its final consequences. Madero's good faith toward the federal army and the científicos, the Porfirian oligarchic elite, had led to his death and created Huerta, a kind of Frankenstein monster with the brain of an alcoholic criminal transplanted onto the powerful body of the Mexican army. Madero's idea of using the armed struggle as a first step toward negotiations was no longer valid. War was now the means of eliminating adversaries and delivering justice, even if that meant sending thousands of soldiers to their death in combat. The leaders who emerged in this second revolutionary phase, from Venustiano Carranza to Álvaro Obregón, were successful in that they were able to organize a war systematically. Initially they controlled local resources and later national ones, in order to combat federal troops and then adversaries from other factions within the revolutionary movement, such as Zapata and Villa.

The new revolutionary armies—including the Zapatistas—paid their troops, occasionally gave them a bonus after a victory, or allowed them to loot. Discussions among leaders led to the unification of the commands of revolutionary divisions and smaller fighting units, with votes held among them to decide who would assume command, as happened in the case of Pancho Villa. From these popular and democratic beginnings, revolutionary military structure and discipline spread and gained importance after the Porfirian army disbanded in the aftermath of Huerta's defeat. In other words, combatants in the movement's largest divisions adhered to an ideology of justice and social protest, but they also weighed up the more immediate potential benefits in exchange for the risk they faced. In Chihuahua, for example, Villa promised to look after the widows and orphans left by his soldiers and he distributed meat to city dwellers. As a counterpart to these personal pledges, combat units became professionalized, forming the core of a new revolutionary army.

These new armies soon took advantage of recently available technologies: trains, artillery, aircraft, machine guns, barbed wire, and trenches. The combat strategies based on surprise and speed that marked the initial phase of the Revolution remained, of course, but now they were complemented by weapons that reduced the need for hand-to-hand fighting. Artillery increased firing range, machine guns helped defend positions, and trains could rapidly move troops and other equipment. Since the uprising against Huerta and during the clashes of 1915 between Constitutionalists and the Convención Nacional Revolucionaria forces, these developments in warfare led to battles with thousands of combatants on each side, like in Torreón and Trinidad. But the guerrilla tactics of fearlessness died hard. The bloodiest example of this strange overlap of military strategies were the cavalry charges ordered by Villa against Obregón in Celaya, in April 1915. Despite being outnumbered, the Constitutionalist infantry neutralized Villa's cavalry from defensive positions with machine guns, rifles, and artillery; they were easily resupplied and were eventually able to launch a counteroffensive when Villa's men became exhausted. This clash between new and old tactics explains Villa's defeat on the Bajío's battlefields. The blind courage of the troops and the surprise factor had lost their effectiveness. The Villistas did not have the tanks or gases that had begun to be used in Europe in trench warfare. Instead they charged, yelling as they went, perhaps inspired by the belief in the infallibility of their leaders. But they were scythed by bullets fired from strategically positioned machine-gun posts hundreds of meters away, or from even greater distances by artillery more effective than that used during the Decena Trágica. Numbers are hard to establish, but the most reliable calculations for the Battle of Trinidad—which ground on for more than a month—indicate 5,000 men were killed, out of armies of tens of thousands.

This deadly clash exposed a vein of revolutionary violence often equated with Villa, although he was by no means its only exponent. I refer to that combination of tactical astuteness and organizational capacity, on the one hand, and unpredictable but always latent arbitrariness, on the other. This erratic behavior manifested itself in his interactions with enemies, subordinates, and civilians, and certain instances became etched in people's memories and in the history of the Revolution, despite being sporadic and less important than the strategic decisions. Villa could fly into fits of rage that frightened even his lieutenants. At other times he was magnanimous and good natured. But as Carranza and Obregón began to gain the upper hand, Villa became more prone to acts of brutality, sometimes personally executing prisoners or his own men when he suspected them of betrayal.

Villa is the best-known example of the same behavioral characteristics displayed by other revolutionaries. The prime examples of this type of violence can be found in anecdotes gleaned from survivors. We cannot confirm the prevalence of these practices with any degree of certainty, nor the truthfulness of each anecdote. By considering a sample of such stories from a broader perspective, we can get a clearer image of the kinds of violence that marked the revolutionary struggle but failed to make it into the history books.

A final scene omitted from the 1936 version of Fernando de Fuentes's movie *Vámonos con Pancho Villa* (Let's go with Pancho Villa) portrays the fear of soldiers who followed the famous caudillo. A farmer who had already fought for Villa, Tiburcio Maya, meets the leader again and tells him that he does not want to reenlist so as not to leave his family alone. The caudillo promptly kills Maya's wife and daughter, taking away his excuse for not fighting. The story is told in Rafael F. Muñoz's 1931 novel *Vámonos con Pancho Villa*. In the film, Tiburcio is killed while attempting to take revenge on the general after the murder of his womenfolk, but in the novel he joins the Villistas, a response that is possibly more shocking. This anecdote contains a significant falsehood, considering that many who joined the ranks of the revolutionaries did so precisely to defend their families, or at least to give them a better future. But in Villa's unspeakable act lies a hidden truth: conscription was inherently violent, and new recruits entered a world in which death was always near, coming either from their adversaries of from their own side. The opening scenes of this movie show the "lions of San Pablo"—a group of friends including Maya himself—who decide to follow Villa and then start singing "La Valentina," a popular ballad or corrido with a lyric that reasons, "If they have to kill me tomorrow, then let them kill me straight away."

The rules of war did not count for much given the arbitrary treatment of prisoners. Nellie Campobello included a famous anecdote in her novel *Cartucho*, also from 1931. When Villa hears that one of his soldiers has been killed, he simply orders, in reference to the one who fired the shot, "Fusílenlo" (Shoot him). A junior officer points out that the shot was fired by a woman, a Villista *coronela* named Nacha Ceniceros, whose gun had accidentally gone off. Villa, showing more concern with grammar than any due process, corrects himself: "Fusílenla" (Shoot her). The historical evidence confirms the essence of this literary vignette. After defeating the Carrancistas in Camargo, in the state of Chihuahua, Villa killed the wife of an enemy officer and ordered the execution of ninety female prisoners.

Many women, like the victims from Camargo, took part in the Revolution as *soldaderas* who accompanied their men on their campaigns but also performed essential duties for the army. In the absence of any conventional logistical arrangements, these women often prepared meals and cared for the wounded. This latter job was particularly important because medical care on military campaigns was otherwise almost nonexistent: medicine was scarce, infections were rampant, and doctors often resorted to amputations as the best option in emergencies. The soldaderas held no rank as such, although some women did earn one by joining in the actual fighting. Coronelas were women who commanded troops, sometimes wearing men's clothing or else without hiding their gender, as in the case of Ceniceros.

Villa's orders to execute Ceniceros and the women prisoners from Camargo illustrated the widespread violence against women during the Revolution. This phenomenon took its most brutal form in rape, a practice more common than official histories of the period are willing to admit. In 1917, Villa ordered his soldiers to rape the wives of the members of the rural community reserves of Namiquipa, in the state of Chihuahua. That act of collective revenge occurred at a time when Villa had already been defeated by the Constitutionalists, and his decisions were born of bitterness rather than any revolutionary ideal. Some years earlier, when he was occupying Mexico City, Villa himself whipped his own soldiers when they were found guilty of rape. He was allegedly a "well-behaved man" with all his wives, not counting other women with whom his affairs did not lead to marriage.

These two sides of Villa (the one who ordered the rape and the other reputed to be romantic and respectful in women's company) are compatible if we consider that, during those revolutionary years, women were seen in patriarchal terms as the victors' spoils, and the most valued possession that the defeated risked losing. Among the abuses of the powerful Porfirian-era hacendados, according to the legends about the underlying causes of the

Revolution, was their droit du seigneur over the wives of their workers. Federal troops punished those who joined the Zapatistas by executing the men and sexually abusing the women. The women of Cholula, in the state of Puebla, experienced the revolutionary years as a period when the abuses already perpetrated by the Porfirian hacendados—affecting their work and personal safety—became even worse. According to Lidia E. Gómez García, when Carranza's troops entered the town in 1918, the local authorities reported rape and pillage. But all factions committed the same abuses. Women hid, especially the younger ones, but when the soldiers abducted them they were forced to provide them with meals and sexual services. And if they returned home with a child, the community rejected them. No group was exempt. According to firsthand accounts, sexual violence committed by rebels could also victimize women from the same side. Rape by revolutionary troops was a widespread fear among the civilian population and may partly explain why many families chose to move to the relative safety of large cities or the United States. Although we can only speculate that this same fear partly motivated women to become soldaderas so they at least had a man's protection, such a supposition would not be unreasonable. This evidence forces us to revisit the idea that the Revolution was also a rebellion against the Victorian era's sexual moral virtues assigned to women, particularly the soldaderas, mobility and independence, and gave them a glimpse of a new eroticism. Urban culture in the immediate aftermath of the war might give this impression, but it certainly does not square with the experience of many women from rural communities for whom the Revolution paradoxically required them to have men's protection in order to survive.

The treatment of male prisoners was the most common sign of arbitrary conduct by revolutionary leaders. The Maderistas and federal troops had generally avoided executing prisoners in 1911, but after 1913 all the belligerents engaged in the practice with increasing frequency. Huerta and Carranza issued two decrees that gave legal footing to something that became prevalent during the second phase of the Revolution: the extrajudicial execution of captured enemy officers. During campaigns, government soldiers could be released if they promised to lay down their arms, or they could be invited to join the rebels, sometimes under threat of execution by firing squad if they refused. The decision could not have been too difficult, since the majority had been press-ganged into enlisting in the army; and they all belonged to the same urban or rural lower classes as the revolutionary fighters. The new soldiers were often sent to the front lines, whether they liked it or not. Revolutionary columns were constantly on the move, making it harder to take prisoners with them. Those injured before their capture were sometimes nursed back to health by neutral women before being executed on the orders of the commanders.

Ample evidence exists of large-scale prisoner executions. Rodolfo Fierro, Villa's fearsome lieutenant from the División del Norte, was implicated in a particularly notorious episode. Martín Luis Guzmán describes how, after one battle, Fierro killed around 200 prisoners using a revolver. He told them that they could save themselves by running and jumping over a wall. Only one survived this desperate attempt to escape, the others were all killed. In 1917, after defeating the Carrancista general Murguía, Villa ordered the execution of 600 prisoners; shortly afterward, Murguía killed 200 Villista prisoners by hanging. There was no tactical reason for these cold-blooded executions, and even noncombatants were victims: counterfeiters, thieves, and spies also faced the firing squad. In the capital, executions became spectacles that drew large crowds.

Civilians were also caught up in the revolutionary violence. Since the first phase of the rebellion, revolutionary leaders sanctioned attacks on Chinese immigrants in Chihuahua and Torreón, where more than 300 Chinese were killed in 1911 in events that included hundreds of executions and mutilations. The only explanation for these acts, apart from looting, was animosity toward this group of immigrants. Villa ordered the attack in Chihuahua. Villistas did not have a monopoly on racism and xenophobia, or on sexual violence. However, legends and evidence connected Villa to many such incidents after his defeats by Obregón's forces. By emphasizing the experience of noncombatants, we should not jump to the conclusion that those who organized or justified the violence for political ends were irrational or incompetent. Villa was an astute, unconventional strategist. Perhaps this explains his ability to instill both personal loyalty and fear through his volatile unpredictability. He was two sides of the same coin: the charismatic defender of the poor and the widowed, and the fearsome commander capable of impulsively killing or abusing civilians and prisoners. Villa was not the only caudillo who veered between such extremes, but his high profile and eventual defeat simply meant that he inevitably gained notoriety.

The fact is that, in the experience of those who lived through it, the Revolution represented a threat that impinged on every aspect and area of life, in the home, the fields, the city streets. Therefore, it is sometimes impossible to distinguish political or military violence from deaths and hardships caused by petty crime, epidemics, and hunger. All of these problems affected urban populations across the country but also rural inhabitants, who constituted the vast majority of Mexico's population at the time.

The Revolution's ideology and official history glorified the new state's political and social progress. Postrevolutionary rhetoric downplayed the war and chaos as people's natural rejection of tyranny, turning those who had been sworn enemies into a unified whole after the fact. The Mexico City monument that now contains the remains of Francisco Madero, Venustiano Carranza, Pancho Villa, Plutarco Elías Calles, and Lázaro Cárdenas is an official attempt to literally cement this simplification, although if people could rise from the dead, many of these figures would continue fighting like zombies on the streets of the Tabacalera neighborhood. By trying to sweep their bitter disagreements under the rug, the monument diminishes the importance of the deadliest war in the Americas in the twentieth century. The violence may have been cruel, according to the official discourse, but it was ultimately justified because it brought about the downfall of the former regime. In the twentieth century, this rationalization tended to blur the boundaries between political and criminal violence, between sexist and racist abuse, and between legitimate and incidental victims. For the state, referring to this murky history meant invoking an ideological legacy which was always vague, and claiming that the involvement of the members of the new political class in the armed phase of the Revolution gave them authority to continue using force, now ostensibly for the good of the nation.

To stop here would be to accept an interpretation of the 1910 Revolution as a simple struggle among elites for control of the state. But the Revolution was far more complex than this: it was a genuine social movement that reached every corner of the nation, involved all members of society, causing a seismic shift in Mexico's class relations, culture, and institutions. The huge demographic impact of the revolutionary violence is undeniable. In the 1910s, 1.5 million people died, mostly as a direct result of the war (battles, executions, accidents, starvation), and a lower number from diseases such as influenza and smallpox, which spread more widely due to the difficulties caused by displacement, hunger, and fear. By 1920, the Mexican population had probably shrunk by more than 2 million from its expected growth in the space of a decade—the 1921 census records a less drastic loss, but compiling it was highly problematic. Apart from the deaths related to the Revolution, around 400,000 people emigrated to the United States. More than half a million births, the figure to be expected based on existing birth rates, did not take place. Robert McCaa records that revolutionary violence caused one in seven deaths, and life expectancy at birth fell to half of the thirty years recorded in 1910. By any measure, the years between 1913 and 1916 were the worst for Mexico's city dwellers, but hardship continued in rural areas for years. However, as Friedrich Katz has pointed out, the Mexican

Revolution did not employ terror on the same scale as the Russian Revolution. Despite massacres of civilians and mass executions due to factional rivalries and repression, the lack of party discipline, operational capacity, or external threat meant that systematic terror was absent both in the early stages and once the new regime was in place.

Patriarchal deference, which had defined social interactions up until the Porfiriato, when relationships were marked by class hierarchies, gender, skin color, and other types of difference, was one victim of this crisis. As noted by witnesses and historians, after the revolutionary decade it was no longer possible to expect obedience from supposed inferiors. Violence played a role in this transformation. Local and regional uprisings, the expansion of revolutionary armies, and the lack of clear boundaries between the political and criminal spheres all democratized access to the material means of committing violent acts. This is paradoxical, of course: democracy rejects the use of force to reach agreements and implies a pacification of the social space. However, after many years of a dictatorship that had used force to exclude most of the population from political and legal decisions that affected their lives, a new cadre of political actors (campesinos, laborers, opposition politicians) now had access to the weapons and organizational capacity needed to counter the official coercion used by Díaz and his regime's supporters. In other words, for better or worse, the Revolution expanded political participation though it did not bring peace to the country. As Arendt wrote, violence's long-term effects are impossible to predict, but its use can certainly be beneficial and foreseeable in the short term for those using it. Picking up rifles and machetes gave the state of Morelos's campesinos a voice that the dictatorship had denied them for decades.

The Revolution also gave many of them access to firearms—smuggled or imported legally into Mexico from the United States, seized from soldiers, recovered from some corner of a farm building where they had been kept since the previous century, or looted from haciendas and private homes. The fact is that anyone, regardless of class, military rank, or official position, could now get their hands on revolvers, automatic handguns, carbines, rifles, and even machine guns. Without this proliferation and expansion of arms, it is conceivable that the Revolution could have been brought under control by the army or one of its factions much sooner. In some parts of Mexico, like in the Chihuahua mountains, people were accustomed to using weapons because of clashes with Indigenous groups living in the region. In most of the country, this newfound access to arms had clear consequences, such as the type of weapon used in common crimes, particularly homicides and grievous bodily harm, but also in armed robberies. The classic *pulquería* brawl during the Porfiriato generally involved two men brandishing knives outside the premises, where they had probably been having a friendly conversation only moments before. After the Revolution, people increasingly used pistols to settle such disputes, even in bars.

As with the knife fights of old, politics was not necessarily a factor in such confrontations. However, revolutionary anecdotes also tell us of apparently arbitrary deaths that, if read in a broader context, say something important about how revolutionary violence changed public life. In Mexico City in 1914 and 1915, a different kind of combatant entered the fray. Some, like the Zapatistas photographed by Agustín Casasola at the counter of Sanborns, behaved properly, even though their clothes and skin color were anathema, in the eyes of the Porfirian elites, to the refinement associated with the famous restaurant at that time. But there were others, particularly during the occupation of the city by the armies of the Revolutionary Convention, who did not behave so well. The democratization of violence was then reflected in unprecedented behaviors in social life, connected with the consumption of alcoholic beverages. Alcohol, for example, altered the personality of Eufemio, Emiliano Zapata's brother, and led to his death in Cuautla in 1917, after he had come to blows with the father of another Zapatista leader, who soon took his revenge. The drunken man firing shots into the air and yelling for joy became iconic in these new times, reflecting citizens' new rights that were inscribed not in any laws but in masculine behavior in public spaces. This formed part of a new claim to freedom of expression by people hitherto forced to lower their voices, but who now showed that they had "red blood in their veins." Cantinas and pulquerías, which nineteenth-century positivism associated with the brutalization of *la raza* (the masses), became spaces where, for example, freedom of expression was guaranteed by the use of firearms. This new level playing field of violence could have tragic outcomes, or so anecdotal evidence suggests, although it was likelier that most revelers were still on friendly terms at the end of their drinking sessions.

The effects of violence, it bears repeating, are never completely foreseeable and, in modern history, they tend to undermine the progress of democracy and civil rights. In the postrevolutionary years, journalists continued to face restrictions to their autonomy and the constant threat of violence. During this period, perilous armed spontaneity in cantinas corresponded to the exclusion of women from public life. Women entering a cantina had to check their honor at the door, and those carrying weapons broke the code of acceptable behavior for their gender. The blatant violence suffered by women during the Revolution was firmly implanted in people's minds.

As we will see in the following chapters, the use of weapons gradually turned into a male privilege linked to official protection or negligence. The police no longer entered cantinas to keep order but to join in the drinking. Officers who tried to apply the law in this masculine and dangerous space ran the risk of being abruptly thrown out by the regulars. As the writer William Burroughs told his friend Jack Kerouac in 1949, in Mexico "anyone who feels like it carries a gun. I read of several occasions where a drunken cop, shooting at the habitués in bars, were themselves shot by armed civilians who don't take no shit from nobody." The "psychology of our race," which worried Mariano Azuela in 1915, had become a violent habit that justified inequality and erratic behavior by invoking the heroic and bloody memory of the Revolution.

CHAPTER TWO

AGRARIAN VIOLENCE

—

THE CIVIL WAR ended in less than a decade, but at its conclusion Mexico was still a rural country marked by stark inequalities in access to land and labor control. What did change, as we saw in chapter 1, was the availability of weapons and the increasing number of voices clamoring for justice. The 1917 Constitution gave the state the prerogative to give back land stripped from communities. It could also request land grants by prioritizing the interests of society over private ownership. The history of agrarian reform is one of the key chapters in the construction of the postrevolutionary state. During the armed phase of the Revolution, the recovery of land was a primary objective of local and regional movements. The Zapatistas, even after their leader's assassination in 1919, were capable of articulating and upholding these demands to make them central to the Revolution. In the following decades, these groups openly organized themselves as agrarian movements. The government began including campesinos in the official party structure through national organizations and an agrarian bureaucracy that acted as a conduit for land claims.

Behind this history of social movements and institutions lies a more complex and less told story. We could define it as the history of the armed struggle for land. This fight included the organized activities of political groups, military operations (albeit on a smaller scale than during the revolutionary years), and clashes between the guardias blancas and communities demanding land, as well as between villages, families, and individuals, where it was hard to distinguish agrarian claims from common crimes. Sometimes the disputes were not over land but over other resources such as water; though it was hard to tell, other problems may have stemmed simply from personal grievances. But in any case, the new uses of violence introduced by the Revolution came into play in conflicts over differing conceptions of land ownership and justice. To understand the armed agrarian struggle that dominated the lives of many Mexicans between the Revolution and the second part of the century, we must therefore consider the violent practices that accompanied it, as well as the norms that justified it and made it so widespread.

This history's chronology is also blurred. In some places, land redistribution had already begun before 1917. Elsewhere, the struggle began in the 1920s or even in the 1930s, during the Cárdenas administration. Some communities rejected agrarian reform while others bet heavily—even their lives—on securing access to new land. By the 1940s, the tide began to turn and agrarian movements became mired in the same local obstacles but received less support from the central authorities. Conflicts continued until the end of the century, sometimes resulting in bloodshed and bearing similarities to the clashes at the start of the century. As we will see in this chapter, this violence was often personal; friendships and family relationships shaped grievances and loyalties. Agrarian violence could be described as sticky: its forms and effects became entrenched in ways that are hard to explain from a purely class perspective.

To make sense of this confusing panorama, narratives tend to focus on the country's presidents as the ultimate arbiters of all land claims and on *amparos* (orders of legal protection), whose strategic preferences determined the pace and scope of agrarian reform. But as we will see, this only tells part of the story, because the evolution of local disputes—even when linked to federal policies—could be either very fast or very slow, settled in a gunfight or dragged out over years of attacks and counterattacks. Presidential policies were largely dependent on local situations. For example, postrevolutionary presidents, despite not necessarily being genuinely committed *agraristas* (supporters of agrarian reform) themselves, found it necessary to associate with some agrarian movements because it gave them the backing of thousands of armed campesinos. Sometimes these governments tried to disarm the agraristas, or alternatively gave them rifles. In 1920, Álvaro Obregón curried favor with campesinos in the state of Morelos to gain power, and once he became president he distributed more land than Venustiano Carranza. As a believer in agricultural modernization, Plutarco Elías Calles was keen to stop agrarian reform in the latter half of the 1920s, but was forced to seek the support of the agraristas in order to defeat Catholic Cristeros and ambitious generals. Even in attempting to establish a disciplined and uncontested army, Calles and his successors were forced to distribute weapons to agraristas and to form alliances with leaders far more radical than was to their liking. Lázaro Cárdenas accelerated the progress of land distribution during his administration and consolidated organized campesino support for the official party; however, he also confronted agraristas he found overly radical in places such as Veracruz with backing from local caciques. Some political parties and organizations such as the Partido Nacional Agrarista (National Agrarian Party, founded in 1920) and the Confederación Nacional Campesina (National Campesino Confederation, established in 1938) claimed to represent campesinos, but it would be an oversimplification to suggest that they could control events across the country at any given time.

State governors had a more direct influence. In San Luis Potosí, Saturnino Cedillo also distributed weapons to campesinos, but the impact of these militias—whose ranks were estimated to number as many as 15,000— was limited by the governor's political ambitions. Apart from fighting the Cristeros and Escobaristas, the militias were part of chaotic electoral processes marred by ballot box theft, acts of intimidation, and gunfights. It was not easy to demobilize them or take back their weapons when they became a threat to the central government. In Michoacán, Governor Francisco J. Múgica's support for agrarian reform in the early 1920s unleashed a wave of violence against campesino groups. Múgica himself was unable to control this fighting, resulting in weakened and more disperse movements in the subsequent years.

While the landless campesinos wanted to benefit from what they believed was the Revolution's promise, the generals and local caciques who had become landowners wanted to make sure that the Revolution also honored its promises to them. The federal government had to make many pledges, depending on circumstances, because it was still too weak to resolve each conflict on its own. The granting of land to communities, on the one hand, and the acquisition of large estates by rich or influential individuals, on the other, were perceived by all actors as a confirmation that the struggle was still worth the cost.

This history is even more complex when we consider tendencies at the state and municipal levels. In Sonora, for example, there were fewer agraristas than in Michoacán. In some regions, agrarian violence claimed thousands of victims in conflicts that included mass murders, destruction of property, and other forms of brutality. But in other areas, agrarian disputes paled in significance when compared to religious conflicts, as we will see in the next chapter, although both are undoubtedly connected. Land ownership structures changed in some places more than others; campesinos took steps forward and backward, and it would be wrong to suggest that more deaths in a particular area correlated with their longer-term progress. The case of the state of Oaxaca—the subject of many excellent studies on violence, *caciquismo* (a locally rooted system of extralegal rule based on loyalty and violence), and *pistolerismo*—shows us that the agrarista-landowner dialectic can simplify the analysis. Cultural diversity and geographical fragmentation partly explain the peaks and troughs in the fighting after the Revolution. The 1920s were a period of instability for the state government, but this did not necessarily increase the number of violent incidents. In some places—such as Juquila, in the state of Oaxaca, according to James Greenberg—this violence abated in the immediate aftermath of the Revolution but worsened again in the 1950s due to rising coffee prices. In San Juan Mazatlán, also Oaxaca, the late 1930s saw a marked increase in the number of murders and attacks by the guardias blancas. In this district and others, fighters carried pistols and Mauser rifles, which had become more readily available, making disputes more deadly despite the absence of an agrarista movement as strong as in Veracruz or Michoacán. Homicide rates remained very high into the 1970s, partly due to clashes between villages. Rule of law was largely absent and impunity rife, leading to some communities to take justice into their own hands.

Campesinos saw the distribution of firearms as the first step toward land distribution. The weapons had diverse origins: some were provided directly by the army or came from the United States, others had simply been hidden and later recovered after the postrevolutionary demobilization. The fact is, as Armando Bartra notes, that the campesinos were armed and tens of thousands of agrarista combatants existed around the country. Occasionally it was necessary to use weapons to obtain land grants, and it was essential to form ejido-based self-defense groups to prevent reprisals by landowners or other communities.

Despite not being a nationally coordinated movement, all the agraristas knew that the state could not simply withdraw the legitimacy of their use of force with the stroke of a pen. They perceived themselves in a "struggle" and were prepared to use these weapons and take risks. It was not simply about stocking up on rifles and recruiting combatants. The success and endurance of some agrarista leaders, such as Juchitán's Heliodoro Charis, was also based on his men's fighting experience and fearsome reputation. This experience could have been acquired during the revolutionary decade or the fighting against the Cristeros and other rebel factions. In any case, it provided political capital. Since 1940, the government tried to limit the campesinos' ability to fight by enlisting the support of the armed forces and caciques, and by slowing down land distributions in order to protect private property. However, it proved hard to quell the unrest in many areas. In San José de Gracia, writes Luis González, many ejidatarios were killed during the 1940s, although the worst years were 1935 and 1936.

As the agraristas went on the offensive in some places, landowners adopted new strategies to defend and expand their properties. Some old hacendados survived and others sold their land to buyers with better political connections and therefore better able to withstand incursions by campesinos. These new proprietors included revolutionary commanders who believed that their participation in the heroic deeds had earned them the reward of becoming the very figure their soldiers had fought against. The most notorious and short-lived of those rewarded hacendados had been Pancho Villa. Obregón and Calles had granted him the Canutillo hacienda in Chihuahua after the fall of Carranza; but Villa did not get to enjoy this property for long, since the same Sonoran politicians ordered his assassination to prevent him from reengaging in politics when Adolfo de la Huerta's rebellion was imminent. For Obregón, it was completely normal, after the Revolution, to return to Sonora to grow chickpeas and other crops on his land, although he soon came back to politics as a presidential candidate.

Many other generals received land or money. As landowners, many proved to be more willing than their Porfirian predecessors to use violence against campesinos who challenged them. For example, Gonzalo N. Santos, in the state of San Luis Potosí, just in 1926 received 2,000 hectares. Managing his land did not prevent Santos from engaging in politics and taking revenge by dismembering the man who had killed his brother Francisco. Cedillo, in the same state, illustrates how agrarista slogans and support for campesino organizations did not preclude the accumulation of possessions. In other cases, landowners continued or expanded forms of coercion that had proved effective since the Porfirio Díaz era, such as the army-supported defensas rurales at the start of the Revolution and the guardias blancas, which did not limit themselves to protecting properties and could go on the offensive.

Across Mexico, the belief began to spread that campesinos and landowners could legitimately use force when fighting over land. Experience appeared to show that coercion was often the opening and closing chapter of any attempt to prevail in land disputes. As they learned this new political culture of violence, representatives from the Oaxacan town of Yiatepec were taken aback by the recommendation of a bureaucrat from the

Departamento Agrario and from an official of the Confederación Nacional Campesina in the capital: to be successful in their demand, apart from greasing the palms of bureaucrats, their first move should be to occupy the land in question. This strategic use of violence had short-term goals. Those taking part in such actions did not see them as a struggle for power; instead, they justified their actions by appealing to class or ethnic identities and to coherent value systems. In practice, though sometimes this was at odds with ideology, the still-fresh experience of revolutionary combat turned into a license to use weapons to defend these values.

The armed struggle for land in the aftermath of the Revolution reflected changes in what politics meant and in the resources employed by politicians, from the highest levels in the capital down to the most modest positions in rural communities. Politics expanded, stoking tensions in people's daily lives and raising the stakes of any quarrel. To return to the example of Múgica in Michoacán: the daily existence of dozens of campesino communities was altered by the "revolutionary script," as Christopher Boyer described it, of ideological radicalism and direct action. This new approach to politics produced agrarista leaders and caciques willing to use force without hesitation; and on an interpersonal level, it manifested itself in defiance and aggressiveness. Finding peaceful solutions to disagreements on matters of shared interest (subdivision of ejido land, control over irrigation canals, etc.) became harder, and violence developed into "an inevitable dimension of politics," to quote Paul Friedrich, an anthropologist who studied this phenomenon in the Michoacán town of Naranja. In Juquila, Oaxaca, Greenberg assumed that anyone involved in politics carried a firearm and that killing or being killed was part of the game.

Such violent agrarian conflict was, in its own way, a new development. Rural confrontations had existed in Mexico since colonial times, but they took a new form in the twentieth century. Unrest was widespread during Spanish rule, but there was no large-scale revolt until 1810. The turmoil unleashed by Miguel Hidalgo remained etched in the memory of the ruling classes, who, regardless of their ideological leanings, worked to prevent or suppress campesino rebellions until massive unrest broke out over a century later.

The struggle for land in the twentieth century was different because the Revolution created a new language to formulate the grievances of rural communities and helped to disseminate new ideas about campesino rights—in other words, it created a different way of justifying the use of force. Article 27 of the constitution expressed an idea about state sovereignty that was both long-standing, given its linkages to the Spanish monarchical system, and innovative, by entitling rural laborers to request the national government to override the inviolability of private property, a principle that until then had been upheld by conservatives and liberals alike. Socialist and anarchist influences fed into this criticism from the second half of the nineteenth century.

Partly because of its novelty, agrarian reform did not have a uniform ideology behind it. According to Luis González, Indigenous agraristas were nonexistent in San José de Gracia and most of the local population took a dim view of those troublemaking outsiders who expected plots of land as handouts instead of being earned through hard work. Aside from the moralistic perspective, which could easily have colored the memory of González's sources, private property was clearly the most legitimate way for the local population to own land. Obregón was being sincere when he said that in Sonora, "we don't have agraristas, thank God." More than an abstract faith in capitalism as a force for good, these attitudes reflected the belief that legal solutions existed for conflicts over land ownership and access to other resources. A long tradition of lawsuits between villages and haciendas existed since colonial times. In San José de Gracia, the agrarian conflict of the 1930s played out largely in court. The public officials in charge were not always honest, but they still enjoyed a certain authority.

The fierceness of postrevolutionary agrarian struggles stemmed from different actors' incompatible ideas about justice. In Juquila, Oaxaca, local people handled informal mechanisms of justice themselves; official justice was extremely expensive and only accessible to the minority who had the means. Apart from money and political connections, the lack of education or command of the Spanish language placed such formal justice even further out of reach than the type understood and applied by inhabitants of isolated communities. This lack of agreement on the legitimacy of norms not only distorted land disputes but also meant that many crimes went uninvestigated. For a father whose child had been murdered, after being falsely accused of another crime, taking up the matter with the authorities entailed an additional risk and no promise of arriving at the truth. In Oaxaca and other states, written legal norms could so fundamentally contradict regulations associated with Indigenous identities that they justified forms of political power, as exercised by some caciques, that navigated between those two conflicting normative frameworks. Tensions between an absolute notion of private property and the communal traditions of some communities gave rise to a different moral value to the one attributed to agrarianism by the people of San José de Gracia. Without a shared set of rules, it was easier to imagine the use of force. Judging such violence right or wrong, as a political or a criminal act, was something that involved a wide range of normative systems. While the penal code focused on the immediate modus operandi and motives of a crime, in some communities transgressions could be judged by taking into account preexisting conflicts, over a longer period and with less harsh punishments, even in murder cases. What may appear to be impunity from today's vantage point in a local context could be a logical consequence of festering quarrels that a judge's sentence could never resolve.

Agrarian violence, in other words, was the result not of supposed backwardness of the poorest or most marginalized rural inhabitants but of the tensions between various normative systems. The difference between these systems was not simply how far back they could be traced. As Alan Knight points out, violence was part of modernization and not necessarily correlated with the underdevelopment of certain places. It did not arise in the complete absence of other conflict-resolution mechanisms, such as justice or elections, but coexisted with them. In mid-twentieth-century Juquila, as in Morelos toward the end of the Porfiriato, the transformations caused by the increasing value of a commodity (coffee in Oaxaca, sugar in Morelos) simply pushed an already-tense situation into conflict. For the Chatino community in Oaxaca, for example, the cycles of agrarian violence were clearly not caused by a capitalist system with which they had successfully coped for generations but by disturbances that combined various causes and actors. The money, arms, and ideologies that had suddenly become available, together with the lack of a reliable judicial process, equally accessible to all groups, upset the delicate balance in which different visions of rights and justice coexisted. These violent conflicts did not necessarily cause clashes between hacendados and campesinos, between the "educated" and the Indigenous peoples; they could also spark confrontations between people of the same social class within a community. In brief, this history cannot be simplified into a dichotomy between good and evil, oppressors and oppressed, without understanding the ideologies that made it possible to consider the use of violence as a rational option that justified the death or dispossession of the enemy. As we will see, no one was blameless.

What did all this mean in practice? New rules regulated the use of force in agrarian conflicts. This was no longer the global and frequently unpredictable danger that had defined the civil war years, though the many civil war veterans continued the fighting tactics that had emerged during the Revolution, using the same weapons. No clear beginning or end was in sight for the armed agrarian struggle, nor were there obvious winners or losers, in contrast to the revolutionary decade. Instead of all-out warfare, there were frequent skirmishes that could be described as personal: adversaries were acquaintances or lived near each other, sometimes in the same town, and it was not easy for them to leave in order to avoid trouble. The fight over land was not a war in which armies were trying to dislodge each other and move forward but a struggle in which both parties asserted their right to remain where they were.

Clashes involved family and friends. In Naranja, adversaries had family ties and the death of one family member had to be avenged, an eye for an eye. The chain of murders was not only an emotive response, it was calculated too. When a group discussed the need to avenge the next murder, the premise was that this act of revenge would trigger a response. Friendship was as important as family to local strongmen, whose routine use of force could isolate them from the community. It was also a very powerful emotional bond that allowed for the distribution of prime public positions among those in the inner circles. Cabals were cohesive in this way, and gained their strength by uniting people from different areas to exert influence at the state level, as Benjamin Smith has described in the case of Oaxaca.

In such intimate networks, hostility and leadership could be expressed in various ways before events came to a head. Talking to possible allies was a valuable skill, even for those most willing to fight. Intrigue was as effective as rhetoric, particularly when talking openly could be risky. Word-of-mouth communication could be a form of aggression. Given the lack of justice for past crimes, rumors pronounced individuals or groups guilty in the public eye. Gossip, gestures, and minor incidents that undermined people's reputations were often precursors to violence. Like any communicative act, homicide, even when motivated by vengeance, still needed to have its reasons.

Material stakes were high, particularly when land could be commercially valuable depending on the type of crop. The campesino leagues that emerged in the 1920s assumed that collective control over land and the means of production could coexist with commercial use—as in the collectivization of sugarcane plantations in Morelos, henequen operations in Yucatán, or cotton farming in Laguna. Conflicts always had an economic dimension, whether they were over the use of water resources and woodland, distribution of land, or access to credit.

To understand the practices and the communicative value of violence, therefore, we cannot focus exclusively on the instant of the machete blow, the gun fired furtively or at point-blank range. All of the actors, from the campesinos to the haciendas' guardias blancas, knew that the legal system and agrarian institutions were ultimately the ones that could provide longer-term solutions. They were also aware of the risk, however small, that a judge or public opinion might punish an act of aggression.

Despite their revolutionary origins, the agrarian organizations formed in the 1920s could not commit the same outrages as in the previous decade without risking the loss of support from governors or allies in Mexico City. To succeed, any local project required the patronage of leaders or factions at the state or national level. In Veracruz, Yucatán, Tabasco, and Michoacán, agrarian movements based their activities on communist, socialist, or anarchist ideologies, and affiliated themselves with political parties or organizations such as the Ligas de Comunidades Agrarias (Agrarian Communities League) or the Confederación Nacional Campesina. In contrast to the direct action of the anarchists, however, they relied on the law, specifically Article 27 of the constitution, and demanded the granting of rights. In their discourses, agrarista leaders did not openly condone violence; nor did they want to attract attention to their methods when these involved the use of force, because it could be counterproductive. Seizing land was part of a bureaucratic and political process that, if successful, would conclude with the president's signature at the bottom of an expropriation order or certificate. The use of weapons was part of the implicit message of this process. Agrarian conflicts rarely feature in the official discourse from the center and from on high. Rural politics was implicitly understood as inherently brutal. The capital's cultural and political elites did not know or did not want to know everything that was going on in the countryside.

This explains the paradox that many acts of rural violence strategically combined secrecy with publicity. Sometimes attacks were clandestine, without witnesses and leaving no obvious tracks. But even crimes taking place in remote areas and at night had an explanation in the unspoken code of cabals. Public opinion did not need physical evidence or witnesses to explain the crimes. Judicial authorities rarely acted because officials followed the logic of revenge, thus validating stereotypes about the brutality of campesinos and Indigenous communities. Witnesses were scarce because anyone reporting an incident or simply informing the authorities risked their life. Outside observers who tried to understand this seemingly endemic violence found themselves dealing with people who did not want to talk about what was happening before everyone's eyes.

Nevertheless, most acts of aggression were deliberately visible. Many attacks took place in public, or else the assailants made sure witnesses were present to spread the word. This publicity could have tactical and propaganda value, harkening back to the revolutionary period, when executing the hacendado's lackeys was a symbolic act of justice. Such methods also warned those who tried to resist that the same fate awaited them unless they backed down, collaborated, or fled. Victims were hanged, hacked with machetes, dragged behind galloping horses: guardias blancas or thugs working for caciques or hacendados were usually responsible for such excessive and public acts of cruelty, but sometimes campesino groups could be similarly brutal. However, the idea was not to wipe out the enemy, as during the Revolution, but to construct an order based on one group's domination. The excess had an explanation: a man from Yaitepec in the state of Oaxaca considered himself particularly macho and took indiscriminate revenge for his father's death; his murderers cut out his heart and placed it in his mouth, as if mocking his bravery. Even in such brutal episodes, some kind of explanation was needed for the act to exist within the framework of a value system, whether that was based on private property, communalism, or shared codes of conduct.

Homicide, inevitably a public act, was the emblematic example of that violence. The killing of a prominent agrarista leader could act as a deterrent to an entire group. The elimination of a hitman who had taken various lives offered hope for a period of calm. These homicides were rarely punished, particularly when they expressed the local balance of power, since this reduced the likelihood of an independent investigation or trial. Perpetrators still took precautions to avoid or mitigate responsibility for their crimes. In Naranja, in the state of Michoacán, agrarian policy may have routinely included killing, but certain rules still applied. Friedrich interviewed a pistolero from Michoacán for whom homicide could be a "moral" act if the hired killer did not torture or talk to the victim. The murderer was often a *luchador* (activist) of some standing, while the victim was on a lower rung of the social ladder, reducing the need for a prior display of ostentatiously macho behavior. When the killer was paid for his services, a close relationship with the victim was not even necessary. A gunman could ambush him from a safe vantage point without witnesses. *Venadear* was the verb used for such killings of unsuspecting targets from a distance with a rifle shot, as if hunting a deer (*venado*). This was the preferred method used by Afro-Mexican pistoleros in Jamiltepec, Oaxaca, according to the anthropologist Véronique Flanet: they would shoot from behind the cover of a tree, without giving any warning or simulating an altercation.

Often, however, an enemy's death was a personal matter that, despite forming part of a political context, still required a specific justification to exonerate the assailant. By reducing the motives for the attack to a basic, individual level, it became possible to invert the importance of the factors and place personal grievances above any political disputes. In such cases, knives, stones, and beatings could be combined with the use of firearms. Such intimate physical contact could communicate three kinds of explanation based on how the homicide was carried out (its "performance"), on the public discussion of the character of the assailant and his victim, and on their respective social networks.

First, some politically motivated homicides appeared to be the result of regular drunken brawls, insults, or apparently spontaneous confrontations in public spaces. The frequency of such incidents indicates that the assailants were in fact following a tried-and-tested script that only simulated a random altercation. The victim could have been drunk and behaving recklessly, firing gunshots into the air before sustaining a fatal knife wound. The assailant could have drunk alcohol to pick up courage and find the right moment to cross paths with the victim. Indeed, alcohol was a key theme in this script, because it was traditionally considered to diminish the assailant's responsibility and to reproduce the same patterns of daily crimes that lacked any political motive. This reached such a degree that some women in San José de Gracia thought that politics was a pretext and that men's drunkenness was the real reason for violence. They were partly right: drunkenness indeed offered a culturally acceptable excuse for violence. In those cases, witnesses to the attack could confirm that the perpetrator was acting in self-defense or to protect his reputation. When a homicide case reached the courts, the files concentrated on the immediate circumstances, and drunkenness was considered a mitigating factor. This interpretation based on the direct context of events referred to an indisputable logic, namely that the reaction to the insult or provocation could not be delayed, lest it appear to confirm the accusations against the integrity of the offended party. After an insult, it was essential to attack without delay. For the killer to be justified by the circumstances, a speedy reaction was essential, even if it was fueled by alcohol. Despite numerous antialcohol campaigns in the twentieth century, the meaning of the association between drunkenness and violent confrontations remained unchanged.

Alcohol was another factor in the second kind of explanation, which referred to the character of those involved. In theory, a drunk man expressed his anger more transparently, converting the real or perceived offense into an inexorable urge to kill. By provoking this impulse, the victim became partly to blame for his own death. This type of aggression (swift, up close, apparently spontaneous) made an implicit statement about the assailant's nature by compounding the victim's susceptibility with the aggressor's brutality. The manner of the attack confirmed the aggressor's manliness and diminished his legal responsibility and the value of witness testimony. In the context of postrevolutionary agrarian violence, this tendency toward violence—which the Porfirian upper classes associated with honor—

became an impulse that could be viewed from a political and moral angle. The agraristas who made a living from this violent propensity were known as luchadores, and their long list of victims attested to their devotion to the cause. Some were marked men, because the law of revenge forced them to seek out their enemies, who knew it was in their interest to strike first. The individual characters of those involved explained homicide as the fatal crossing of two destinies.

The third way of justifying homicide was expressed through family ties or friendships connecting those involved. In these cases, preexisting quarrels provided the pretext, and homicides could be explained as a link in the chain of acts of revenge that went beyond the perpetrators' personal responsibility. The evidence for these cycles of vendettas comes to us from ethnographic studies that identify honor and family bonds as the basis for actions that might otherwise appear to be knee-jerk responses: If you kill one of my relatives, I'll kill one of yours. Families living together in a community could become ensnared in long-lasting retaliatory violence, with homicides becoming commonplace and carried out with increasing cruelty as confrontations escalated. Agrarian disputes were fueled by this thirst for vengeance and leveraged for material gain. A local official who used force to attack an enemy as part of an interfamily dispute was not, strictly speaking, committing an act of political violence. Oaxaca's state authorities decided not to intervene in the clashes in San Juan Mazatlán between pistoleros and Indigenous Mixes because, according to the governor, the violence was motivated by interfamily vendettas. Even though this was not quite true— the pistoleros of a cacique, Luis Rodríguez, were also stealing and raping women—the governor's argument worked because it referred to the supposed brutality of rural customs. The stereotype became self-perpetuating if violent crimes went unpunished. Performance, personal character, and social links tended to combine in order to give homicides various overlapping explanations that made them appear inevitable and justified.

Not all agrarian violence fits the mold of these explanations. In some periods and places, such as in mid-1930s Veracruz, the deaths were too numerous to be attributed to interpersonal disputes. In the district of Yaitepec, around the middle of the twentieth century, the homicide rate was twenty-nine times higher than the national average. During the same years, Paul Gillingham writes, the homicide rate in Ometepec in the state of Guerrero was comparable to that of Colombia during the civil war period, known as La Violencia, between 1948 and 1959. Homicide figures considered by the judicial system do not provide a perfect indicator because many cases were never officially reported, let alone investigated, and because the data available to us do not break down figures by district but are combined to provide a statewide count. These limitations notwithstanding, states such as Veracruz and Michoacán clearly had far higher rates than elsewhere in the country during the critical decades of the 1930s and 1940s.

Quantity says something about quality. We can cite examples of incidents with several victims that lack any of the explanations described above: entire families killed, rapes, looting, agraristas mown down by a machine gun during mass, a rival group picked off at long range while passing through a ravine. These acts may have been cowardly but they were nevertheless effective, at least in the short term, achieving their goal of eliminating the enemy and spreading a message. Agrarian disputes displaced entire populations. A figure named Manuel Parra was said to have ordered the simultaneous killing of twenty-two men in Veracruz, and according to one journalist he was behind a total of 2,000 deaths. Aware that they were unlikely to face punishment, anti-agraristas and agraristas alike could get away with indiscriminate and blatant homicides.

To understand the magnitude of the accusation against Parra (court documents do not help corroborate this information), we need to analyze the situation in Veracruz more closely. This state experienced different types of agrarian violence and their far-reaching effects. The agrarian reform movement was powerful, but it triggered an equally strong reaction. The Revolution introduced many actors who could use force, including campesinos who attacked haciendas to seize land. Governor Adalberto Tejeda (1920–24 and 1928–32) armed the agraristas and supported them in their fight against their enemies within the state. This intensified campesinos' clashes with federal troops, who often obeyed local interests rather than orders issued from central or state authorities, and with landowners and their private security guards.

Agraristas in Veracruz became more powerful by supporting Obregón and Calles in their conflict against Adolfo de la Huerta's faction in 1923, and, by the middle of the decade, according to Romana Falcón, 150 agrarista guerrillas were active in the state. Despite their autonomy, armed campesino groups in Veracruz could respond at the national government's orders. Apart from fighting against the Delahuertistas and then against the Cristeros, in 1929 they provided 4,000 combatants to put down the rebellion organized by José Gonzalo Escobar and other generals. But the agraristas were unruly: their modus operandi included homicides, robberies, and various acts of revenge. Occasional attempts to disarm them were thwarted by the groups' dispersion. In late 1932, the government deployed more soldiers to Veracruz to disarm the agraristas, whose numbers were estimated to have reached over 20,000.

Parra was particularly aggressive in his land acquisitions in Veracruz. In coordination with other landowners, he personally armed and led a network of guardias blancas and pistoleros called La Mano Negra. This name may refer to the Sicilian Mafia, which had already attained mythical status in Italy and the United States as a secretive and vengeful organization (two contradictory qualities, since vengeance was pointless without people recognizing the assailant's affiliation). A victim of a kidnapping in 1931, Parra (and his allies) saw the threat of the armed agraristas as a justification for what Antonio Santoyo has called "anti-agrarista terrorism," which purported to uphold law and order and punish thieves. In Veracruz, Tlaxcala, and Puebla, La Mano Negra killed agraristas and took part in moves to facilitate land acquisitions or to prevent resistance by organizations or families. From his hacienda in Almolonga, Parra had hundreds of loyal men, many of them employed on his farm. Perhaps to set an example, he even carried out homicides himself. Parra's pistoleros could operate near their base or travel to cities to eliminate adversaries or candidates who threatened their power in the state. This was how governor-elect Manlio Fabio Altamirano was killed in the Café Tacuba in Mexico City in 1936. Parra found a way to remain on good terms with Presidents Lázaro Cárdenas and Manuel Ávila Camacho, who generally preferred to avoid confrontation with caciques. Hundreds of people were murdered in the region, land was redistributed, and crimes often became intertwined with political confrontations. Parra was so effective in organizing his pistoleros to attack the agraristas that he began to sell his services to other landowners, who now viewed the illegal use of force as the only way to hold on to their property. The amount of land distributed in the state diminished, and the overall agrarian structure ultimately did not change as radically as might have been expected given the power that the agraristas had enjoyed. A spate of killings after Parra's death in 1943 avenged the Mano Negra's abuses, as its members lost their protection from above. According to Santoyo, throughout the 1930s and until the early 1940s, the death toll on both sides was very high, reaching the tens of thousands.

The presence of private security guards was not a new phenomenon. Since the Porfiriato, haciendas might employ a number of armed men, either defensas rurales, soldiers deployed by the government, or guardias blancas hired by the landowner. As we saw in chapter 1, in many cases abuses by these employees had driven the rebels to take up arms. Revolutionary veteran Gonzalo N. Santos—never one to dwell on life's ironies—remembered in his memoirs how some years after the Revolution he began using the guardias blancas employed by oil companies and other landowners to enforce law and order in the Huasteca region in the state of San Luis

Potosí. Thieves were executed by firing squad and, if the culprits were Indigenous, their hands were cut off. In the early 1930s, the guardias blancas in Veracruz went beyond protecting private property and killed hundreds of campesinos. In the states where the fighting was fiercest, the guardias blancas helped revert the tendency toward land distribution. Unsurprisingly, agrarista groups killed many hacienda foremen. These workers and their hired thugs represented an owner who lived elsewhere and did not want to dirty his hands to control the campesinos. Even in San José de Gracia, where no hacienda existed to commit such abuses, resentment led to revenge attacks and "pure evil."

The guardias blancas could act with impunity in some particularly flagrant cases, but the landowners and caciques also used the services of other experts in the use of violence, such as hitmen. These could be local or hired from other parts of the country. Evidence exists of this practice in the second half of the century in particular, when the national government become more concerned with covering up the most egregious types of conflict. The Afro-Mexicans of Jamiltepec, in Oaxaca's Mixteca region, were notoriously effective and charged less than their counterparts in Acapulco. As I will detail in chapter 4, skill at handling weapons, specifically to kill, facilitated certain kinds of business that were not necessarily political.

Men such as Parra, Cedillo, Santos, and Charis were often called caciques. In many regions of the country, agrarian disputes produced violent leaders. Such figures were deeply rooted in their areas of influence, motivated by personal gain but also by maintaining a type of informal and only partially coercive political representation. Their power derived primarily from controlling access to land but also from an ability to connect different levels of the state. Caciques are generally imagined as figures with pistols tucked into their belts, mobilizing political militants and hired guns to establish their own version of stability within ejido communities and in areas with haciendas and farms. But caciques also had connections to governors and presidents, and they could adapt to, and mediate, orders coming from central authorities. Armed agrarian struggles strengthened their hand, whether this meant leading or oppressing campesinos: caciques were not necessarily distinguished by a particular class identity or by coercive practices. Some caciques started out as agraristas and then became as tyrannical as the worst hacendados. They acted as intermediaries between the community and the government with a more personal than institutional approach, and their power was essentially incompatible with the existence of an independent judiciary. In the state of Puebla's Sierra Norte region, locals supported Gabriel Barrios's swift and informal administration of justice to rapists and thieves. His summary executions reflected the gap between official state and local forms of justice. This gap expressed the many normative systems that fueled agrarian disputes, requiring caciques to play a mediating role. In specific contexts, their actions could be legitimate but not legal.

The caciques' authority derived not solely from violence and their ability to mobilize their followers but also from their power of persuasion, using rhetoric or gossip as necessary. As Boyer points out, part of their legitimacy stemmed from the fiction that their communities were unanimous and perfectly adjusted to the campesino class identity—when in fact those communities could be diverse and divided. Just as Barrios introduced infrastructure to a remote part of the state of Puebla, rural *cacicazgos* were not opposed to modernization, and were instrumental in bringing benefits such as education to their followers. They simply exploited a moment in the process of state formation in which law and coercion had taken on a personal quality. As we will see in chapter 4, the type of informal leadership that defines the caciques could also be found in urban settings, such as in trade unions, where the pistoleros' ability to use violence connected the world of politics to illicit businesses.

Caciques also allowed the federal state authorities and the country's intelligentsia to maintain their deliberate ignorance about the methods and meanings of violence in rural areas. This disregard could be reduced to a formula that enabled them to sidestep the contradictions between normative systems: "That's just how campesinos are: they only understand bullets and machetes, it's better to leave them to those who know how to handle them." Caciques became the prototype for the injustices and ills of rural Mexico; iconic examples are the performances of Carlos López Moctezuma in movies like *Río Escondido* (Hidden river) (dir. Emilio Fernández, 1948) and *El rebozo de Soledad* (Soledad's shawl) (dir. Roberto Gavaldón, 1952). Although it would be easy to classify them as a moral archetype, caciques were in fact never a clearly defined group, like a hereditary caste; instead, they gained and lost power with equal ease, and in some cases, such as that of Regino Sandoval, the cacique in *Río Escondido*, they met a grisly end. Caciques practiced a routine brutality that, from the perspective of higher rungs of power and highly educated urban audiences, was antithetical to progress. Juan Rulfo's fictional works, particularly *Pedro Páramo* (1955), presented the world of campesinos and caciques as separate from that of his readers. Death and rape were part of a narrative that belonged in the past and was told by the dead themselves, but which had no before or after, and made little reference to the Revolution or the Cristero rebellion. In this way, Rulfo connected the physical distance of Comala and other remote locations where the stories took place with a temporal distance created by his narrative, as if Mexico had two historical temporalities: one modern (inhabited by the reader but not mentioned by Rulfo, unlike Azuela) and another that was always in the past, even if it happened in the present. This provided an aesthetic key to contrast urban modernity with a rural life that was radically different and where violence remained inexplicable yet deeply entrenched.

Agrarian violence did not come to an abrupt halt in the 1940s, but, at least in the states where it caused most deaths, such as Veracruz and San Luis Potosí, it began to diminish. In Veracruz, state police began to take over control from the guardias blancas and agraristas. In the Pisaflores district, in San Luis Potosí, many people remained armed but the violence began to recede after negotiations resolved decade-long disputes between rival factions, and as many local inhabitants became more conservative. This tendency spread. In San José de Gracia, the local population wanted the army to maintain law and order, but people urged to surrender their weapons during the famous *despistolización* campaign refused to do so. Perhaps, in a symbolic interpretation of the campaign's objectives, they feared it would threaten their manhood.

Although violence continued after the 1940s, its immediate causes and related strategies gradually altered. As Elisa Servín notes, since the 1950s various local electoral conflicts ended in repressive acts that in turn spawned armed movements and the occupation of land. While in some places prosperity reduced conflict, in others the new money could be used to buy weapons and continue the violence, only now in ways that were so personal that they seemed to be driven by selfish reasons rather than class identity. Struggling for campesino causes continued to come at a high personal cost, in what could now be called "repression." As the story of Rubén Jaramillo illustrates, the line between agrarian struggles and revolutionary guerrilla movements was blurred in places such as the state of Morelos. The repression of rural movements around Juchitán, sparked by the land distribution pledges of Luis Echeverría's presidency (1970–76), included paramilitary groups in which the police, caciques, the PRI, and the armed forces collaborated systematically if not legally.

Pacification was possible partly thanks to new political systems that channeled conflicts. In the corporate structure of the Partido de la Revolución Mexicana (Party of the Mexican Revolution), the political party established by Cárdenas in 1938, campesinos constituted a sector from the outset. This meant greater influence and benefits for the larger organizations, such as the Confederación Nacional Campesina, and the emergence of a cadre of politicians who claimed to be agraristas but who in fact had no quarrel with private property. They worked less to achieve class harmony than to capitalize on the tensions that always threatened to boil over. But corporate organizations never held a monopoly on campesino struggles, nor could they prevent outbreaks of violence: land continued to be seized by force, people rebelled against being drafted into military service and against the campaign to euthanize cattle in order to eradicate foot-and-mouth disease, and gunfights continued to explode in the aftermath of elections. If nothing else, the party's corporate organization offered an additional and less violent resource for the groups seeking to advance their cause, invoking Article 27 and campesino identity.

Fatigue also helped to diminish the violence. Though impossible to measure, this weariness undoubtedly set in following the experience and memory of the tumultuous years described here. By the mid-1920s, in parts of Oaxaca, local inhabitants tired of feeding the Zapatistas still roaming the countryside. Sometimes they even turned on them. In San José de Gracia after the Cristero War, acrimony, hatred, and resentment festered, poisoning a community that, according to Luis González, had once been more harmonious. According to Greenberg, it was the women of Yaitepec who successfully took the initiative in the 1980s to limit the still-deadly combination of alcohol and firearms. This response to the chaos excused summary executions by caciques and the army.

However, this response did not necessarily undermine rights and public liberties. Benjamin Smith argues that the public sphere's expansion (through the press, urban protests, and other means of venting disagreements without resorting to weapons) was another factor in the lower death toll after the 1940s. In Juchitán, memories of the repression of other popular movements influenced the methods chosen by the Coalición Obrera, Campesina, Estudiantil del Istmo (Worker, Campesino, and Student of Coalition of the Isthmus) from the 1970s to counter caciquismo. In Oaxaca, as in other states, women played a more prominent role in urban protests. Men's fear for their masculinity during despistolización campaigns was not only symbolic, as the use of weapons was in fact a male privilege.

Although the answer is not simple, it is important to ask about beginnings and ends in the history of agrarian violence. While Mexican campesinos are not essentially violent, the agrarian disputes that broke out with the Revolution and intensified during the following two decades deserve their own explanation. We must challenge the notion that things never change and even the idea of a sharp distinction between rural and urban environments. The struggles over land in the twentieth century cannot be understood without considering the availability of weapons or the organizations and ideologies that emerged from the Revolution and the new regime. The ambitions of a new group of landowners and their greater propensity to use force, alongside vigorous campesino demands for land reform, reveal the existence of a kind of rural violence that we might call modern. This phenomenon seems to have crept into an increasing number of everyday spaces, to the point that, in numerous episodes, any apparent connection with a confrontation over land was lost. Perhaps this lack of clear limits turned agrarian violence into a thorny conceptual problem for intellectuals and academics. While the difficulty of telling those stories can be seen in Rulfo's work, the films mentioned earlier in this chapter found a solution in a romantic celebration of its heroines. The disregard of Mexico City elites, based on stereotypes about campesinos, was one cause of the violence. This disdain led, for example, to deadly but rarely reported interventions by the army, and to other types of crime going unpunished. As we will see in the following chapters, the impunity that characterized agrarian struggles would become the common denominator of other forms of violence in the twentieth century, connecting rural and urban spaces in a way that myths cannot explain.

RELIGIOUS VIOLENCE

T HE LINK BETWEEN religion, intolerance, and violence was a characteristic of twentieth-century Mexico. The Cristero War was the largest and most costly manifestation of this phenomenon, but it was not exceptional. Claiming that anticlericalism was the cause for this conflict would be insufficient, however, to explain the other factors and forms of violence that are integral to the history explored in this book. The connection between violence and religion does not mean that Catholicism is inherently violent or, conversely, that only Catholics have been victims of state violence. As a vast network of beliefs and practices, Christianity in Mexico absorbed various perspectives on what was sacred, and it affected every aspect of people's lives, from gender relations to political affiliation. Faith in divine unity and the exalted mission of its earthly representatives also added an inflexible logic that placed these beliefs above secular laws and legitimized violence. This combination of the mundane and the divine is not intrinsically violent or pacifist. But it infused the tensions between believers and secularizers in the aftermath of the Revolution with a bitterness hard to find in other areas of life in Mexico. It was another clash of conflicting ideas about what was legal and permissible, as seen in chapter 2, which the actors tried to resolve through force. Anticlericalists resorted to symbolic and physical violence to counter what they saw as fanaticism. Catholics contemplated martyrdom but also took up arms against the enemies of an authority they considered to reign supreme. The conflict was not confined to the period of the Cristero War, and it included forms of collective violence such as lynchings and intolerant ideologies linked to fascism. This history shows the persistence of specific violent practices linked to religion, and their effects on collective identities, political ideologies, and gender perceptions.

The clash between anticlerical ideas and Catholic fundamentalism implied a confrontation between two incompatible value systems. This opposition came to be conceived as a battle in which the one adversary perceived the other as radically different, either as an enemy of the state or of God. The struggle shifted from the arena of controversy, debate, and legislation to military and police operations. At certain critical junctures, violence reached extreme levels, as if confirming the impossibility of any reconciliation.

Violence and religion were never far apart in Mexico. At least since the Classic and Postclassic pre-Hispanic periods, and continuing with similar intensity after the arrival of the Europeans, war was about religion. For the Aztecs, for example, it was part of a worldview based on an idea of conflict and sacrifice as the driving forces of history. The "Flower Wars" between the Aztecs and Tlaxcalans provided a supply of captives for sacrifice to the gods, although these confrontations also served strategic purposes. In this religious context, the destruction of bodies was not limited to combat and included rituals such as human sacrifice off the battlefield. Aside from tactical and economic considerations, the fighting between Aztecs and Spaniards was centered on their respective sacred entities, some of which were representations of war itself—such as the figures of Huitzilopochtli and Santiago Matamoros. As David Carrasco writes, the natural order was also a violent one, marked by combats and ruptures over time.

If we accept the view that there are continuities in the role of violence in social life, we can say that the centrality of war and human sacrifice in Mesoamerica during the Postclassic period is not radically different from the Catholic notion of a just war and from practices of mortification on the bodies of believers and heretics. Although conversion to Christianity could only be voluntary, coercion was constantly used to evangelize and root out heresy. The destruction of Tenochtitlan's Great Temple was an example of the Europeans' practices in the service of another god. Execution, torture, and other types of psychological coercion were used to eliminate idolatry in colonial times. These methods were designed to extract confessions that would furnish irrefutable proof of the transgression of practices suspected of masking idolatry or witchcraft. Judicial and ecclesiastical authorities used symbolic violence by destroying icons and books, and meting out physical punishment on those who persisted in their pre-Hispanic rites or beliefs. The Inquisition lacked jurisdiction over the Indigenous population. However, it was sufficiently active in New Spain to instill fear in the hearts of anyone engaging in unorthodox religious practices—whether out of their personal mystical experiences or because they wanted, secretly or otherwise, to keep alive the flame of a tradition that the Reconquest and Counter-Reformation had sought to extinguish. Men and women, many of them nuns, who experienced a different relationship with the divine, or entire families of Jews and Protestants, lived with this threat constantly hanging over their heads. The colonial state's various officials also faced rebellions when communities' shared religious beliefs stirred protests against abuses committed by those representatives.

In the nineteenth century, the religious question—specifically the Catholic Church's economic and institutional might—lay at the heart of the bloodiest civil wars. Conservatives sought to maintain the social order and its religious structure as it existed in colonial times, and they accused liberals (or "Jacobins," as they called them) of being fanatical, just as blind to the revealed truth as the heretics. Both conservatives and liberals, however, were careful not to mobilize their forces by invoking mystical or messianic arguments—the memory of the brutal violence triggered by the 1810 revolt was still fresh in their minds. Under the standard of the Virgin of Guadalupe hoisted by Hidalgo, thousands of rebels rose to fight against "bad government" and to defend a king betrayed by French heretics. The royalist response was equally violent, justified in the name of the primacy of the Catholic religion against assailants who attacked it from below and from outside the empire.

For conservative Catholics, and in particular those closest to the church hierarchy, liberals were committing an abuse in their campaigns to expropriate the funds of religious corporations, to secularize nuns, and to destroy buildings to open up streets. Liberals—most of whom were also Catholic—viewed the church's opposition to the 1857 Constitution and the Reform Laws as an equally threatening form of civil war, which included excommunication, ostracism, and the use of military force by conservatives and foreign invaders. Porfirio Díaz managed to reconcile these differences among the elites but failed to prevent the millenarian rebellion that took place in Tomóchic, in the state of Chihuahua, between 1891 and 1892. Federal troops had to repeatedly attack and virtually exterminate settlers in a remote mountain area, leaving more than 200 dead. The rebels were fighting for their community's political autonomy but framed their (physical and symbolic) resistance in religious terms. They expressed the coherence of a daily life in which it was hard to clearly tell apart religion, identity, and political structure. That daily life included the habit of using guns against Indigenous groups. To the central government, the Tomochitecos were just like the Apaches, who were fearless of death and never surrendered. Tomóchic rebels were inspired by a faith that combined anticlerical Christian aspects with the belief in the redemptive powers of a religious figure, Teresa Urrea, from Cabora, Sonora, who healed people, practiced spiritualism, and preached against the venality of priests and for a direct communication with God.

The Catholic hierarchy could not intervene in the rebellion because of its heretical and rebellious character. As we will see below, the hierarchy's lack of control was the common denominator of twentieth-century religious uprisings. The fear of a revolt from below gripped the elites in the late 1800s as powerfully as it had after the 1810 movement and, like then, it was shared by the ruling class regardless of ideology. The state's repression of the Tomochitecos reflected, in its brutal violence, a basic fear of an internal enemy—labeled as fanatics—who seemed completely anathema to the modern nation. In the view of critical observers such as Heriberto Frías, this use of force to uphold the law became the pretext for the excess that characterized other interventions by the army in reaction to social unrest. However, the state did not learn the lesson from Tomóchic that intervention in local religious practices always led to conflict.

The history of anticlericalism is more interesting than the notion of a binary religious struggle in twentieth-century Mexico suggests. To begin with, the Revolution cannot be described as a religious or antireligious movement. Some rebels, such as the Zapatistas, adopted Catholic symbols in their struggle against bad government, but this did not define their program. Despite not being essentially anticlerical, the Revolution was also a cultural movement that contemplated using coercion to achieve its aims. As Carlos Martínez Assad points out, religious and agrarian conflicts had contrasting dynamics. The revolutionary leadership was secular but included beliefs as diverse as Carranza's Freemasonry, Madero's spiritualism, Felipe Carrillo Puerto's deism, and Calles's Protestantism.

The influence of anarchism, scientific socialism, and the tradition of the liberal Reform movement introduced actively anticlerical militants into the revolutionary leadership, most notably Tomás Garrido Canabal. From the 1920s until the mid-1930s, Garrido imposed in Tabasco the most aggressively anti-Catholic laws, including the establishment of alternative rites for marriages and baptisms. He staged public burnings of saints worshipped in churches and homes, and named some domestic animals after religious figures. As in Michoacán, Veracruz, and Yucatán, many priests were expelled from the state. These actions formed part of a broad program designed to "regenerate" the Mexican people; in other words, to replace habits and beliefs deemed antithetical to modernity and even to rationality. The idea was to compete with a culturally influential opponent on its own turf, infusing iconoclastic public events, like the change in street names and the demolition of important buildings, with a ritualistic tone, sometimes to the rhythm of a march. The destruction of icons mimicked, to an almost absurd degree, the punishments inflicted on humans: in 1938, San José de Gracia's parish priest accused the local schoolteacher of the perplexing feat of decapitating a Sacred Heart. Public spaces became battlegrounds. The government not only banned processions but also appropriated places of worship. Some officials turned churches into brothels, or ate communion wafers with carnitas. As this chapter shows, both sides unwittingly resembled one another in their efforts to destroy or produce images of sanctity and death.

In parallel to these "cultural" events, Garrido deployed a paramilitary organization, the Red Shirts, against Catholics and political opponents in the state. The young members of this group, not all of whom were recruited voluntarily, beat up their adversaries and also carried Colt and Smith and Wesson pistols and Star submachine guns. In 1935, when Garrido traveled to Mexico City as a member of Cárdenas's first cabinet, the Red Shirts shot and killed five Catholics in Coyoacán. This led to a retaliatory lynching of a Red Shirt, criticism in the press, and Garrido's exit from the cabinet, where he was actually representing former President Calles.

Anticlericalism was neither uniform nor stable. Its most violent manifestation in the revolutionary years was not the inevitable result of its history, which can be traced back, in Mexico, to the enlightened liberalism of the pre-Reform period. Since that time, and throughout the struggles of the nineteenth century, one of its core arguments was that religion, when taught badly, dumbed down the people. For liberals such as Ignacio Ramírez, this called for a struggle on a symbolic level. He mocked priests for their venality and stupidity in satirical and carnivalesque invocations of the devil in poems and plays. Following the liberal victory, socialism, anarchism, and communism embraced the reformist tradition and radicalized its arguments. Positivism gave scientific weight to their arguments. With a few exceptions, such as in the case of Ramírez, who denied the existence of God in 1838, the issue was less about attacking religious faith than how the Vatican distorted it. The excessive luxury and colonialism of the church were frequently contrasted with a vision of faith that referred to the primitive simplicity of Christianity. These ideas circulated in the press, political meetings, trade union headquarters, and classrooms, generating grassroots support. Despite the exaggerations spread by leaders such as Garrido Canabal, anticlericalism was not always top-down: it could also be a popular persuasion within communities whose belief systems were less homogenous than they might have seemed from a distance.

The Revolution adopted and emphasized different potentialities of anticlericalism. The most intransigent liberal figures within the revolutionary coalition viewed Díaz's reconciliation with Catholics as a betrayal of Juárez's legacy. Albeit on a smaller scale compared to subsequent events, anticlericalism became aggressive from early on in the revolutionary period. The Catholic Church hierarchy sided with Victoriano Huerta in 1913, triggering retaliation in places such as Guadalajara, where the Constitutionalist proconsul, Gen. Manuel M. Diéguez, began to order the desecration of figures of saints and execution of people, and in 1914 he also closed newspapers as a way of punishing the city's reactionary elite, rather than out of any desire for redemption. In other states, revolutionary bosses made arrests, seized property, imposed fines, and ordered expulsions.

Article 130 of the 1917 Constitution allowed the government to regulate religious activities, and even to reduce the number of priests in each state. This was a key moment. From this point on, the government officials' use of force was no longer merely anticlerical Jacobinism but was enshrined in law. The various displays of renewed anticlerical aggression, both symbolic and physical, could no longer be downplayed as cultural Jacobin subversion. The aim had become to uphold the law through the use of force and also, in the revolutionary context, to make the law. Or, as Walter Benjamin would say, to use divine violence as a foundational act. Outbreaks of revolutionary violence, from this perspective, are the foundation of a new order and, to this end, the more destructive the better.

We can therefore surmise that there was something almost religious in the government's anticlerical zeal. First, the idea was not to eliminate all religion but to destroy the Catholic monopoly. Paradoxically, this radicalized the resistance of bishops and Cristeros. In the 1920s, the government supported a schismatic church that consisted of a group of Catholic priests and deacons. Despite not attracting many followers, these figures were able to express an internal dissent within the church that, as Matthew Butler shows, had popular support. The Mexican Apostolic Catholic Church's appeal to patriotism had a xenophobic dimension, but it also supported the Revolution's agrarian and labor reform program. The Catholic hierarchy had always struggled to regulate religious practices that were firmly entrenched yet not entirely orthodox. Adrian Bantjes shows that revolutionary anticlericalism was not simply antireligious but marked the beginning of a new pluralism in which the state confronted the Catholic Church, and also supported or protected other religious expressions. Catholic resistance to those other beliefs would continue justifying violence for several decades to come.

The clearest example of the religious aspect to the antireligious movement can be found in the language used to attack and defend religion. It was not enough, or even a priority, to expel or execute members of the clergy; it was necessary to challenge the representations of divinity in acts that believers could understand directly. The difficulty of disassociating the physical from the symbolic was exacerbated as the conflict escalated and the leaders on both sides lost control of their rank and file. Violence ensued: bombs were planted in places of worship and clashes broke out between protesters who no longer followed orders from their superiors but expressed the indignation of believers or local resentments connected to land disputes or ideological differences. The bishops who were forced into exile during those years had to use all the leverage that the uprising had given them and, at the same time, steer the rebellion of their own flock. This loss of control on the part of the leadership did not mean that the nature of the fighting on both sides lost its meaning. At every level, the performance of violent acts had its own justification.

The parallels between rivals and the unbreakable connection between symbolic and physical violence gave the confrontation its defining masculine character. Since the nineteenth century, liberals saw religion as something for women—and particularly those who were aged, ignorant, and unproductive. This enduring anticlerical prejudice explains the delay in enfranchising women, who only legally gained the right to vote in federal elections in 1953. Anticlerical forces not only thought that Catholic priests would control women's choices at the ballot box, but they also resented how domestic and public forms of worship gave women visibility and initiative— something they lacked in the political sphere. Indeed, women who played leading roles in the Catholic resistance did not receive any chivalrous treatment from the government. In 1918, several women were killed while participating in a protest against the Constitutionalists in Guadalajara, where Catholic women's organizations had gained prominence since the late Porfiriato. Finally, secularizing revolutionaries considered women responsible for stultifying children's minds with superstitions, even though they also entrusted many female teachers with the mission of raising awareness of new ideas through education. Women's lay organizations, which gained some prominence in states such as Michoacán, were vulnerable to the same kind of violent attacks facing male activists, yet without receiving any special protection from the government.

Catholics also sought to protect male dominance. Within the resistance movement that challenged the government, prominent women's brigades faced suspicion. Opposition to secular state education in the 1930s led female teachers employed by the federal government to become prime targets for harassment and mob violence. Catholics—from bishops down to local priests and their parishioners—defended a moral order in which women should remain subordinate, demure, and humble. This vision of male supremacy was no more coherent than the government's: the rebels' Christological emphasis, with its explicit focus on establishing the unforgiving kingdom of Christ on earth, coexisted with other Marianist forms of worship that stressed intercession and forgiveness through the Virgin Mary and the saints rather than punishment.

Two visions of women emerged, reflecting what Carlos Monsiváis called the bifurcation of patriarchal culture in the twentieth century: on the one hand, a state that refused to consider women as individuals but instead saw them as stereotypes of maternity or exaggerated religious devotion; on the other, a church that claimed to control them and make them upholders of moral and religious tradition. A shared trait of both visions was to render women objects instead of actors in history, making them easy targets for violence.

The century's bitterest religious conflict was thus the result of an accumulation of old processes and attitudes. When the hierarchy closed churches in 1926 after Calles refused to compromise on the interpretation of the 1917 Constitution's articles and a 1926 law that prohibited public acts of worship and reduced the number of priests, the Catholic faithful considered that government repression had gone a step too far. The lack of representatives of divinity, in the form of priests or sacred images, disrupted the daily practices that allowed many Catholics to receive the sacraments and request succor from the saints and the Virgin. The Cristero rebellion, which developed mainly in western parts of the country but spread widely, was just as surprising to the bishops as it was to the government. While Catholics in the cities began to organize in secret, campesinos and rancheros took up arms to attack the agents of a state they saw as a distant enemy attacking their most intimate rituals and beliefs. In some places, miraculous signs reinforced the obligation to respond to the government's provocations and to dust off the Winchester 94s and Mauser rifles. After the first stage of this initial conflict in 1929, tens of thousands were killed, injured, or displaced.

The revolt was initially spread out. Rebels attacked government officials or barracks, railroads, bridges, and prisons. In Michoacán, Catholics had been organizing protests since 1925, with women playing a prominent role. These protests led to street battles and fatalities among protesters and army officers, as in Ciudad Hidalgo or Zitácuaro. The outbreak of the Cristero rebellion in these rural parts of Mexico reveals that, once again, the causes of the violence defined its form. In Chilapa, Guerrero, a group of women stoned the municipal president to death while he was taking an inventory of the church. In Torreón, a mob attacked police using stones, knives, and bags of chilies. After these incidents, the attackers generally fled straight away to evade official retaliation. In some cases, they gathered weapons and ammunition from wherever they could and began to operate as guerrillas, moving in small groups, ambushing the enemy, launching attacks, and then hiding as a means of countering the numerous but more cumbersome government forces. Armed but with little ammunition, the early Cristero rebels attacked only when they had the advantage, picking off federal troops from a distance. Such tactics aside, the Cristeros had little military experience. Some priests did stir up revolts, however, and even took up arms themselves. Father Federico, of San José de Gracia, had read about the doctrine of the just war and was in contact with Catholics in the cities who were organizing a resistance movement. The uprising combined—without much coherence—various visions about the appropriate method of fighting. The rebels allegedly believed that bullets would not touch them if they shouted "¡Viva Cristo rey!" or wore a scapular—a certainty that turned them into fearsome adversaries in the eyes of the federal troops. In his 1944 novel *Dios en la tierra* (God on Earth), José Revueltas described the mutual and irreconcilable hatred between both sides.

The government's counteroffensive attests to the confusion sown by these fanatics, whose tactics resembled those of the revolutionaries sixteen years previously but lacked any clear political or economic logic. The immediate official response was similar to that of the Porfirio Díaz regime: tens of thousands of infantry and cavalry troops were deployed, along with artillery that now included new military hardware such as aircraft and Thompson submachine guns. What was new in this confrontation was the evident resentment of these seemingly implacable enemies. During the Cristero War, the postrevolutionary government forces used extreme physical violence against rebel Catholics. In this way, word would spread to other Catholics and act as a deterrent. Anticlericalism took the short step from the symbolic to the physical through orders to execute, torture, and rape the regime's enemies in the name of the law.

This threat was initially expressed in the language of executions. As we saw in chapter 1, these became a central part of the revolutionary experience, exemplifying the arbitrariness or chaos of the period. Within the context of the religious conflict, the death of an individual punished a group. A priest's execution led to suffering among his flock, who no longer had his protection. Many priests, perhaps more than a hundred, were executed, even though the church hierarchy had forbidden them from taking up arms; they were supposed only to give spiritual succor to the rebels. Religious sculptures continued to be shot, mocking the belief that inanimate objects could have human attributes. Threatening execution proved an effective form of extortion for military commanders in need of resources.

Death by firing squad produced images that proved useful for both sides. The photographs of the Catholic facing the line of soldiers or agraristas became a new type of icon representing the moment of martyrdom. The images of Agustín Pro, who attempted to assassinate Obregón in 1927, standing before the firing squad and then crumpled on the ground after the shots were fired, circulated among fellow Catholics to confirm the martyrdom of the faithful. Renato González Mello has noted how, in one possibly touched-up image, Pro's soul could be seen rising up from his body at the moment of the bullets' impact. Cristeros' bodies were left hanging from trees and telegraph poles, sending a message to those traveling on passing trains. This display of executed bodies was a more extreme reflection of what Ben Fallaw has called "barracks anticlericalism." The photographs of Cristeros hanging by their necks carried a crystal-clear message: the punishment was collective, the government had the tools of modernization at its disposal, and those executed had no individuality. On the government side, dead teachers, agraristas, and soldiers also acquired a martyr-like aura. While photographers documented much of the revolutionary violence, it did not generate as many widely circulated images as the Cristero War did. During that conflict, both sides used photographs of the violence to create propaganda and support their cause.

Federal troops attacked the Cristeros, knowing that they enjoyed popular support; public displays of brutality therefore were part of the combat strategy. In Zacatecas, Generals Eulogio Ortiz and later Maximino Ávila Camacho used a combination of tactics that ranged from negotiating with the Cristero leaders to rounding up local populations and taking hostages. Torture was useful to extract information, but it was also undoubtedly part of an aggressive modus operandi that included verbal violence, looting, summary executions, and rape.

The Cristero conflict is remembered for the army's abuses against people, corpses, churches, and objects. The Catholics in urban resistance movements reported attempted rape by policemen and even sexual attacks on nuns. Jean Meyer collected testimonies that referred to torture methods such as flaying, burning, quartering, being dragged behind a horse, electrocution, and hanging by thumbs. Cristeros also abused their adversaries' property and women. On both sides, the type of torture preceding the captives' actual death was a sadistic mockery of the reasons for fighting. Agraristas crucified the Cristeros and left them to die in the sun. In a cruel synecdoche, Cristeros strapped bags of earth around agraristas' necks or genitals, or made them carry bags of earth as they walked barefoot on a bed of thorns.

The government resorted to the use of agrarista militia fighters because it soon realized the limitations of the army, especially its indiscipline but also because of its slow progress through unknown or difficult terrain. Agraristas were no less brutal than the soldiers; they assumed that the Cristeros were allied with the landowners who opposed agrarian reform. In some places, in fact, the early Catholic protests in the mid-1920s targeted agrarista leaders identified as members of the tyrannical regime of President Calles. From today's perspective, it appears bizarre to see tens of thousands of Cristeros fighting similar numbers of agraristas; they all lived similarly rural lives, often in the same regions where the fighting was taking place; their clothing and social class were of a kind. Some even switched camps, or chose sides for local or personal reasons rather than ideological ones. Yet this proximity between enemies did not prevent the use of extreme violence against each other. Perhaps it even encouraged it.

However, each group clearly demanded a different type of right: one side called for government intervention to secure access to land, the other rejected it to maintain religious autonomy and to protect property. In Michoacán, according to Christopher Boyer, most of the early Cristeros were ranchers who resented the agrarian land reform actively supported by Governor Múgica. The official historiography classifies the Cristero War as a counterrevolutionary movement manipulated by the clergy, but simplifying it as a rejection of agrarian reform would be a mistake. Anticlericalism was only one part of the Revolution's ideological program and the Catholic hierarchy had only tenuous control over the rebellion. Religious autonomy did not need additional political justification, such as the bishops' conservatism, to be defended at gunpoint. However, autonomy and local practices went beyond religion. As Jennie Purnell points out, various political identities came into play, determined by different local political experiences, but no less authentic for that diversity. Agraristas and Cristeros knew that rifles, by this stage familiar tools, would settle the conflict.

In parallel with the battles in rural Mexico, middle-class Catholics in cities organized themselves into secret societies that defined their own set of combat strategies. The Vatican and the church hierarchy kept their distance, at least publicly, and ostensibly rejected the use of violence. The National League for the Defense of Religious Liberty—an organization with thousands of members including Pro and José de León Toral, Obregón's assassin—was the largest organization in this other, urban wing of the anti-government movement. The league's aim included supporting the Cristeros, a term generally used for the rebels in rural Mexico, but also maintaining its own independence by using different tactics. Its work was not based on local community identities, and it had more ambitious views about the links between politics and religion. Other clandestine organizations also existed, including women's and youth groups, with a total membership in the hundreds of thousands but without any central coordination. In class and gender terms, the movement was fairly heterogenous. Women's organizations played an important role in moving money, correspondence, and munitions; nursing combatants; and, in some cases, killing adversaries. Women had greater capacity to infiltrate enemy spaces and use their social capital. This largely unconventional activism explains why the women's brigades clashed with male-dominated organizations, such as the league.

The members of the league and other organizations did not fight alongside the Cristeros in the countryside but took initiatives that reflected ideas about direct action already well known in Europe and the United States. They used explosives, poison, and assassins prepared to martyr themselves to take the life of their victim. Pro was executed for participating in an armed assault on Obregón as he was traveling by car to a bullfight in 1927; Toral succeeded in in 1928, assassinating Obregón as the former president and president-elect was eating a meal in San Ángel. At his trial, it came to light that some female members of the resistance were preparing to inject poison into enemies of the cause in apparently neutral venues, such as dances. Concepción Acevedo de la Llata, "Madre Conchita," accused of Obregón's assassination alongside Toral, exemplified the potential threat posed by Catholic women. Explosive devices had been used since 1926, such as the bomb planted on the route taken by Portes Gil when he was traveling aboard the presidential train in 1929. Although these methods had already been used by anarchists and other terrorists against President William McKinley in the United States and other high-profile figures in Europe, in the context of the Catholic resistance in Mexico their justification was based on long-held Catholic views on the legitimacy of regicide to defend the faith.

The Catholics' armed resistance was driven by a time-honored Christian tradition that associated violence with divine justice. From the earliest days of Christianity, martyrdom was a way of bearing witness to the human suffering of Jesus, who in turn had to atone for humanity's original sin. A number of interpretations for this phenomenon existed within the church. However, the definition of martyrdom eventually required a voluntary sacrifice when taking down a tyrant—whether this meant the Roman emperor, the caliph on the Iberian Peninsula, or the emperor in Japan, to give some examples that led to beatifications and canonizations. Warrior saints and martyrs played an essential role in the Christianization of America as devout examples and icons of local identities, and symbolic Christian violence was a favorite instrument for converting Indigenous populations. In the narratives and images of martyrs, shedding blood was not a punishment but a reward that, like asceticism and other forms of physical suffering, offered a path to salvation.

This long and diverse tradition, which in practice could contradict official doctrine, was appropriate to the circumstances in which Catholics confronted the Mexican government from the 1920s. At the start of the conflict, some thought that the martyrs' blood spilled passively (as victims of government persecution) was enough to regenerate Mexico. Eventually, the idea prevailed that blood could also flow actively in combat, as when warrior saints participated in the Crusades. Becoming a martyr while fighting against federal troops and agraristas was a collective route to salvation which, as in European hagiography, exalted virgins, deacons, bishops, and soldiers. Some bishops affirmed that it was a just war, a use of armed force that, as during the Conquest, did not contradict Christian principles, since the goal was to ward off a greater evil and to attack enemies unworthy of rights. For the hierarchy, the armed struggle was licit but needed to emerge from the conscience of the faithful.

For many Mexican Catholics, the war gave an opportunity for people to approach salvation and the kingdom of God with their hearts full of joy, by bringing justice to the enemies of the faith. Like the early martyrs of the Roman era, the Cristeros and urban fighters were tortured to bear witness to the suffering of Jesus. During his trial, Toral drew the positions in which he had been tortured after his arrest and showed them to members of the jury, not to deny the charges or retract his confession but to demonstrate his sincerity when explaining the reasons for his actions. By connecting martyrdom with political violence, the members of the resistance possessed additional conviction (what their enemies called fanaticism). The fighters' craving for martyrdom was something that the government could not match among its own troops or agrarista fighters. This apocalyptic idea was incompatible with secular values and legality.

Another aspect of this legacy of religious violence was the idea that killing a tyrant was a righteous act. In 1920s Mexico, tyrannicide summarized a hard-to-define political project. During his trial, Toral stated that when Calles asked him why he had killed Obregón, he answered, "I did what I did for God to reign in Mexico." Then the president, after thinking about his second question, said, 'And what kind of reign is that?' To which I replied that it is a complete and absolute reign over people's souls. No half-measures." Official church doctrine forbade regicide, but the idea stemmed from a powerful narrative, the story of Judith beheading Holofernes in Ecclesiastes, which Toral cited as inspiration during his trial. The hierarchy denied the legitimacy of this interpretation, but the rebels paid no heed to theological details and were so adamant about seeking martyrdom that they were prepared to commit murder. Those who chose this path offered their own lives in exchange for those of their enemies in order to free the Catholics and bring about the kingdom of God. In doing so, they also invoked a natural right to resist tyranny.

We know about these aspects of the Catholic resistance because Toral was prosecuted under criminal law. President Calles wanted to strip the defendant of the aura of sanctity given to Pro after his summary execution the previous year. This allowed Toral and Acevedo to describe and explain the resistance movement's doctrinal and tactical premises, directing their message to a wide audience following the trial on the radio and in the newspapers. Toral's lawyer argued that his client had simply carried out the obligations of his faith as a good Catholic, an argument aimed less at securing a pardon than using the trial for propaganda. Despite the lack of evidence linking Acevedo directly to the assassination, the charges brought by the Ministerio Público (the public prosecutor's office) and the defendant's witness statements revealed a political network in which nuns who had been secularized by the government but still lived in their religious communities, as well as other middle-class men and women, supported prisoners, organized social events attended even by government officials, and possibly coordinated attacks. According to the allegations, Acevedo and other conspirators kept the secret and ensured loyalty through rituals that included branding parts of their bodies as a sign of their commitment to the cause. This information is hard to prove (although Acevedo never denied it), but the prosecutors still used it to describe the perverse religious extremes of these sophisticated fanatics. Gonzalo N. Santos and other Callistas accused Acevedo of fostering promiscuous behavior among her nuns, revealing the discomfort caused by women's involvement in politics, particularly when it involved the use of violence—the supposed privilege of men.

Toral was executed and Acevedo was sent to serve her sentence in the Islas Marías penal colony, where she remained until President Manuel Ávila Camacho ordered her release. The church hierarchy had excommunicated her as part of a broader effort to distance itself from rebel violence. This effort contributed to an agreement reached between bishops and the government that ended the conflict in 1929, allowing acts of worship to continue in churches and some exiles to return. Many former fighters felt humili-ated by these accords and in places such as San José de Gracia a legacy of destruction, depopulation, and simmering resentment remained. Catholic resistance continued, especially in rural areas, and the violence inspired by faith persisted for the rest of the century.

This ongoing conflict was due to the failure of high-level negotiations to resolve the grievances that had surfaced during the fighting. One difference between the Cristero War and the Revolution was the greater importance given to the victim in the records of the religious conflict. Unlike the passive subjects who had suffered injustices at the hands of the hacendado elite and judges during the Porfiriato, the martyrs sacrificed themselves voluntarily and became examples of a kind of virtue that was contrary to the values of the regime. From the Catholics' perspective, this exacerbated immorality, women's disobedience, and the tolerance or spread of false beliefs; it also constituted an attack on the material goods and symbols that enabled a daily relationship with the divine. Those who met a violent death, actively shedding blood (their own and that of others), set an example for the fight-ers who came after them. The memory of religious resistance, mainly in regions such as the Bajío, was based on the images and narratives of such fighters and paved the way for new rebellions on a smaller scale, but which lasted longer than the 1927–29 conflict.

The second phase of the Cristero War, in the 1930s, was marked by rebel-lions that were more isolated and resistant to negotiation. The government was wary of sparking another mass movement through military anticleri-calism and the type of collective punishment it had meted out in previous years. Thanks to renewed land distribution under Cárdenas, the govern-ment was better equipped to make rebellion less appealing and was pre-pared to negotiate directly with local leaders. As a result, Catholic violence in the 1930s was more reminiscent of the guardias blancas and pistoleros who attacked agraristas and trade unionists in an ostensibly apolitical way.

However, this new wave of violence did have a political dimension that we could call anticommunist and patriarchal. First, it was a reaction—fueled by the conservative press and from the pulpit—against the ideological rad-icalization detectable within the government's six-year plan in 1934 and particularly obvious after Cárdenas's break with Calles in 1935. During the middle phase of his period in government, Cárdenas accelerated land dis-tribution, supported the workers' movement, incorporated Communist Party groups into the state apparatus, and continued an education project that emphasized secular and collectivist values. For Catholics, a particularly provocative aspect of this part of the revolutionary program was the new school curriculum, which included sex education and introduced gender roles that were less traditional than those commonly practiced by Catholics in their daily and religious lives.

Public education, promoted by the federal government, was a frequent target of this violence at a local level during the second phase of the Cristero War. Hundreds of federally appointed teachers were killed in a wave of violence that peaked in 1935. In the regions of the country hardest hit by the Cristero War, as well as in other states where the Catholic Church was particularly influential, such as Puebla, attacks on rural teachers were common from the 1930s onward. Many of these victims were women who saw the teaching profession as a means to have a professional career and to develop their progressive political ideas at a time when almost every other area of public life was off limits to them. These teachers were sent to remote regions to give lessons on new educational content but also to change people's customs, from organizing ejidos to preparing food and raising children. In Guerrero and other states, maestros and agraristas were often victims of sexual abuse and mutilation. These Cristeros argued that socialist education weakened families and enabled the sexual abuse of minors, even though many of the teachers who were attacked were women. The teaching of sports in schools was said to undermine gender and age hierarchies. As with the just war, defending these hierarchies was a natural right that transcended secular laws. The result, in Guerrero, was a decline in the literacy rate during the decade. Elsewhere, as in Hidalgo, this religious aggressiveness led to new cacicazgos, in cahoots with a government that was no longer anticlerical and willing to turn a blind eye to local abuses.

Behind this reaction was a project that still used violence for righteous ends. Since 1926, the church hierarchy had blamed the erosion of female virtue for the difficulties facing Catholics. Although the government did not have a feminist agenda (exemplified by Cárdenas's refusal to extend suffrage to women in 1938), socialist education altered domestic roles through initiatives, ostensibly to promote hygiene, for teaching mothers modern techniques to feed and keep their children healthy, and implicitly to show that women, like teachers, could occupy a prominent place in public life. The Catholic reaction included women's organizations that were effective to a certain degree in counteracting government interference; it also engaged in practices that combined ideological approaches akin to fascism, with outbreaks of that persistent violence that remained latent in rural parts of the country, and that justified the federal government's indifference described in chapter 2.

Armed Cristero groups were not responsible for all of these attacks on teachers. Often they were collective, apparently spontaneous acts, or instigated by the local priest or some other figure of religious authority. Such incidents could only be described as lynchings. These could reflect internal tensions within the community, but their common denominator was publicity, a lack of punishment, and extreme violence against female victims labeled as outsiders. Gema Kloppe-Santamaría has researched the history of lynchings in Mexico from the beginning of the past century to the present. Teachers were mutilated and their bodies left out in public. Their schools were destroyed, just as some churches had once been. It was not unusual for ears to be cut off, similarly to the mutilation of Chinese immigrants during the Revolution. The code of brutality carried a political message. Lynchings of teachers and other officials sent from the central government was an attack on representatives of the same regime that had deployed soldiers and agraristas during the 1927–29 Cristero War. Religion's central role in community life legitimized the use of violence in the eyes of its perpetrators, beyond any legal considerations.

The lynchings were highly coherent, as if each incident repeated the previous one, despite lacking any actual coordination. As with the attacks on teachers, these actions often had religious underpinnings. The practice persisted in the gap between different regulatory systems that the government and educated classes preferred to overlook. Unlike in the United States, where congressmen from southern states defended lynching and blocked federal legislation to prevent it for decades, the Mexican press and politicians almost always criticized it as a barbaric act, yet they accepted its recurrence like any other local vendetta. Despite this blinkered attitude, as Kloppe-Santamaría writes, publicity was a central theme in the narrative of lynchings. Frequently, the tolling of church bells summoned local residents to a public place to begin proceedings. The authorities' complicity was not limited to abstaining from prosecuting culprits; in some cases it extended to handing over victims to the crowd. The victim would be accused of various transgressions (child theft, attempted rape, witchcraft) and the only evidence required was the accusing finger of a few participants, often women. In front of the assembled group, and with as many people as possible taking part, the lynchings followed a tried-and-tested pattern: the mob would tie up, beat, insult, spit on, humiliate, mutilate, wound, and burn the victims. Knives, guns, and hanging were all used to punish alleged culprits. Bodies were left out in a public place to reinforce the message of the punishment. This is a characteristic of lynching: the punishment was chosen to fit the crime. It was not a legal relationship, of course, because lynchings were never formally allowed, but a supposed proportionality existed between the seriousness of the transgression and the cruelty of the punishment. This implied a critique of the state's inability to impose appropriate punishment.

The importance of this practice was often downplayed and attributed to a spontaneous and traditional custom of isolated communities. However, and although they expressed a rejection of the state, these Mexican lynchings were a modern phenomenon and had much in common with the original lynchings, in name at least, that emerged as a practice in the United States during Reconstruction in the aftermath of the US Civil War. In the United States, supposed acts of collective justice were fundamentally political. Terror sought to reduce the influence of Black people now that they were citizens with the same (constitutional, if not practical) rights as the white population. A semisecret organization, the Ku Klux Klan, invented a set of rituals associated with lynching, though it never held a monopoly over this practice. Lynching basically was an expression of racism carried out under circumstantial pretexts, often with Black men accused of disgraceful attacks on white women. In Texas and other states, lynchings also targeted "Mexicans"—referring to immigrants as well as US citizens of Mexican origin. Nevertheless, some publicists in Mexico praised this practice. One example was Querido Moheno, a prominent lawyer and former Huertista, whose speeches and articles, including one from 1932 in *La Prensa* of San Antonio, Texas, defended lynching as a higher, spiritual form of punishment: "[It is] true justice, which does not exist in the letter of the law but in the depths of the soul," thus superseding the formal justice of a corrupt state.

Moheno's argument was also racist, but it alluded to a different past than that of the United States. Since Madero's period, when Moheno was a leading advocate for the Porfirio Díaz regime in Congress, the Revolution was characterized as an invasion of barbaric hordes. The political cartoons of those years depict revolutionaries with the features used in Mexico and other countries to animalize Black and Indigenous people. Moheno and other counterrevolutionaries praised the self-defense of "civilized" society against such mobs. As in the United States, symbolic violence was the first step toward material violence. The link between US and Mexican lynching was also found in the process itself: the script, the excessive and public violence, and the impunity. Although religious motives were more common in Mexico, they also existed in the United States, where some victims were targeted for their Catholic faith. The history of lynching in Mexico, in other words, has enough in common with that of the United States to be considered a shared experience with historical and regional variations.

During the rest of the twentieth century, even after the suspension of the socialist education program, religiously motivated lynchings continued in Mexico. Victims included women and men suspected of witchcraft or desecrating images, as well as Protestants. The history of attacks against Protestants is particularly long. In 1944, Archbishop Luis María del Río felt compelled to call upon Catholics to repudiate these heretics with the collective and illegal use of force. In 1952, an archbishop declared a "holy war" against infidels—referring to Protestants and believers of other religions such as Jehovah's Witnesses and Mormons. Hundreds of Protestants were targeted, thrown off their land, or lynched in Puebla, the state of Mexico, Guanajuato, Oaxaca, Veracruz, Guerrero, and Chiapas. They were accused of not being true members of their communities and of weakening the integrity of a supposedly Catholic nation. These attacks, which sometimes went beyond lynchings and included the displacement of dozens of families, murders, and the destruction of churches, continued despite—or perhaps because of—the marked increase in religious diversity among the population. A well-known incident of this kind took place in Canoa, in the state of Puebla in 1968, when a local priest and others accused five university employees of being communists. In Chiapas, PRI and Zapatista groups continued to attack Protestant communities. As Monsiváis mentions, the authorities did little to protect them, in part because of the indifference of the rest of society and the attitude of some intellectuals and academics who associated Protestantism with US interventionism.

Lynchings still take place, both in rural and urban areas. Victims are supposed criminals targeted by spatially well-defined groups, such as local residents or communities, although not everyone takes part. Implicitly criticizing the lack of security and justice, these attacks use the same types of excessive and public violence against offenders. Tacitly, they claim that some social norms override legal regulations, while continuing to benefit from the same impunity they denounce.

Another aspect of Catholic violence stemmed in part from the wide dispersal of the Cristero War's second phase, and the lynchings of teachers and Protestants. Acción Revolucionaria Mexicana (Mexican Revolutionary Action), a group of Villista veterans established in 1931 whose militants were known as the Camisas Doradas (Gold Shirts), adopted antisemitic and anticommunist ideologies and used violent tactics in the streets. The Unión Nacional Sinarquista (National Synarchist Union) called for violence to defend religion and attack communism, Jews, and Cárdenas's policies, in a combination similar to that used by the Camisas Doradas. The Sinarquistas were not so much pro-Nazi as anti–United States; adhering to the church discourse, they believed that Luther had instigated all subsequent hostilities against the true faith, a mantle taken on by the liberals and then by the communists.

Sinarquismo most visibly represents what Luis Herrán has called the post-Cristero Right. This movement could apply political pressure more openly and effectively than the Cristeros. It had half a million members in the early 1940s, although it did not attempt to challenge the government at the ballot box. The Sinarquistas also participated in the 1944 lynching of protesters in Puebla and other acts of violence. By that stage, however, their public activities had become awkward given the new entente between the national government and the church. The defeat of fascism in Europe made their style of mobilizing in squads less attractive. Moreover, the lack of an equivalent leftist force reduced their usefulness, and they were easily demobilized by the government itself.

The Camisas Doradas and Sinarquismo were a Mexican version of what was known in many other countries simply as fascism. As a political movement, fascism was defined by the creation of an enemy that was both internal and external, and whose elimination justified the use of extreme force. In the case of fascist governments, the state used technology and propaganda to support this movement. Paradigmatic examples can be found in Mussolini's Italy and in Germany's National Socialist regime, where fascism took control of these nations' entire state apparatus and unleashed large-scale violence through war and genocide. In both Italy and Germany, fascism began as a movement that used violence, initially on a personal and symbolic level on the streets; it mainly targeted communists, whose influence on the working class and other sectors of the electorate grew after the First World War and the triumph of the Russian Revolution. Germany provides the clearest example of a country that attempted to exterminate an internal enemy framed in racial terms, embodying Jews as a threat to the nation's "body." The defeat of the Axis powers in the Second World War led to the mistaken belief that fascism ended in 1945, surviving only in a few countries. However, as Federico Finchelstein has shown, movements in many countries—including Mexico—were sympathetic to German and Italian fascists. The Sinarquistas employed similarly nationalist rhetoric and engaged in practices similar to those of the fascists and Nazis before they gained power, including beating and killing workers. Like the Nazis, they sought to militarize their movement, but unlike the Germans they failed. However, the Sinarquistas criticized Nazism for its atheism and highlighted their affinities with Spanish Falangismo and the concept of "Hispanidad." In collaboration with exiled bishops, Sinarquistas used violence against "internal" enemies, as defined by a vision of a national community based on religion.

Other Mexican fascists had the support of Spanish Falangistas and Hitler's representatives, but they never came close to winning elections or posing a genuine threat to the postrevolutionary regime. Mexican fascism even failed to prevent Mexico from supporting the United States in the Second World War. The armed forces, born of a revolution after all, did not support it, while trade unionists and agraristas proved that it was not going to be straightforward to displace them with bluster and beatings. Workers' organizations were able to counter this aggressiveness because they were already familiar with *la lucha* (the struggle). These right-wing militants clashed with left-wing trade unionists, leading to the death of some militants in shootings and beatings. The most notable clash took place during the parade commemorating the Revolution on November 20, 1935. The Camisas Doradas took part on horseback and carrying firearms, but they were attacked by trade union members who objected to this right-wing, nationalist appropriation of the revolutionary legacy. The violence proved that a taxi was more effective than a horse in skirmishes on paved roads.

After Mexico entered the war, it became more difficult to openly support a fascist ideology, with its racist, anticapitalist, and ultimately destructive ethos. The Mexican government adopted many aspects of anticommunist ideology espoused by the right-wing, post-Cristero movement. A few political organizations survived. Unlike in Italy and Germany, but similarly to Argentina, such groups combined Catholicism with the ideology of hatred of the "enemies" of the nation and the true faith. They had to act discreetly, however. Some of the founding members and ideologues of the Partido Acción Nacional (National Action Party, or PAN)—a political party founded in 1939, and which from the outset proclaimed itself to be the defender of democracy against the authoritarianism of the regime—were sympathetic to the Axis powers. Some right-wing intellectuals, such as José Vasconcelos and Jorge Prieto Laurens, were former revolutionaries who had become profascist, antisemitic, and anticommunist and spread their ideas through national newspapers and magazines.

A good example of the intersection of Catholicism with fascism in Mexico can be found in public antisemitism and migration policies from the 1920s. A long Catholic tradition existed of persecuting and marginalizing Jews, peaking in the colonial period when dozens of crypto-Jews were punished by the Inquisition. The eighteenth and nineteenth centuries saw a continuation of the narrative that blamed Jews for Christ's death and defined them as a culpable people, though Mexico did not experience the collective violence of the European and Russian pogroms. In the twentieth century, this tradition reemerged with the onset of scientific racism, feverish conspiracies about the supposed global power wielded by the Jews, and then fascism. By 1930, the Jewish population had risen to about 10,000, thanks to an influx of migrants that the government could not entirely stem. This new phase of antisemitism in Mexico encouraged forms of discrimination that were published in the press but which were also evident in the restrictions placed on the immigration of refugees from Europe—despite the support of diplomats such as Gilberto Bosques, who issued Mexican passports in occupied France to Jews seeking to escape imminent deportation to the concentration camps. The Camisas Doradas abused and extorted Jews and their property. Cárdenas expelled the head of the organization, Nicolás Rodríguez, in 1936, and clearly deplored antisemitism, though he did not lift migration controls on Jews desperate to leave Europe for Mexico.

The Camisas Doradas were one of various nationalist organizations that attacked Chinese and Jewish immigrants during this period. Jews did not face the same deadly violence as the Chinese had suffered during the Revolution, but the symbolic aggression and antisemitism remained latent. This is documented in the pages of the official newspaper *El Nacional* and the letters sent by citizens to the Ministry of the Interior complaining about Jews and demanding their expulsion. Some Jewish businessmen were hounded out of their stalls in La Merced, a sprawling market in downtown Mexico City. The religious basis for this phobia did not disappear either. The authorities deemed Jews difficult to "integrate," implicitly linking religion to national identity. The bishop of Guadalajara had been preaching antisemitism since the 1920s. During the Second World War, the Catholic hierarchy continued to blame the Jews for killing Christ but also for supporting the liberal cause and financial capitalism.

Mexican postfascism emerged during the second half of the century in different ways but constantly associated with the use of violence and intolerance. The extreme right movements of the 1970s were a reaction to the new types of radicalization in the country's universities. Los Tecos (The Owls), the secret organization at the Universidad Autónoma de Guadalajara—Mexico's first private university, with close ties to the city's Catholic hierarchy—was an early illustration of this phenomenon. The Frente Universitario Anticomunista (Anticommunist University Front), active in Guadalajara, Puebla, and Mexico City, and supported by Los Tecos and members of the Catholic Church, also clashed with left-wing students on the streets. Their antisemitism and attacks on leftist activists, while comparatively ineffective compared to the government's acts of repression against guerrilla organizations, helped Los Tecos update or at least imitate Nazi violence against communists and Jews.

It is hard to know to what extent this idea of using the enemy's body as a vehicle for acts of violence as a nationalist or religious purification remains. Mexico has not yet seen the emergence of the postfascist populism found today in the United States, Hungary, the Philippines, Brazil, and Italy. What does survive in Mexico is a nostalgia for fascism. Popular expressions of this can be found in stalls selling Nazi paraphernalia in Mexico City's Lagunilla market, and in reprints of the 1953 book by the pro-Nazi Mexican author

Salvador Borrego, *Derrota mundial* (Worldwide defeat), which suggests that Hitler's downfall resulted from a conspiracy between international Judaism and Soviet communism. Borrego produced an unusual blend of antisemitism with Catholic nationalism, and thousands of copies of *Derrota mundial* were still being sold in the 1960s. This nostalgia has more subtle effects today, through racism and calls for a "firm hand"—as examined in more detail below—against criminals.

This brings us back to the initial question posed in this chapter. After our analysis, we can affirm that the Catholic religion was associated with violence during the twentieth century in Mexico, although we cannot say that religion itself caused the violence. The government's absence or hostility was instrumental in the use of force examined here: first, by taking anticlericalism and the reformist urge to the verge of a break with the church hierarchy, in an approach that hit the faithful hardest of all; second, by failing to punish certain kinds of violence such as lynching. From the 1940s, the central government's position moved closer to the conservative anticommunism of the Catholic hierarchy, which ended up weakening potential rebellions from the right. Some beliefs continued to exist on a local scale. This no longer appeared to pose a threat to government or the educated urban population, who could see rural Mexicans as fanatics predisposed to brutality and easily manipulated by priests and religious women, a population for whom justice was a mere fantasy. The evidence of lynchings during the century shows, contrary to these opinions, that calls for justice have constantly mobilized people. The state's neglect allowed lynching to substitute for formal justice. We should recall that lynching-related practices are modern, rather than the expression of traditional ideas about community justice, and also that religion articulated and justified such violence. Otherwise we risk overlooking an undeniable aspect of this complex and wide-ranging phenomenon that is religious faith.

There are two ways to succinctly analyze the history explored in this chapter. First, as an irreparable confrontation between two forces, church and state. Second, as a complex and violent web in which these supposed rivals actually had more in common than the first means of analysis might suggest. From this latter viewpoint, the persistence and brutality of this history can only be fully understood from a gender perspective.

In the first analysis, the clash between normative systems during the revolutionary anticlerical period and the Cristero conflict was based on two different—but equally radical—understandings of the law. On the one hand, there was the law of the state, specifically the articles of the constitution, and laws regulating religious worship, education, and land distribution. Observing these laws justified the use of violence, first symbolically but soon physically too. To defend this secular law, state agents engaged in numerous illegal practices and abuses. As the heirs of a revolution, they were prepared to use (frequently brutal) violence in a wide range of situations. The extremes to which the government went suggest that its goal was not simply to comply with the law, but to establish it. Executions and the public display of bodies, torturing and abusing citizens, and also desecrations, were intended to form a radically new law, a clean break from a past in which the liberal tradition had been betrayed by Porfirio Díaz in collusion with the bishops.

The Catholics were fighting for a law that they believed was above the constitution or any other human legislation. The word "resistance" was often deployed to characterize the use of weapons by Christians, a group that in principle should have rejected violence. The memory of the Cristero War has kept that idea alive, portraying the conflict as communities defending themselves from the regime's anticlericalism. The Catholics' mobilization did reinvigorate their faith, however. Martyrdom reaffirmed the supremacy of Christ. The blood of the faithful and their enemies purified the nation. Violence against teachers, communists, witches, and Protestants reinforced the integrity of an imaginary Christian community that was at once local and spiritual. In their struggle for Cristo Rey, Catholics were fighting to impose a new regime to transcend the division between natural and celestial laws, speeding up the dawn of a divine city on Earth, a new Jerusalem. However, the laws that would then be applied were incompatible with those the government sought to impose. Ultimately, this notion of justice was centered on divine grace. And to achieve that vision of a new government ruling the world, controlling bodies and souls, Catholics also allowed themselves to use extremely brutal force. Although they did not defeat the government militarily, the violent acts of the Cristeros, lynch mobs, and nationalist groups show the extent of their radical convictions.

This first interpretation of the link between violence and religion helps explain the fighters' motivations and their use of force. However, it does not elucidate their impact on the broader landscape of Mexican history during the twentieth century, which involved a wider range and greater numbers of actors. This is because both laws failed. The postrevolutionary state was unable to establish an unchallenged legal framework, as we will see in the following chapters and was already discussed briefly in chapter 2. Instead, it consolidated on the understanding that there were many ways of interpreting the law and other customary norms, and that little could be done from Mexico City to transform reality throughout the country. Or, to put it more simply, impunity and the embezzlement of public funds were not necessarily an impediment to a program of national modernization. The Catholics also failed to impose Christ's law. The secularization of people's lives and the diversity of beliefs increased during the twentieth century. However, there is one aspect of this project that we cannot consign to the past.

This brings us to the second analytical approach referred to above, and which connects to this book's final chapter. A common denominator exists in the destruction and death wrought by all the actors in this history; in the simplest terms, it was about keeping women in a subordinate position within society. We have seen in this chapter how anticlerical forces associated women—and particularly those of a certain age—with religious worship. Fanaticism, they thought, was something women injected into children's minds. And because the priests manipulated them, it was preferable not to give them the vote. Catholics, meanwhile, were fighting to defend an idea of family and society in which both were linked to a patriarchal hierarchy. They saw secularism both as an effect and a cause of the loss of young women's chastity. Fascism was also based on an exclusively masculine idea of politics and on limiting women's role to the reproductive service of the nation.

Violence itself, in practice, illustrated these masculinist attitudes more accurately than any discourse: sexual abuse and symbolic and physical attacks on Catholics' daily practices, where women played a more socially prominent role than in politics, were part of the government's offensive strategy, while women schoolteachers were targeted by Cristeros and lynch mobs. The paradox of this patriarchal violence is that it unwittingly created forces that challenged it: on the one hand, women schoolteachers, who reminded the government of the enormous importance of their participation in the postrevolutionary regime's project of improving education and hygiene; on the other, women fighters within the Catholic resistance demonstrated their ability to organize and stand firm against the government, even when this meant going against the hierarchy's dictates.

CHAPTER FOUR

PISTOLEROS AND OTHER CRIMINALS

—

B Y 1940, with the end of the civil wars and decline in agrarian violence, Mexico appeared to be entering a period of peace. History
books describing the country's newfound political stability and
economic growth during these decades offer this image of Mexico during
the country's urbanization. City populations swelled, while the number of
Mexicans living in rural areas also increased in absolute terms. More than
6 million people, most of them from poor communities, migrated from the
countryside to cities between 1940 and 1970. This economic boom came to
an abrupt halt in the mid-1970s.

An analysis of this period from the perspective of most Mexicans, particularly in the cities, reveals a new type of violence, one motivated by profit
rather than ideology. Common crimes became a daily concern; violence was
no longer seen as a clash of value systems. At around the midpoint of the
century, a range of attitudes emerged in relation to criminal offenses, and
the state's response to them. A sliding scale of values could be seen along

two axes: one running from the prohibited to the allowed, and another from the violent to the peaceful.

Figure 4.1 gives the axes of this historical analysis. There are no clearly defined parties; no universally accepted borders between the good and the bad. The state is not even a reference point for drawing any dividing lines, since it never achieved a monopoly on the legitimate use of force. In fact, state agents often used force for illegitimate purposes, so most Mexicans did not clearly distinguish between criminals and the police. This was a period of ambiguity, as opposed to the firmly held convictions that led to so many fatalities in the first decades of the twentieth century.

From the perspective of the history of crime, the paradox of these decades is that while violence became less prevalent, Mexicans' experience suggested that crime was an inevitable part of life. For the generations who had not experienced the civil wars of earlier decades, it became harder to know where danger came from, and cities no longer offered a safe haven. The result was something I have called "criminal literacy"—an empirical knowledge of crime and justice, separate from any moral judgment, something everyone needed in order to navigate the labyrinth of danger and opportunity that was modern life. People gleaned this knowledge from *nota roja* crime news, movies, and rumors, and used these insights into the practices of criminals and the police to avoid them.

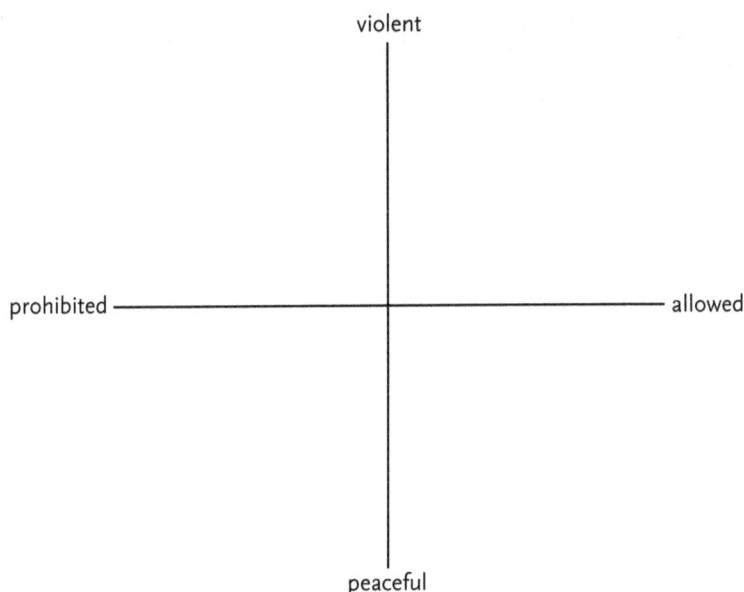

FIGURE 4.1. Attitudes toward violence.

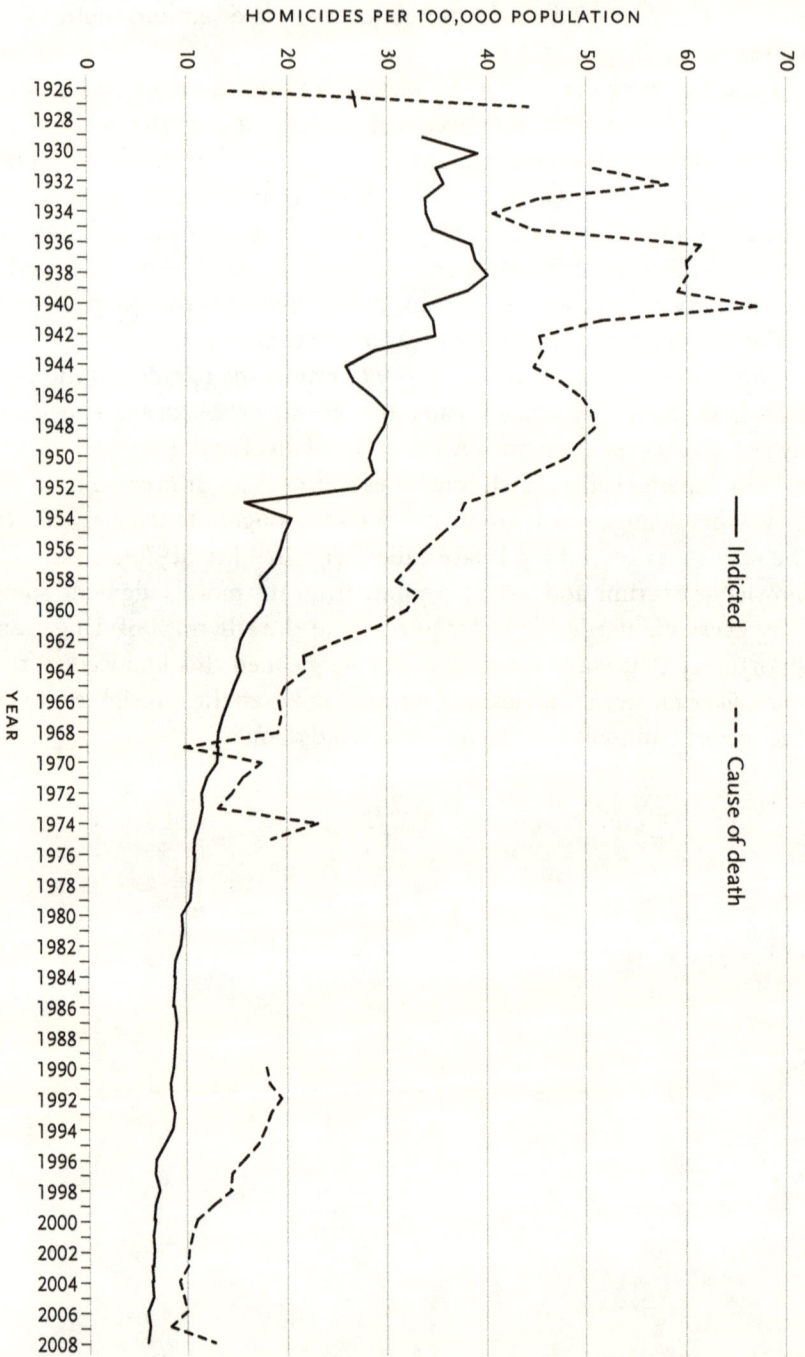

HOMICIDES PER 100,000 POPULATION

— Indicted

- - - Cause of death

FIGURE 4.2. Homicide, indicted, and as cause of death (1926–2007). Source: Pablo Piccato, "Estadísticas del crimen en México: Series históricas, 1901–2001," 2003, www.columbia.edu/~pp143/estadisticascrimen/EstadisticasSigloXX.htm.

Criminal justice statistics reveal that violent crime was on the decline. Based on how many cases were brought to trial, homicide rates fell after the 1940s, even after factoring in population growth (see figure 4.2). The number of people appearing before a judge is always lower than the number of crimes actually committed. Many offenses are not reported or investigated. However, the number remains a useful indicator because at least it tells us whether crime rates are rising or falling. In the late 1930s, the national rate of court cases for homicide (the number of those standing trial per 100,000 inhabitants) was about 40. The downward trend started in the late 1930s, though a few years later in Michoacán, Nayarit, Morelos, Mexico City, Guerrero, and Nuevo León. Figure 4.2 also shows the homicide rate calculated by the medical authorities, in other words by cause of death, a number that includes cases not brought before a judge. The figures clearly reveal that, in every region, the 1950s were less violent than the preceding two decades, marking a tendency that would continue for the rest of the century. By 1980, the rate of people brought to trial had dropped to 10 per 100,000. States reached this level at different points: Yucatán and the Federal District in the mid-1940s and early 1950s, respectively, while Sinaloa and Oaxaca only managed to do so—and only briefly—in the early 1980s. It was not until the 1990s that the rate began to climb again in some states, such as Sinaloa and Baja California, while the national rate kept falling. In 2015, the homicide rate was 11.92 per 100,000 inhabitants.

This is no longer how we measure the number of homicides. Today, the figure is not based on court files but on the more comprehensive information from police and forensic authorities. The gap between homicide investigations and actual homicides has widened considerably in recent years. The vast majority of cases do not go to trial, let alone lead to a conviction. In late 2018, Mexico's homicide rate according to the new counting hovered at around 25 homicides per 100,000 inhabitants, a high figure compared to most other countries around the world, but no higher than the number recorded in Venezuela (89), El Salvador (60), or Honduras (55). In the historical data presented in figure 4.2 I use the number of cases brought to trial because, despite being imperfect when making comparisons to the present or to other countries, it is the only indicator used over a long enough period to reveal long-term trends.

In a country where the arm of the law can hardly be described as long, we should keep in mind that the decreasing number of people brought to justice for violent crimes could be a misleading statistic. It could be argued that fewer homicides were registered in the second half of the century simply because the police and the Ministerio Público (public prosecutor's office) were less interested in investigating such crimes. However, that is unlikely because the authorities are legally obliged to investigate a crime that leaves such solid evidence (a dead body). We could also contend that fewer people became homicide victims because of improved healthcare services, and a wound that might once have been fatal due to an infection or a lack of proper medical care was now listed as an injury. Antibiotics had just such an effect in other cities, such as New York; and in the second half of the century, Red Cross ambulances were a common sight in city streets and on the pages of the nota roja. However, injury rates—a statistic that even the best medical treatment should not be able to affect—decreased in parallel with the homicide rate during the same period. The number of homicides fell as a proportion of all deaths recorded by medical institutions, a significant piece of data since it comes from official sources other than court files. The decline in violence cannot therefore be simply attributed to improved medical care or a waning interest on the part of the police and courts in prosecuting these crimes.

These figures were not available to people at the time, nor did they reflect their experience. Everyday observations in press reports, movies, works of fiction, and other sources are focused more on a new type of criminal behavior, one that posed a greater threat because it seemed to benefit from official protection. People still felt that danger was constantly lurking. News stories and rumors spread by the media and word of mouth contradicted any notion that urbanization was synonymous with security and justice. Criminal violence ranged from routine domestic frays and attacks by individuals or gangs on unlit streets to cases of notorious serial killers and bank robbers. The best-known example was Gregorio "El Goyo" Cárdenas, who killed four women in 1942 (a number that might seem trifling to us today) and spent the following decades in La Castañeda psychiatric hospital and the Lecumberri prison. His grisly crimes earned him celebrity status; however, sex workers faced similar dangers on a routine basis, as we will see in chapter 7. The true danger, as anyone with criminal literacy knew, was not posed by pathological individuals such as Cárdenas. An article published in *Revista de Policía* in 1965 referred to how "new types of evil" were organized as a "collective crime" committed by mafias and youth gangs. *Últimas Noticias* contrasted Cárdenas with a more common figure: "The pistolero is the natural-born criminal. . . . His job is to kill and when his boss tells him to take someone out, he'll calmly go about his business; and then he'll commit the same crime again when ordered to do so."

Exponents of this type of criminal danger were men who specialized in using firearms, instilling fear and avoiding punishment. Initially the word "pistolero" was used, like in other Spanish-speaking countries, to refer to common criminals who both robbed and killed. The term became more common in Mexico in the 1930s, and began to be associated also with political violence, to the point where *pistolerismo* was almost considered a trade. The ideal Mexican pistolero was an expert in violence and had the support of other men with high-level connections. All kinds of dangerous characters existed, including regular, small-time criminals who tried to pass themselves off as big fish. But pistoleros embodied the intersection between crime and power. A 1947 newspaper article published in Apizaco, Tlaxcala, described pistolerismo as "one of the scourges of Mexico, and, as a terrible legacy of our internecine wars, it has firmly taken root within the collective consciousness, morally corrupting many individuals who could otherwise be useful to society but whose unrestrained bestial instincts have instead brought grief into people's homes." Since the early 1930s, at least in Tlaxcala, murders seem to have been committed more often in cities by pistoleros at the orders of caciques and electoral candidates. "Politics" maintained the negative connotations it acquired within the context of agrarian conflicts, only now it was associated with the activities of those experts who prospered at the expense of citizens' safety.

Our contemporary perspective can be misleading when we try to comprehend the anxiety felt by opinion piece writers in *Don Paco*, the Apizaco newspaper quoted above. "Politics" was not the same as the state or the law. From the municipal to the federal level, significant leeway existed to make the most of the new economic opportunities offered by stability and growth. Gonzalo N. Santos's memoirs openly expressed this sentiment: "I don't know what the moralists think, but for me the *moral* is a tree that gives mulberries, and I also know that the politician needs to make a living from politics and to assign himself emoluments in proportion to his strength, because the stronger he is, the greater his commitments and responsibilities." Santos is a prime example of the generation of postrevolutionary politicians prepared to use force to achieve their goals as soldiers of the regime but also as ambitious individuals. Unlike Santos, most of those involved in "politics" did not accumulate large properties but responded to the same incentives that lay behind real-estate speculation or the embezzlement of pension funds practiced by others at a higher level. Illicit enrichment enjoyed a certain legitimacy. Santos recalls, for example, that when he worked as a customs agent in Tampico, some local politicians tried to bribe him. In response, he showed them all the money that he kept in his office: "I've earned this through my cunning and bravery. No one has bought me with this money. It's rightfully mine and I didn't steal it from anyone. It didn't rain down on me from the heavens but it's something I've earned, like I said, as a just reward for my victories."

To describe such practices as "corrupt" would be anachronistic, given the contemporary moral connotations of the word. The term was already being heard within the Partido Revolucionario Institucional to describe the greed of the Alemán government, but it became central in the public discourse in the final decades of the century, lending a negative tone to the perception of "politics" on all levels during those years. Government officials applied broad discretion to interpret, distort, or ignore the law for commercial benefit or to obtain bribes. But many such practices deriving from that discretionary behavior were not deplored by the public. Bribery, for example, could facilitate some economic activities and reconcile legality with established social practices. The idea was not to subvert power or class hierarchies; a malleable bureaucratic apparatus was simply preferable to a vertical and repressive one, just as it was better to avoid paying taxes and, as religious violence had shown, to follow the law to the letter. These arrangements were predictable (everything had its price) and allowed for the stability of illegal businesses that would otherwise have required the use of force. One example was drug trafficking, a widely tolerated business activity. Official protection allowed drugs to be consumed and profits made without the need for the violent confrontations that came decades later, when the pacts between government officials and criminals were disrupted (though not eliminated) by militarization and the alternation of parties in power at the turn of the twenty-first century. The quip that no general can resist a 50,000-peso cannon shot is attributed to Obregón. What we read today as a blatant celebration of corruption was a rational means of avoiding military coups in the 1920s. After the civil wars and chaos of the early 1900s, violence was administered by a new political class without any qualms about "assigning themselves emoluments" as Santos put it. Applying the concept of corruption to these moments imposes a retrospective moral perspective that took years to develop.

Corruption as a category also makes it difficult to understand the postrevolutionary decades since it is vague and can be confused with impunity. Avoiding punishment was undoubtedly a benefit of being part of the system. Public officials accepting bribes knew that they faced almost no risk of being charged with a crime. But impunity also applied to other illegal activities. Apart from the bribes that criminals could pay to stay out of police cells or jails, the inability of the judiciary, police, and prison systems to deliver justice was also fundamental. Impunity was guaranteed for anyone who could pay off the police, the Ministerio Público, or a judge; however, escaping justice was also likely if you calculated the probability of these institutions even becoming aware of the case. According to *Cuidado con el hampa* (Watch out for the underworld), a 1950s radio program, people hung around the Ministerio Público offices claiming to be friends with law enforcement officers, promising detainees that "their problem could go away" before the case reached the judge in exchange for a sum of money. These deals protected anyone who could pay, regardless of their crime. When Antonio del Moral was taken to the police station in 1970 for killing a woman in a traffic accident in Puebla, the tone of his words spoken in the police station illustrated this practice: "I'm influential, very influential. I've got enough money to pay off anyone. My lawyers will soon get me out of jail. Why all this fuss over nothing?"

For anyone without such influence, impunity was directly related to violence. Pistoleros could go about their business knowing that they would not be punished. The idea of impunity as the nexus between crime and politics took root in the late 1920s, when democratic opposition movements proclaimed civil rights that challenged the power of caciques and army generals. The 1929 elections—when dark electoral arts led to the defeat of José Vasconcelos—would be etched in people's minds because of the intervention of armed men who killed with impunity on the orders of their superiors. Santos, who participated in that presidential campaign and again in 1940 against Juan Andreu Almazán, explained with characteristic eloquence why this crime was necessary: "It wasn't a combat between French and Spanish knights of the Middle Ages, it wasn't a swordfight. We were fighting as Mexican revolutionaries against Mexican reactionaries in the usual Mexican way." Democracy found its antithesis not in dictatorship but in an ethic of "the struggle" in which the means were irrelevant.

In the postrevolutionary decades, when bribery seems to have become increasingly prevalent, under-the-table deals and other types of extortion by state agents corresponded to fewer violent crimes, as noted above. Impunity in the mid-twentieth century did not cause a spike in homicide rates and injuries, but it did encourage a specific type of criminal behavior. At the core of this criminal conduct was the link between the use of force and the illegal economy. "Politics" and crime were part of this connection. Violence was inherent in all prohibited activities where material gain was possible: it could involve not only the direct use of force in armed robberies or a contract killing but also a wide range of activities where the lack of formal contracts required the threat of force in order to seal mutual obligations.

To understand Mexicans' perceptions during those decades, we can locate the actors of this history in the coordinates of figure 4.1. Figure 4.3

shows the reality that I will describe in the rest of this chapter on the abscissa, now defined by the law, a frame of reference that is more relevant in the case of state agents, although without a strict moral equivalence for most people, given the acceptability of some illegal activities. As gunmen, pistoleros were in the violent quadrant of the diagram, but they acted on both sides of the divide between legal and illegal activities when working for politicians. Police officers were close to the pistoleros but their activities could be less violent, although they occasionally crossed over the line into illegality. The line between the pistoleros and the police could be blurred, and their intersection was at the center of the vertical line. Police activity extended down and to the right, to include members of various units less prone to bribes, to reach—in theory, at least—the technical investigative officers. Common criminals, or *rateros*, are on the left-hand side of the graph; they displayed different levels of violent behavior. Men who beat or killed their wives, a type of violence analyzed in chapter 7, are in the upper right-hand corner because their violence was legally sanctioned.

These axes detailed the danger in a way that all criminally literate citizens could understand; all members of society had to live within this space, whether they liked it or not. Understanding the law was useful in order to deal with bribery. The distinction between police officers and pistoleros vanished when observed up close, but a failure to understand this separation

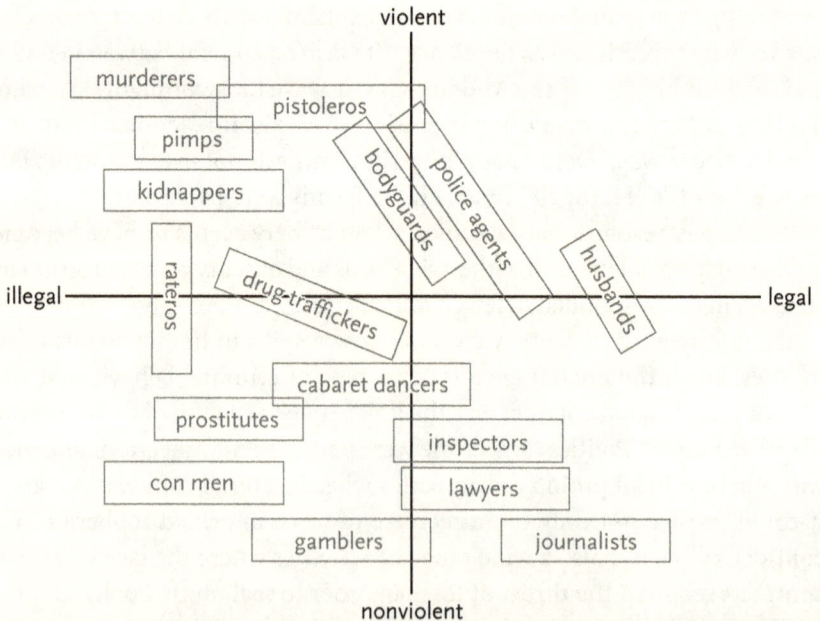

FIGURE 4.3. Actors in the history of violence.

was perilous. In a letter sent to President Miguel Alemán, Manuela López stated that her husband's problems started as the moment when, after his arrest in Tlaxcala, he was summoned to a meeting with Apizaco's mayor. She was not allowed to enter the room, which was filled with "various pistoleros including . . . the police chief Ignacio Alarid." Some days later, López tried to rescue her husband, who had been forced by those present to commit a political assassination, but she was beaten and raped. It was in her best interest to "know" her place because otherwise she risked being victimized and left destitute by this unholy alliance between pistoleros and policemen.

Understanding "politics" is therefore essential to comprehending criminal violence. The postrevolutionary peace meant a new use of force. The regime's consolidation around a single party and strong presidential authority brought a new generation of local and regional leaders to the capital. Many of these new public officials had fought for one of the factions in the Revolution. In chapter 2, we discussed the appearance of caciques in rural areas. While some of them transitioned into national politics, Congress, or the cabinet, others made their presence felt in the capital while barely leaving their home turf. Men such as Gonzalo N. Santos, in San Luis Potosí, and Manuel Parra, in Veracruz, used armed groups in their employ to amass power and eliminate potential threats from campesinos and former landowners. Santos placed these resources at the service of presidents and the party. Parra used them to expand his reach into the capital. Both were flexible enough in their use of force to respect the law if possible, or disregard it when necessary. As shown by the case of Saturnino Cedillo, who was killed in a surprise attack in 1939 by the federal forces pursuing him for rebelling against Cárdenas, there were limits to caciques' power: they had to know how to exchange electoral results and peace at a local level for tolerance of their misappropriation of public and private property.

Violence was a resource that defined caciques, something that they themselves identified with "politics" or the "struggle." From the point of view of civilians who began to confront local and state cacicazgos during electoral processes in the 1950s (such as Salvador Nava in San Luis Potosí, against Santos), caciques' use of force was actually antipolitical, a form of violence that eroded values and institutions. For Santos, however, democracy did not preclude violence. When describing the municipal elections in San Luis Potosí in 1923, in which his men used firearms to seize control of the voting booths to ensure the victory of his candidates, he claimed that the elections "were genuinely democratic and 'pistoleristic.'" This was the case in the PRI's primaries, which were properly competitive in the 1940s despite the lack of real competition in the federal elections. The caciques' distance from the central government allowed them to use illegal violence. As Paul

Gillingham also notes, the weakness of the judicial system and the police created a market for violence, supplied by the pistoleros and controlled by the caciques. The army, as the only force capable of controlling caciques in the regions, only stepped in when violence got out of control.

Homicide was consubstantial with these struggles. In his memoirs, Santos was blunt: "I've given detail in these memoirs about those I've put away. I've still left many others out. I'll mention them when their turn comes." In the end, "I'm not going to lose any sleep over one lousy dead more or less." Santos had a group of loyal employees ready to do anything for him, including assassinating adversaries in San Luis Potosí and elsewhere. Santos called these henchmen his *gargaleotes* because he recruited them in his ranch called El Gargaleote in Tamuín, San Luis Potosí. Their weapon of choice was the Thompson submachine gun. Associated in the United States with 1920s-era gangsters, these firearms could quickly fire rounds of .45-caliber bullets. They lacked accuracy, but at close range they spread terror and destruction. The gargaleotes did not need to conceal themselves from their victims or witnesses because they could count on their boss's support. Fondly remembering his cousin Braulio, his partner-in-crime, Santos described the ideal mix of brutality and loyalty that defined the good pistolero: "He was very smart, incredibly cruel to his enemies but loyal to his friends, his group, his party, and particularly to me."

Parra could also order hits in his region or in Mexico City. Like other caciques who were less attention-seeking than Santos, the weapons did not need to be so ostentatious. To kill Manlio Fabio Altamirano at Café Tacuba in downtown Mexico City in 1936, one of Parra's men used a .38 Special pistol loaded with at least one expanding bullet. Far from the city, pistoleros could use blatant and brutal violence against their enemies, and express their power more effectively. In Altamirano's case, the Mexico City press was surprised that the assassin was not a "ranchero" used to "complete and utter impunity." On the contrary, "the pistolero who killed Altamirano, ... looked like a city gangster, well versed in violent North American films." After Altamirano's murder, several anonymous letters referred to the background of Parra's pistoleros, some of whom had "committed more than twenty murders." In Veracruz, as noted above, the violence of Mano Negra's "antiagrarista terrorism" claimed thousands of lives between the 1930s and 1940s. When Parra died in 1943, his pistoleros lost political protection and "revenge broke out" among the relatives of those killed.

Rural pistolerismo shifted to the cities, first as a frightening yet distant image and later as a series of violent practices. Whereas few witnesses of this violence were prepared to speak up in rural areas, it was harder to hide from the gaze of city dwellers. These accounts of cacique brutality cast a threatening shadow at a time when many saw the country moving inexorably toward modernization, urbanization, and industrialization. An opinion piece in *Excélsior* in 1939 described "an atmosphere of unruliness and insecurity that stokes fear, clearly evident in the frequency of premeditated, cold-blooded murders, by individuals of certain local notoriety, friends, or partners-in-crime of leaders or public officials, or at least, their pistoleros; people who think that they can get away with their crime." In 1954, *La Prensa* expressed the same fear incited by the urbanization of political violence, in this instance following the murder of trade union leader Alfonso Mascarúa: "Does this mean that pistolerismo considers itself so strong, or public authority so weak, that it plans to impose the law of the jungle in the capital of the Republic?" An extreme example that few dared to write about was that of Maximino Ávila Camacho, the president's brother, who came from Puebla accompanied by "a small private army of assassins," according to journalist Roberto Blanco Moheno. This enabled him to become minister of communications and public works, where he skimmed 10 percent of all building contracts. Maximino's arbitrary decisions, such as forcing impresarios to use inferior bulls from his own ranch for bullfighting in 1943, sparked a public backlash that became hard to control. As Gillingham shows, the bullfight scandal was an effective means of reining in Maximino's excesses and showing that people in the cities were prepared to protest against the worst abuses of caciquismo.

In the cities, pistoleros had to adapt to the risk of publicity. Santos warned his gargaleotes not to use Thompson submachine guns during political campaigns because they could cause a massacre if fired into a crowd. Several murder cases also appeared in the newspapers. Altamirano, for example, was killed in front of many witnesses, including Diego Rivera and Frida Kahlo, who were eating in the Café Tacuba at the time. The man who fired the shot escaped from the crime scene in a getaway car. No one could identify him because, as it later transpired, he was one of Parra's pistoleros and came from Plan de las Hayas, Veracruz. His name was Rafael Cornejo Armenta. Neither was punished for the crime, and Cornejo Armenta was killed for unconnected reasons in 1952. In 1948, a similar modus operandi was used to assassinate Senator Mauro Angulo: shots fired in a public place in Mexico City, an escape in a waiting vehicle, suspicions centering on local politics, this time in Tlaxcala. In this incident, the shooter also shot a witness and the investigations led to other "superpistoleros." Three of them, including Armando Armenta Barradas and Marciano Armenta, were killed by the police on a road in Veracruz, victims of ley fuga while investigations were still underway. The difference in the outcome of these two cases, separated by twelve years, shows that disputes in the capital were beginning to be settled differently than during the period of agrarista violence in the 1920s. During his cross-examination, Marciano Armenta boasted of being a "close friend" of President Alemán. He was also allegedly implicated in the assassination of Altamirano. Perhaps his brazenness led to his downfall. Force had to be used more discreetly. Filiberto García, Rafael Bernal's character in his 1969 noir novel, *El complot mongol* (*The Mongolian Conspiracy*), said that the murders he committed while carrying out orders from his superiors "are unfit for newspapers."

We know about these cases because the victims were high-profile politicians. Just as in the scandal of Maximino's bulls, the unexpectedly large public outcry, first expressed in the press, surprised those who were used to getting their own way in their fiefdoms. Police investigations into the murders of Altamirano and Angulo would have probably stalled if the newspapers had not pointed to the "intellectual authors" based on information about local conflicts. Although legal process was not followed in either case (Parra went unpunished and the superpistoleros were eliminated in an extrajudicial execution), both illustrated the perils of exposing the caciques' violence to the critical eye of public opinion. There was something strange, in people's eyes, in this type of ruthless use of force, something that had made it even more troubling than the brutality of "El Goyo" Cárdenas, the famous woman killer. Cárdenas was eventually caught and his motives explained in traditional police procedures; pistoleros only faced justice when political pressure was brought to bear. Letters sent to presidents, stored in the national archives, offer many examples of citizens complaining about individuals with state connections (members of the army, police officers) committing murders and then being freed from jail without ado. One missive from 1958 referred to a military pilot who "loudly boasted to anyone who would listen that the President's office explicitly instructed the newspapers not to report on his case."

The authorities eventually became so concerned that they tried to implement despistolización campaigns. *Excélsior* claimed that these initiatives were doomed to fail, arguing that regular Mexicans did not carry guns because of the difficulty in obtaining them. "Therefore, only two groups in society use firearms: politicians and their bodyguards, who are not required to have a gun license; and criminals, who, as you would expect, do not apply for licenses to carry their weapons." The permission to bear "regulation" weapons could only be granted by the armed forces, which meant that influential contacts were needed in order to get one. Pistols, particularly large-caliber automatics (9 mm, .45, .38) became the instrument and symbol of the pistoleros' power. It is clear that, despite the opinion expressed in *Excélsior*, many obtained these weapons by various means. One campaign, in 1946, sparked protests because the police took away the weapons from the "peaceful patrons" of Apizaco's cantinas and cabarets, depriving them of their means of "legitimate self-defense."

After the 1940s, pistoleros began to embody a troubling type of violence that was modern yet primitive. Official sources make few references to this figure in society, but judging from the press and cinema they were a notorious presence in certain parts of the city. Pistoleros dressed in a peculiar way, slightly exaggerating their attempts to appear fashionable by wearing large shoulder pads, cowboy hats, or dark glasses. Occasional mentions are made to pistolerismo as such a specific type of job that, according to slightly ironic reports, the city of Oaxaca held the "First Congress of Pistolerismo" in 1943. José Martínez de la Vega's detective and satirical stories referred to "Matías, el pistolero," a man described, with more than a hint of racism, as "an uncouth fellow with a moustache trimmed above thick lips. Swarthy, well-built, and wearing a light-colored raincoat." Movies often featured criminal characters who evoked pistoleros but rarely alluded to "politics." One exception was Julio Bracho's 1943 *Distinto amanecer* (Different dawn), which portrayed the darker side of trade union struggles in an astute take on everyday reality. Pedro Armendáriz plays a trade union activist on the run from "one of Governor Vidal's pistoleros," a sinister character with dark glasses and a soft but threatening voice. Darkness predominated in Gabriel Figueroa's cinematography, in contrast to his movies with rural themes. For the audience, the reference to trade unionism gave the story an even more sinister realism. The word *charro* usually refers to a traditionally dressed Mexican horseman, but around this time it began to be applied to union bosses, after the nickname for Jesús Díaz de León, a leader imposed by the government on railroad workers in 1948. Firearms had been a part of trade union struggles since the 1920s. What changed in the mid-twentieth century was the urban population's growing intolerance of the more brutal manifestations of violence.

Pistoleros adapted to this new context in various ways. They continued to be used by the ruling class for political ends, only now in a more orderly fashion. The bodyguard, or *guarura*, was a figure who derived and was virtually indistinguishable from the pistolero. Bosses needed personal security in a world where politics was a dangerous occupation. It required the use of weapons that could also be put to other uses, such as intimidation or illegal businesses. Pistoleros also threatened and beat up journalists who jeopardized their political reputations. Roberto "El Güero" (The Blonde) Batillas was the bodyguard for underworld figures such as Graciela "La Bandida" (The Lady Bandit) Olmos, a notorious madame in Mexico City;

for movie stars involved in union activities, such as Jorge Negrete; and for various politicians. Tony Espino, whom Batillas beat up so he would relinquish control of the famous Waikiki cabaret, was another bodyguard for politicians. Later he formed his own criminal gang and ended up dying in the Lecumberri prison. Despite the loyalty expected of them, bodyguards often moved between jobs.

Batillas's story illustrates the vicissitudes of the occupation. He ended up selling cigarettes outside public toilets. In an "Autobiography" published by *Sucesos* in 1966, Batillas defined himself as a criminal, the product of a difficult childhood and poverty. "I've had a career. . . . . I've been a criminal; I don't deny the crimes I've committed. . . . I've lived outside the law, outside the laws made and unmade by the rich and powerful as they saw fit." Apart from his involvement in gangs, thefts, and attacks, Batillas was also a talented boxer. His story does not distinguish between apparently gratuitous acts of violence from crimes committed for business reasons. As a child in San Antonio, Texas, he forced other youngsters selling newspapers or shining shoes outside a hotel to pay him a "weekly fee for working on *my* turf." Becoming a pistolero was part of this same dynamic of fighting and stealing. He denied being the true culprit and laid the blame instead on "our venal and unscrupulous authorities, from lowly policemen in uniform to the high-ranking public officials, [who] mock the law." After managing the Waikiki, Batillas became an assistant to Negrete, who advised him not to go back to his criminal ways, invited him to act in a movie (Batillas turned down the role), and once scolded him for punching a man who had insulted Negrete. When he began to experience life as a respectable member of society, the police accused him of a crime he had not committed and he spent five years behind bars. During those years, the prison's governor appointed him "leader" of his sector, in charge of keeping the other inmates in line. Batillas had already sent the former leader and his assistants to the infirmary. In this position he received a kickback from everyone bringing drugs into the prison, but "I warned them that if there was any bloodshed the deal was over." His earnings, however, amounted to little, according to Batillas at least, compared to the millions that Lecumberri's warden earned through various extortions and embezzlements.

The most significant moment in the institutionalization of pistolerismo was the arrival in Mexico City of gunmen from Veracruz under the protection of Miguel Alemán. Alemán, whom Cárdenas had selected as governor of Veracruz after Altamirano's assassination, brought a group of his men with him when he was appointed interior minister by Ávila Camacho in 1940. Several of these pistoleros were siblings, and never left Alemán's side. Later, as president, he placed them in the Dirección Federal de Seguridad (Federal Security Directorate, or DFS), a government department established in 1947 to combine the work of investigating and acting against organized crime and possible sources of political instability. In theory, the DFS was meant to operate like a Mexican Federal Bureau of Investigation (FBI), scientific and powerful, but in reality it was a means to facilitate espionage and to ensure political control—which was in fact how the FBI's long-serving director, J. Edgar Hoover, conceived his bureau's operations. Over the years, discipline began to erode. DFS agents' badges were generously distributed as presents or forms of payment to "honorary" members who used them to protect themselves from arrest by other police forces. The generation of civilians who controlled the country's politics were uncomfortable with an overly visible use of force, but they were still happy to use their political influence to enrich themselves when the opportunity arose.

The line between pistolero and police officer was often blurred. For example, "many fake cops" used their badges to avoid arrest after committing a crime. They partnered with *madrinas* (godmothers), male police informants who helped them with their investigations and arrests. Showing the badge was part of a performance in which the owner combined displaying the ID, revealing the weapon, insulting and handing out a beating in order to stop "suspects"—essentially any defenseless citizen—in their tracks. Figure 4.3 shows police officers alongside pistoleros because of the connection between the protected use of violence and the interest in illegal businesses. To tell them apart, we could say that whereas pistoleros used the badge for self-protection when they needed it, for police officers it was a full-time occupation. As the pistolero in Bernal's novel ruminated, in reference to a pimp he had to kill: "If you want to work in pimping, armed robbery, and the like, you need a police officer working alongside you." Access to weapons and impunity meant that enterprising pistoleros and police officers looking for extra income could engage in lucrative activities such as prostitution and drug trafficking. The structure and fragmentation of law enforcement agencies, in which officers could be assigned to different jobs, enabled that flexibility. Police officers were rarely punished, even when witnesses testified against them.

It is therefore unsurprising to find that the difference between pistolero, police officer, and common criminal was not always clear cut. In Españita, Tlaxcala, three men killed Manuel Maravilla in mid-1946. The police arrested them and sent them to jail in Calpulalpan, but they walked free a few days later after giving fifty pesos to the Ministerio Público agent. There was no way of knowing, from the perspective of members of the public following the case, whether the fifty pesos amounted to a routine extortion paid by three common criminals or part of a network of favors and complicities that signaled that these three pistoleros enjoyed some kind of protection from higher up. In any case, no one expected them to be rearrested. The brothers Hugo and Arturo Izquierdo Ebrard, with links to caciques from the same region and the assassinations of Altamirano and Angulo, were a case in point. After spending a few years in prison (they were arrested after bragging about their jobs too loudly) they were released "under murky circumstances" and joined Fidel Corvera Ríos's gang of armed robbers. Arturo Durazo Moreno, chief of police in Mexico City in the 1970s, was the brother-in-law of the Izquierdo Ebrards. How can we classify Alfredo Ríos Galeana, who began as a police officer in the state of Mexico and became famous in the 1980s as a bank robber, often using lethal force? According to him, he was captured only because he could not afford the amount of money a senior official demanded for protection. Ríos Galeana calculated that armed robbery was more profitable than extortion or bribery. Therefore, he could not be classified as a pistolero, even though he enjoyed impunity for years and escaped from jail twice, until he was eventually captured in California in 2005.

This blurring of police officers and pistoleros, of legality and illegality, affected civilians' experience of danger. Even though the likelihood of falling victim to a violent act committed by a common criminal was less than it had been in the early 1900s, people knew that they could also suffer violence at the hands of those in charge of fighting crime. This did not mean that the distinction between pistoleros, police officers, and criminals had disappeared. What we can see in these years is the appearance of a logic that, from the citizens' perspective, gave a structure to the dangers. Money and connections meant you could feel safe even in dangerous places. In cabarets and dance halls, unruliness and insults were commonplace, making armed protection in these places a constant requirement. But according to one chronicler of nightlife, "in Salón México, a secret code obliged patrons to behave decently, or else within a couple of minutes a burly employee, a seasoned boxer, would show up and restore order." On the street, people knew that a bribe could resolve any awkward situation.

While citizens could not expect too much in the way of moral scruples from the former boxer, they were less impressed by police officers' readiness to accept bribes. Dishonesty aside, police officers' illegal behavior went in parallel with, or one could say required, their ineptitude at basic law enforcement duties. Throughout the century and across the country, particularly in working-class areas, people demanded security in public spaces and complained about petty but costly crimes like larceny or fights.

Arturo "El Negro" Durazo Moreno was the most scandalous example of the amalgamation between police officers, pistoleros, and criminals. He started out as just another thug, hovering around Mexico City's "scuzzy cabarets and cheap dance halls." He progressed naturally and rose to become a police officer; he was a childhood friend and bodyguard of José López Portillo, a DFS agent, and was eventually appointed chief of the Federal District police when López Portillo served as president from 1976 to 1982. During his tenure as police chief, police and criminals became virtually indistinguishable. When thirteen bodies bearing marks of torture and execution were found in Tula River in 1982, the initial investigations and suspects pointed to a link between criminal gangs and the police. His propensity for extortion, drug trafficking, and the simple expropriation of public property was an open secret. José González González, one of Durazo's bodyguards, wrote *Lo negro del Negro Durazo* (The dark side of "El Negro" Durazo), a best-selling book since its publication in 1983. This true epic of pistolerismo can be misleading since the majority of those involved in the trade— including González González himself—never acquired Durazo's power and wealth. The chief of police's greed and brazenness speak volumes about the exceptional opportunity given to him by his close relationship with López Portillo, and are in sharp contrast to the past. The fact that Durazo ended up serving an eight-year sentence signaled not the end of impunity but rather the need to respond to pressure from the public, for whom Durazo was the prime example in a long history of police involvement in illegal business activities.

Since the early postrevolutionary years, the police were known for their tendency to engage in illegal business. Gendarmes committed extortion, negotiated fines, and protected petty criminals, swindlers, and drug dealers. They had to share their take with their superior officers, obliging them to maximize what they extracted. These practices were fairly open and normal, a part of the job. For citizens on lower incomes, gendarmes were the most resented state representatives, frequently subject to insults and violence, particularly during the Revolution. Uniformed police officers always had low salaries and they frequently left their jobs. It was no secret that most police officers had negligible investigative skills and sometimes needed help from the public to solve cases or catch suspects. The nota roja regularly reported arrests of low-ranking officers for theft and rape.

Municipal police chiefs and agents representing other corporations who enforced the law through coercion were similarly despised, although people could not express this sentiment as easily. From the citizen's perspective, the common denominator was the threat posed by any law enforcement agent. This ranged from direct physical violence, which the policemen and higher-ranking officers could use without the fear of any reprimand, to the simple threat of arrest. No crime was necessary for someone to be detained or shaken down. Regular dragnets of dive bars and sleazy nightclubs produced a varied harvest of suspects, defined by their perceived membership in a particular social group rather than by anything they might have done: "the whole spectrum of urban crime in the underworld." The police could also fabricate charges, plant evidence, or simply falsify statements. Being arrested meant spending hours or days in a police cell or in a jail, places that posed all manner of threats. Torture was regularly used in police stations to extract confessions. Such techniques included beatings, strangulation, sleep deprivation, and threats to family members. The police's frequent denials of the use of torture seemed to confirm its prevalence. In jails, prisoners themselves robbed and attacked other inmates. Avoiding such a hellish experience required a payment—the amount depending on whether the individual receiving the bribe was a street cop, an investigative officer, or a judge. Over time, "the fraternity" within the Federal District police became apparent, a network of complicities that structured the Federal District police force, the pyramid of fees that its members needed to keep paying "upward," and the frequency of torture and car theft, among other activities in which the capital's police played a central role. Beginning in the 1920s, efforts were made to train agents and improve the administration of the capital's police force, but its professionalization was uneven and its reputation always weak.

In the Mexican capital and other cities, police units were found to be a revolving door for elements who might have criminal records, routinely get drunk, and find employment through bribery. Police officers' tendency to threaten coercion for their own profit was both cause and effect of the fragmentation of the different law-enforcement agencies. The twentieth century was marked by the appearance of a multitude of institutions under different commands and in theory with specific functions: the banking and industrial police, linked to the private sector; the Mexico City police force, in turn divided into secret service, traffic, and antiriot divisions; judicial, state, and federal criminal investigation units; the narcotics department, later replaced by federal judicial agents; and intelligence services such as the DFS. The main reason for creating new, unconnected police agencies was the lack of trust generated by the existing ones. This mistrust was very clear in the case of crimes where public pressure made it necessary to uncover the truth. Parallel investigations often undermined each other. Positions in the new agencies and units also created new opportunities to sell badges or offer positions based on friendships rather than qualifications.

In Mexico City, where the position of mayor was a presidential appointment from 1928 to 1997, the most usual response to addressing this mistrust was to designate a general as chief of police. When Obregón was assassinated, Calles used the Mexico City police to demonstrate the seriousness of the investigation. Since Obregón supporters mistrusted the police chief, he replaced him with an Obregonista general, Antonio Ríos Zertuche. For much of the century, the vast majority of police chiefs were soldiers. Durazo's appointment caused tensions among the military's top brass because López Portillo had promoted him to general despite his total lack of military credentials. Another response to the police's lawlessness were regular "purges," in which officers were fired en masse. The trick's effectiveness wore off over time. In 1970, there was a campaign in Ciudad Juárez. According to the nota roja magazine *Alarma!*,

> Various local media outlets insisted on the fact that [agents] had been dismissed for arbitrariness and extortion, although the termination of their employment was perhaps just a smokescreen, because as often happens in these cases, police officers disappear from one department only to pop up again in another one as unpaid "interns," forcing them to extort everyone in order to cover their costs and those of their family, while the municipal authorities just look on with their hands tied because they do not pay them a salary.

A persuasive explanation is that disputes within the state were behind the creation of these multiple police forces working in parallel. Each force represented the political needs of different groups. For those who controlled these agencies, a coordinated approach to fighting crime was less important than direct access to means of state coercion. This model, put forward by Diane Davis, presents the police as the product of the consolidation of the postrevolutionary regime. But if we consider the perceptions discussed up until this point, we could surmise the existence of another factor as important as high-level politics: generalized distrust of the police. Politicians and citizens alike approved of creating new institutions. They clung to the hope, inevitably dashed, that new structures would put an end to clumsy investigations and rampant bribery.

Distrust of the police extended to their role in politics. Beginning in the 1920s and throughout the rest of the century, the government used the police from Mexico City and other urban areas and the armed forces to suppress political opposition, often classified as criminal by the government. The urge to fine-tune this role led to the creation of the Servicio Secreto in the 1930s. The Dirección de Investigaciones para la Prevención de la Delincuencia (Investigative Directorate for the Prevention of Delinquency) was a crime bureau that operated during Durazo's period as head of the capital's police, while the DFS played the same role at a federal level. All of these new agencies would be better equipped to investigate and have greater operational discipline in tackling criminals and political rivals. But that capacity, generally deployed in a gray area of the law, was also used for less respectable purposes. Evidence shows that these political duties did not remove the substrate of illegal activities that permeated all levels of policing; if anything, they reinforced it. The careers of police chiefs such as Durazo, José Antonio Zorrilla Pérez, and Miguel Nazar Haro show that going after guerrillas was compatible with other activities such as stealing cars, distributing drugs, and kidnapping.

Pistoleros and police officers converged on the line separating the legal from the illegal because representing the law offered a significant advantage in collecting rents and making profits. Their motivation was not simply entrepreneurial but also the chance to earn a steady income with minimal effort, exploiting the complicity of other public officials and the sanctioned use of violence.

The threat posed by the police was a basic factor in planning any business activity, particularly if state representatives might question its legality. For example, what was the risk of an officer charging his "fee" or, failing that, expropriating the trader's merchandise? The risk was higher for a drug dealer than for someone selling legal goods on the street, and so was the price. Protection was necessary in both cases, either in the form of PRI-affiliated traders' organizations or through regular bribes paid to the political authorities. Police protection from high-ranking officers worked not only for the threat of violence they posed but also because it was preferable to pay them than to rely on the unpredictable appearance of lower-level cops. The latter were bribe-hungry because they in turn had to pass on some of their take to their superiors. Therefore, they could create awkward situations in which all the goods could be lost. In some businesses, like cabarets, pistoleros (whether they were genuine police officers or simply had badges and connections) offered the promise of order within this sliding scale of threats. It was preferable to be in their good books because, unlike lower-ranking officers and criminals who lacked protection, they were predictable and averse to scandal. This reveals a paradox also observed in other countries: unofficial actors (criminals) could be more reliable than their official counterparts. Pistoleros benefited from their political connections but they also made sure to keep their own interests and those of the government separate, because the latter were less dependable and more treacherous from the perspective of citizens who felt vulnerable due to their business activities. In other words, the resilience of extortion and protection rackets was not a problem that could be solved simply by purging public officials and police officers. The actors inhabiting this complex world of crime and impunity were part of social networks that involved their victims, who knew that, in order to survive, they had to learn to accept and navigate such practices, because they could not disentangle themselves from these webs.

A brief look at the illegal businesses that attracted police officers and pistoleros helps us to understand how violence was a constant possibility, even if its overt use was limited. In these businesses, actors with close connections to the state operated according to the same principles as criminals: trust was always personal, agreements were verbal, secrets valuable, and punishments for transgressions brutal.

Prostitution, drug trafficking, and gambling were some of the businesses in which pistoleros' talent could be profitable but the intervention of local police officers was essential—in the words of Bernal's pistolero, Filiberto García. This was because many of those activities were concentrated in parts of the city that were both appealing and dangerous. Businesses that existed on the fringes of legality, such as cabarets where there was illegal prostitution and drug dealing, were mainly found in urban areas where the local police could exploit their jurisdiction. This was common practice on the other side of the border between the Federal District and the state of Mexico, such as the "vice belt" in Ciudad Nezahualcóyotl that *Alarma!* deplored in 1970. Even in places like Apizaco, Tlaxcala, men such as Eustaquio Sánchez, the suspected killer of Senator Mauro Angulo, ran sleazy cabarets and trafficked women and girls. Red-light districts were a well-known but unofficial part of any urban area. They proliferated especially in the 1940s, partly due to the reforms in regulations on prostitution which, as we will see in chapter 7, led to the rise of new players in the business and more danger for sex workers.

If we begin with this industry, we see how sex work was linked to violence, despite the state's permanent obsession with regulating a business it perceived as a threat to the public health (of men). Prostitution was regulated since the 1860s. The legislation was designed to improve health and hygiene but had the effect of subjecting prostitutes to surveillance and extortion. They had to be registered, and legal brothels were set up around them to offer protection. The prohibition of brothels and pimping in the 1940s and 1950s merely fragmented the business, driving it completely underground and into that gray zone where the discretionary interpretation of regulations gave greater powers to state actors and their middlemen. Local police officers collected regular rents by exacting bribes (*mordidas*) from street prostitutes and their clients caught in the act. A US academic,

Norman Hayner, observed in 1946 that prostitutes were plying their trade on some of the most central streets in downtown Mexico City, such as Cinco de Mayo, San Juan de Letrán, and Madero. If a prostitute charged a client six pesos, she had to hand over two pesos to the police. The police also ran protection rackets that controlled brothels with official protection, particularly in urban or suburban areas notorious for illegal practices, such as Tepito and La Merced in Mexico City.

Prostitutes were particularly vulnerable to violence. Pimps acted as middlemen with the police and gave protection from abuse by clients. The 1929 regulations prohibiting their work were largely ignored. These men also used violence against the women they were protecting. For example, in 1942 Eusebio Martínez Cantonell (a.k.a. "El Cinturita" [The Pimp] or "Tarzán") killed the woman who maintained him, Elvira Baeza Baeza. *Novedades* described her euphemistically as a "cabaret dancer." In his confession, Martínez said he killed her because she insulted him in public. Relations between prostitutes and pimps were defined by informal agreements. Apart from protection, these arrangements were about instilling fear, access to drugs, and perhaps occasionally romantic relationships. Beyond the glamour of nightlife, the parallels between these relationships and those that led to domestic violence will be examined in chapter 7. Threats against prostitutes and partners were based on police control over, or abandonment of, certain urban spaces: streets were dangerous for any woman after dark, and avoiding danger meant accepting occasional abuse from a pimp or partner.

The consumption of prohibited substances was an illegal business highly conducive to the intervention of these "violent entrepreneurs"—the pistoleros. In the 1920s and 1930s, despite some resistance within the state, a prohibitionist attitude took root, prioritizing policing over health considerations. The Policía de Narcóticos (Narcotics Police) was set up in 1931, and from the outset its agents were accused of abuses against consumers and small-time dealers. Although the science behind prohibitionism alleged that drugs caused aggressive behavior, government agents were the ones who beat up and threatened suspects. Various federal and local authorities took payments in return for offering protection or selectively targeting an activity that was well-known and concentrated in certain nightclubs, opium dens, and other places where drug users could avoid risks by obtaining informal support from public officials.

In 1935, Cárdenas stripped the Narcotics Police of its powers, leaving the federal Ministerio Público and the Procuraduría General de la República (General Prosecutors Office of the Republic) in charge. But the abuses continued. Moreover, from that point on, the belief took hold that the justice system, even at the federal level, was incapable of taking on drug traffickers.

It was more common for the police to enter the business themselves. For example, Jesús Fernández Palacios, "a drug-trafficking kingpin and former chief of the Narcotics Police" in Tijuana, killed another trafficker, "El Chivo" (The Goat) Carbajal, in 1959. That same year, Leopoldo Salazar Viniegra, medical authority and critic of prohibitionism, published in *Excélsior* a letter to Dolores Estévez Zuleta, a.k.a. "Lola la Chata" (Lola the Flat-Nosed), acknowledging her talent in earning the favor of police officers: "As a generous distributor of bribes, you have become a national figure. No one has been able to resist your handouts, which I have heard are splendid." From the outset, as Sergio Aguayo shows, DFS agents were interested in the drug business; although it was still not a high priority for this bureau, it was already a parallel activity that helped supplement the salaries they received from the federal executive and the armed forces.

A type of exchange then appeared that marked the subsequent history of drug trafficking, as studied by Benjamin Smith: the inspectors, judicial police, and other law-enforcement agents who "caught" traffickers or users generally kept some of the impounded drugs, which they later sold through the traffickers with whom they had the closest ties. On the premise, perhaps, that someone stealing from a trafficker deserved forgiveness, drugs were an ideal commodity to be put back on the market for a 100 percent profit. In the early 1930s, in Baja California, for example, Governor Carlos Trejo y Lerdo de Tejada appointed a health inspector who was a trafficker in Tijuana, fought off competition, and resold confiscated drugs. The same thing happened in another important city, Ciudad Juárez, where the Quevedo brothers controlled local politics and appointed loyal men to public positions with responsibility for drug trafficking, such as the police force and the public health and welfare office. The system expanded from the border region in the following years. Under the protection of Durazo and other public officials, Francisco Sahagún Baca was a police officer who specialized in seizing and reselling drugs.

Producers and traffickers also fell victim to theft and extortion by pistoleros posing as police officers. In some municipalities of Sinaloa, including Badiraguato, these attackers pretended to be state judicial agents in order to rob traffickers, at least until the legitimate owners of the product reacted violently. Others, "passing as federal agents," extorted a trafficker in Monterrey, also in 1970. Implicit in the reports of these exactions was the fact that the culprits were pretending to be police officers, because the real ones had a closer relationship with the traffickers.

The connection between drug dealers and police officers was based on the threat of violence rather than the open conflict that, to cite a well-known example, had characterized the clashes between gangsters over the sale of alcohol in Chicago during Prohibition. The fact that many of the early traffickers were women, and that some spent decades in the business, indicates that firearms did not have the importance they acquired by the end of the century. Lola la Chata, for example, ran operations out of La Merced in Mexico City and consolidated her drug trafficking business in the early 1930s. She married a former police officer, and various high-ranking officials and admirers attended her burial in the 1950s. The heir to her empire in La Merced was a man whose violent crimes seem to have had a negative impact on the business. Ignacia "La Nacha" Jasso, a trafficker in Ciudad Juárez, married Pablo "El Pablote" González, a particularly chaotic pistolero who was killed in 1930. As Elaine Carey has shown, despite these dangerous beginnings and after being arrested and declared "wanted" by the US authorities, Jasso remained a key figure in international drug trafficking until the 1980s. She achieved this by forming an alliance with the Quevedo brothers' gang, probable culprits in the death of her former husband. Jasso continued operating for years after the Quevedos lost control over Juárez and the city's drug trafficking networks. The drug business at that time created a perfect space for the pistolero as an expert in discreet violence connected to the worlds of legality and government. El Güero Batillas is one example, having worked for Estévez Zuleta but without direct involvement in trafficking, except for during his time in jail.

By its very nature, drug trafficking spilled over from the urban spaces of tolerated vices and established more distant connections. Since the Alemán administration, police involvement in drug trafficking was the kind of graft that most worried the US government representatives in Mexico. Smuggling took place in border towns, although by 1931 Sinaloa had already been described as "one of the world's most important centers for the smuggling of all kinds of drugs, with the law turning a blind eye." As Carlos Pérez Ricart has shown, US collaboration and intervention shaped Mexican drug enforcement efforts from the first half of the century. In chapter 6, we will look at how the business metamorphosed from this relatively low-key, domestic business into an extremely violent transnational industry. As Ricardo Pérez Montfort and other historians remind us, viewing the history of drugs from a contemporary standpoint exaggerates certain aspects of an activity that did not necessarily have to develop into the monster that it became by the end of the twentieth century.

Other illegal businesses offered opportunities for those able to move between the licit and illicit worlds. These included illegal gambling and betting. Santos, for example, was already receiving money in the 1920s to protect these activities. We know about makeshift casinos in private residences, as described in Rodolfo Usigli's *Ensayo de un crimen* (*Rehearsal for a Crime*). This novel, published in 1944, was a veritable guide to Mexico City's nightlife—for Usigli a different place than the criminal underworld, because it attracted high society as well as hoodlums. Roberto de la Cruz often plays poker with politicians and members of the elite in the house of "El Gordo" (Fats) Asuara, until Asuara is appointed Supreme Court judge. In real life, Lázaro Cárdenas outlawed gambling and ordered the closure of casinos at the start of his presidency. This did not eliminate betting altogether, but it did make it less visible. This prohibition was a blow to his predecessor in the presidential office, Abelardo Rodríguez, who profited from gambling licenses for establishments that included the Agua Caliente casino in Tijuana, set up during Prohibition in the United States, with investors linked to organized crime north of the border.

Disputes over the control of casinos could turn violent. A clash with other organized crime groups also involved in drug trafficking claimed the life of Enrique Fernández Puertas, husband of La Nacha Jasso, whose businesses included the Tivoli casino in Ciudad Juárez. In that instance, the conflict was with other organized crime groups also involved in drug trafficking. Fernández Puertas was killed by pistoleros sent from Chihuahua to Mexico City. There were no political or judicial repercussions for the crime at a federal level, although it was well known that there was a conflict in Chihuahua between Fernández Puertas and the Quevedo family group, which led to more than thirty deaths between 1933 and 1934 alone. In Tijuana, as in Ciudad Juárez, casinos were a major source of revenue for local tax offices, and their operations were linked to drug dealing.

Other forms of gambling continued throughout the century, though without reaching the same economic importance as drug trafficking. Brazil's *jogo do bicho*, Argentina's *quiniela*, and US sports betting involved large amounts of money, but Mexico had no equivalent market. Those illegal activities were based on sprawling webs of buyers and sellers, networks in which consumers had the same or more confidence in each other than in state institutions. Mexico's National Lottery was a legal scheme that provided the government with considerable revenue, as well as patronage for the local administrators of the lottery and street vendors. President Adolfo Ruiz Cortines, for example, awarded the journalist Enrique Borrego the national lottery concession in Ciudad Juárez as a wedding gift. Betting at jai alai games and at horse races were sufficiently formal, despite being associated with certain illicit activities, so it is not clear whether it required the protection of pistoleros. Therefore, in addition to the lack of large networks of trust and the political importance of the official lottery,

Mexican pistoleros confined their operations to clandestine casinos. In any case, violence in this area was only useful if it was discreet, since the main beneficiaries tended to have cozy relationships with political authorities.

Abortion was one type of illegal activity prone to extortion by the police and racketeering by pistoleros. Terminating a pregnancy was a criminal offence; however, it was still available, and under better medical conditions for those of sufficient means. If reported, both patients and doctors faced high costs if they wanted to stay out of jail. Under Durazo, the police controlled a wide network of doctors and midwives who paid off the police with large kickbacks. The history of police protection of abortion in Mexico is still poorly documented, despite this procedure posing significant social and medical risks for the women involved, and being performed by a wide range of practitioners, from traditional healers to professional doctors.

Urban growth offered many opportunities for violence and officials' discretional use of the law. Migration from various parts of the country to the cities, especially the capital, created a sudden demand for housing that was met through the creation of neighborhoods in which the ambiguity over the ownership of lots existed in parallel with land grabs. The growth of cities such as Acapulco or suburbs like Ciudad Nezahualcóyotl created a clientele for violent leaders who supported and protected illegally occupied land. Construction projects, especially those that involved large contracts, were particularly vulnerable to such activity. At the time of Angulo's assassination in 1948, the DFS was already investigating aggressive behavior and fraudulent business practices in the construction of Hotel del Prado in the capital by one of the pistoleros implicated in the murder, Marciano Armenta. Other urban services created a new class of entrepreneurs who used legal and illegal methods. According to one complaint filed by three workers who did not know how to sign, in 1947 a police corporal from the Federal District controlled the Magdalena Mixhuca dumpsite and used pistoleros and union workers to control the sale of products extracted from garbage collection. The supply of food to cities led to new leaders who used force to collect high rents. Their control was concentrated in specific areas, similarly to the vice industries, and sometimes existed in the same spaces, such as La Merced market. The paradigmatic example of this combination of urban space, illegality, and official protection is Mexico City's Tepito neighborhood. Since the early decades of the century, this area was the center for trading stolen items, contraband, prostitution, and other illegal businesses. The fact that these activities were able to continue was due not only to the local residents' notorious aggressiveness but also to the organizations of traders and residents who controlled the protection racket in coordination with the municipal authorities.

The work of the pistolero found its most fearsome expression in the riskiest and most lucrative business of all: hired killing. Here, violence was not only a means of production but also the product itself. Hitmen could charge large amounts for their services and still remain affordable. In the 1970s, according to Veronique Flanet, in Acapulco a hit could cost up to 20,000 pesos, while on the Oaxacan coast you could find someone to do the same job for 1,000. The price varied depending on the target's importance. In 1954, Alejandro Ponce de León was accused of offering 75,000 pesos for killing cinematographers union leader Mascarúa, although in the end he managed to negotiate a price of 20,000. In 1959, *Detectives* described a certain Sabino Zermeño from Tamaulipas as "a professional hitman of grim notoriety in the pay of the region's caciques." According to this report, Zermeño was protected by the authorities of the Ministry of Hydraulic Infrastructure and its incumbent, Alfredo del Mazo. Batillas was a bodyguard who also killed people on the orders of politicians.

These are just a few examples. The shortage of studies on the history of the illegal economy is another result of pistoleros' dark arts: to be effective, they needed people to keep quiet. Discretion was particularly important in this regard. As confirmed by Filiberto García, the hero of *El complot mongol*, pistoleros had to be discreet and carry out orders regardless of ideology: "I'm just a pistolero. I don't care what party the dead man belongs to." They could use their weapons and badges and not expect to be punished, but they had to avoid public or brutal acts of violence since that might force their bosses to withdraw their backing, as Negrete did with Batillas. Filiberto García understood this, although he did not fully comply: "You need orders before you go around killing people. Once I went rogue and killed without orders. I had my reasons to kill her, but I acted on my own."

The illegal businesses described here had continuity and made economic sense, and they involved a very selective use of violence. They were often compared with the organized crime that existed in countries such as the United States and Italy since the early 1900s. In Mexico, people talked about "mafias" and were very aware of the example of gangsters. Apart from cultural influences, there were connections and parallels, especially around the prohibition of alcohol and drugs. But there were also major differences. In Mexico, illegal businesses had been flourishing in a similar way since the 1920s but without requiring the violence that the gangsters of Chicago and New York used to control their territories and settle their disputes. An enormous illegal market did not immediately spring up when alcohol was prohibited in the United States in 1920—an equivalent ban was proposed for Mexico by the 1917 Constitutional Congress, but it was rejected. One could argue that the protection and participation of government officials in these illegal businesses was a more important factor in Mexico than in the United States. However, we cannot say that the state took the place of organized crime, since, as we have already seen, the illegal economy and use of violence was distributed among a range of actors who did not follow orders from a center.

Reading the nota roja press and crime fiction, or watching movies with urban themes from this period, gives the impression of a country overrun by criminals. Mexico used stories and even words from other countries to talk about local crime. Even though it was not a case of imitation, images and reality went hand in hand.

The gangster figure appeared in US popular culture in the 1920s. Piggy-backing on the fame of Al Capone, John Dillinger, and others, Hollywood created an attractive yet ruthless cast of villains. This was achieved through a dynamic visual style: urban scenes shot at night, the acting of James Cagney, Paul Muni, and Humphrey Bogart among others, and scripts centered on the protagonist's rise and fall, with romantic liaisons, shoot-outs, and death. The characters' appeal was magnified by being based on real-life events and characters reported in the news. These movies were screened in Mexico; comic books and novels were also published on the same themes. The Mexican film industry also produced its own films. *Luponini, "El terror de Chicago"* (Luponini, the terror of Chicago) (dir. José Bohr, 1935), told the story of the shifting fortunes of a Chicago-born bank robber, whose gang members toted Thompson submachine guns and posed as police officers. Toni Camonte, played by Paul Muni in *Scarface* (dir. Howard Hawks, 1932), also used these firearms. In *Gángsters contra charros* (Gangsters versus *charros*, 1947), by filmmaker Juan Orol, who made other movies in this genre, the clash between the two stereotypes was probably an involuntary reflection on the dilemmas of Mexico's modernization. In both films, the subplot of romance revolved around the cabaret. The gangsters offered a stylistic lesson that went beyond cinema.

The lexicon of criminal literacy in Mexico reflected the impact of events in the United States. In a letter sent to President Miguel Alemán in 1948, Luis Ramírez de Arellano reported his uncle's killers: "*raqueteros* and pistoleros" who pretended to be members of the police from the state of Mexico. Mexican magazines translated articles by journalist Herbert Ashbury on the US underworld. In 1932, *Detectives* reported "Detroit in the Grip of Pistoleros." In Mexico, *el hampa* traditionally referred to the criminal sphere and imbued the spaces of danger and illegality with a coherence that they lacked in reality. In the world of contemporary gangsters, unlike visions of crime in the late 1800s, danger was no longer confined to specific parts of the city. The threat now came from shadowy organizations that not only occupied the underworld but also dwelt in places associated with luxury and with connections beyond the city and the country's borders. "Mafia" (often spelled "maffia") was the most commonly used word, especially in nota roja articles.

The Mafia emerged as a regional phenomenon in eastern Sicily. To use Salvatore Lupo's definition, it was a network of criminal groups involved in legitimate and illegitimate business. Internally, it was based on the secrecy shared by its members, cemented by initiation rituals as well as family structures, ethnic solidarities, and a supposedly inviolable code of honor supported by the threat of punishment. The capacity for using violence was based on the combination of extortion and protection that enabled these groups to extract money from almost any economic activity. The mechanism was straightforward: the mafiosi offered a service to "protect" people from other criminals but mostly from the threat they posed themselves. Some of the kingpins went on to acquire properties and administer their own businesses, but they never cut ties with their group.

The Sicilian Mafia began to develop transatlantic connections from the late 1800s following the migration of Italians to the Americas. In the United States, criminal organizations with links to the Mafia soon incorporated different ethnic groups, and they eventually received a more generic name: "the mob." A common simplification based on racist stereotypes affirmed that organized crime in North America was simply a result of waves of migration reaching the major cities since the nineteenth century. Italians, Jews, and African Americans fleeing Jim Crow segregation in the Southern states were blamed for the growing illegal economies that involved the entire population. Nevertheless, the lack of political representation and segregation helped create networks that exploited the spaces of illegality created by the carelessness or complicity of police forces—which in turn had a strong ethnic coherence, only a Northern European one in this case. More than the criminals' ethnic background (which was always diverse), the emergence of violent, organized crime was the result of spatial and social divisions created by the growth of cities like Chicago and New York, and by new economic opportunities in poorly or overly regulated areas, such as alcohol.

Organized crime grew in the United States as a result of the ban on the production and sale of alcoholic beverages that followed the constitutional amendment in effect between 1920 and 1933. Given its illegality, the production, import, and sale of alcohol had to be based on relations of mutual trust for businesses to prosper. This was the only way to ensure the efficiency of the thousands of informal daily transactions that were the bedrock of the illegal economy. The meteoric rise of the business led to the most successful bosses trying to become Americanized in order to distinguish themselves from the poor Sicilian immigrants initially associated with the Mafia, and to diversify the identities of organized crime networks. The gangsters of Italian origin, especially those most in the public eye, began calling their association La Cosa Nostra (Our Thing). But regardless of the name, their activities included loans, betting, extortion, prostitution, drugs, and incursions into legitimate businesses such as transportation and construction. In some cases the control of trade unions provided an entry point for criminal bosses to become capitalists, as happened with Jewish mobsters in New York's textile sector.

Violence in these structures was inevitable. It was necessary when someone failed to honor agreements over debts or rents, or did not observe a gang's turf. The most notorious example was the 1929 Saint Valentine's Day Massacre in Chicago. Four men, two of them dressed as police officers, executed seven rival gang members in a garage using shotguns and Thompson submachine guns. The crime may have been a collaboration between the police and Capone's group, which was trying to control territories in the north of the city. But the cooperation between gangsters and state agents was never entirely harmonious. On the one hand, there was the implicit racism in the authorities' discourse on law and order; on the other, there was the mob bosses' dislike of the police, politicians, and judges on their payroll. Perhaps this revulsion betrayed the uncomfortable reckoning that they, the outlaws, were victims of the same type of extortion that formed the basis of their own businesses.

Gang violence in the United States diminished in the 1930s. This did not mean, despite what FBI director J. Edgar Hoover wanted to believe, that organized crime had disappeared after Al Capone was sentenced to prison for tax evasion in 1931. The reduction of violence coincided with the consolidation of "families" who coordinated the division of territories (for illegal gambling, loans, extortion, and construction) around the country. However, their power continued to derive from their capacity to use violence. The difference was that their threat was now more credible than before, enabling them to use it with more discretion. Corruption remained rife among municipal and state authorities, while the negligence of federal government continued up until the 1960s, abetted by Hoover's rabid anticommunism. At this point, after US congressional investigations and confessions by repentant criminals such as Joe Valachi, La Cosa Nostra reclaimed the place in popular culture that it had enjoyed in the 1930s, spawning new books and films, notably Francis Ford Coppola's *The Godfather* series.

Nota roja articles often decried Mexican "mafias" but no such networks existed in the mold of the Italian and North American criminal organizations. Various organized crime figures from the United States, including Benjamin "Bugsy" Siegel, invested in Mexico, enjoyed the warmth of Acapulco and participated in drug distribution, but they did not create a binational criminal organization. One difference was the smaller scale and fragmentation of the groups running illegal businesses and protection rackets. "Mafia" was the word used to describe criminal groups that enjoyed some level of protection from a powerful figure and therefore benefited from silence. The term commonly referred to networks within the police forces or to pistoleros with political connections. In 1948, *Policía Internacional* complained that the "terrifying mafias of organized pistoleros, nurtured by political interests, have become powerful in the provinces, and the local authorities mostly turn a blind eye." But the word was also used in 1957 to describe petty crimes such as those committed by the "mafia of ruffians and thieves that have organized a gang of pickpockets" around Calle Palma in downtown Mexico City. The lack of a famous homegrown gangster may explain why Mexican cinema's mafiosi characters were comically stylized, like in Orol's films. A realistic representation of organized crime in mid-twentieth-century Mexico would have been impossible in isolation from the role of pistoleros and the support they received from above, something that few films, such as Bracho's *Distinto amanecer*, dared to portray.

The stories of El Güero Batillas (based mainly on real-life events) and of Filiberto García (fictional yet true to life) can help us understand the disconnect mentioned at the start of this chapter: in the mid-1920s, criminals carrying badges were responsible for the most visible violence. Citizens could accept this state of affairs up to a certain point as long as life continued to appear more peaceful, which it did. Punishment was less important to criminally literate citizens, who knew that prisons did not prevent crime and some of whom considered impunity a price worth paying for some peace in their daily lives.

Although the trade-off may have been positive in the short term, it proved costly in the long run, as we will see in more detail in the remaining chapters, and as already mentioned twice in this one: the blurred line between the police's political uses and its officers' criminal behaviors combined with the potential of drug traffickers to alter the precarious balance of violence. The history of pistoleros is marked by the appearance of an expanding space in social life in which violence can be both legitimate and illegal, less frequent but posing a wider threat. Hannah Arendt's observations are apt here: the long-term effects of violence are unpredictable, even when carefully meted out; the use of force for political ends and financial profit exposes a state's weakness, not its strength.

Homicides and injuries may have diminished during these decades, but it would be a mistake to understand the process in purely quantitative terms. In this chapter, the period between the 1920s and the 1970s saw the emergence of new actors and practices related to criminal violence. This new phenomenon was defined by the fact that each criminal act was located in the coordinates of figure 4.3. In other words, even those forms of illegal conduct that did not involve the use of force (like embezzlement) were linked to those that did (such as kidnapping). The connection existed in the discretion practiced by the police representatives, Ministerio Público agents, or judges who decided whether or not to enforce the law. As a result, all criminals could be reasonably confident that they ran a minimal risk of being punished for their illegal actions. This did not translate into more frequent crimes, despite what one might expect by taking a perspective that assumes punishment to be the best way of preventing crime. What did happen, as we have seen in this chapter, was that criminal violence ended up being defined by a small group of actors who were experts in the use of force and fear. The power enjoyed by the pistoleros, the corruption of the police, and the lack of punishment of criminals were closely related from the citizens' point of view. Anyone with criminal literacy knew to keep a safe distance from these actors, police stations, and courthouses.

The trade-off was never permanent. The criminal violence described in this chapter became less accepted over the course of the decades in question. At a local level, scenes that years before were routine now became objectionable, as those in 1963 when the mayor of Escuinapa, Sinaloa, Mateo Camacho, regularly got drunk and behaved abusively toward anyone around him, "brandishing his super .38 Special and bragging about his power." The case of the bodies in the Tula River and other outrages committed by police officers under Durazo's command contributed to the fact that police corruption could now be considered a human rights violation, in a language that eventually became slightly more effective in defending civil society against the threat of pistoleros and police officers, and in defining the state's negligence toward common crime.

CHAPTER FIVE

GUERRILLAS AND REPRESSION

THE HISTORY OF POLITICAL VIOLENCE of the 1960s and 1970s in Mexico cannot be told in a linear fashion but rather as a complex web of memories and silences, historical legacies and visions of the future. Even the concept of time varied for the different actors: some guerrillas thought their cause would require decades of gradual progress; others wanted to precipitate events to achieve what they thought was an inevitable future. The government was perhaps the most rushed of all; it saw repression as the quickest way to resolve matters, at the same time trying to deny the existence of armed groups and to wipe them out. Violence was seen as inevitable and effective by both those seeking revolution and those trying to prevent it. However, it would be a mistake to see a symmetry between the two sides, or even refer to the existence of two sides at all. While the guerrillas never came close to taking power, the state forces always enjoyed a strategic advantage. During this period, both the revolutionaries and their repressors had to form alliances and negotiate with, or break from, other political and social actors who chose the path of nonviolence. Therefore, it would be misleading to describe these events as a series of strikes and counterstrikes; instead, this chapter surveys the main actors, episodes, and places in a process that still awaits a comprehensive narrative.

As Carlos Montemayor notes, rural guerrilla movements were an enduring feature of Mexican history. The same can be said about the counterinsurgency methods and abuses of state power that will be described below. However, for almost two decades, from the mid-1960s to the early 1980s, clashes between these opposing forces, and including armed urban groups, created a nightmare for many and probably changed the course of Mexican history.

When Rubén Jaramillo, his wife, and three children were killed in Xochicalco in 1962, something seemed to have changed. Decades earlier, Jaramillo had taken up arms to fight for agrarian and labor rights in Morelos. He had also laid them down again on several occasions, but this time the government was unwilling to enter into talks or offer concessions. This change in approach may have been the result of events in Cuba three years earlier, after a guerrilla movement formed in another mountainous region had overthrown the Batista dictatorship. Washington had become obsessed with this development on its doorstep. In Mexico, as in other Latin American countries, the idea that an initial *foco* (literally, "focus"; roughly, a localized small group) of guerrilla activity could trigger a political crisis and defeat the national armed forces was a source of inspiration for many who also admired figures like Jaramillo. For President Adolfo López Mateos (1958–64) and his interior minister, Gustavo Díaz Ordaz, these same possibilities were grounds to use violence against the threat of communism.

The figure of Jaramillo, however, had evolved in the context of the postrevolutionary politics described in the previous chapters. He had been a Zapatista and later played an important role in organizing campesinos and sugarcane workers in the state of Morelos. He was forced to take up arms after being targeted by pistoleros working for local caciques and other PRI leaders, or by army units taking orders from the federal government. He led uprisings in 1946 and 1952 as a continuation of protests against fraudulent elections in which he was candidate for governor. He first took up arms after surviving an assassination attempt, initiating a period of several years of armed self-defense rather than revolutionary offensives. In 1952, the rebellion continued with the momentum of the Henriquista movement, which had broader aims but was still confined to the state of Morelos, calling for the governor's resignation among other demands. Despite failing to seize control of towns through the use of arms, Jaramillo's supporters executed pistoleros and authorities linked to abuses that had gone unpunished.

Many communities supported Jaramillo, whose mobility and knowledge of the local terrain made him hard to defeat militarily. His story was representative of many others in which rebels championing workers' rights fought against brutal experts in violence who acted with impunity, targeting individuals rather than creating widespread terror, as described in the previous chapter. The attackers who came to his home to kill him were a representative sample of his long-standing enemies: soldiers, pistoleros, and judicial police officers, according to one daughter who survived. Ultimately, Jaramillo was a figure who had emerged from that brand of postrevolutionary politics that combined violence with negotiation: Lázaro Cárdenas's protection had extricated him from difficulties more than once; he had never had close ties with the Partido Comunista Mexicano (Mexican Communist Party, or PCM); and, since he already had strong local support, he was not an outsider arriving to light the fuse of a nationwide revolution and had no plans to lead a Cuban-style guerrilla uprising.

Jaramillo worked hard to give political expression to campesino demands, but as Tanalís Padilla points out, his group's radicalization was largely due to cycles of repression that did not end in 1962. On the contrary, in the history of subsequent revolutionary movements, the Xochicalco massacre was the first chapter of a story of state repression that broke the old rules. For those who came after him, this was the initial strike that justified, with all its brutal force, the decision to take up arms. First, it revealed that the political channels that Jaramillo had used as an organizer were now closed off, and that the local, state, and federal authorities were in lockstep when using illegal violence. But it also served as a warning: Jaramillo had allowed his enemies to take him by surprise, perhaps thinking that campesino demands could be resolved through traditional politics. From this point forward, it was important to gain a tactical advantage by taking the initiative, instead of relying on negotiations as the best possible alternative to the use of arms.

Changes were afoot. The presence of soldiers in the 1962 operation against Jaramillo, an assassination that local agents could have carried out unaided, suggested to many that the federal government, even President Adolfo López Mateos himself, was willing to become more directly involved in resolving conflicts. Whereas previously, for example, trade union leaders could control union rebellions through heavy-handed but discreet measures, the large-scale operation against the railroad workers union in 1959 was another sign that anticommunism was introducing new ways of using state power. It was no longer just about the personal brutality of pistoleros, judicial police officers, and secret police. Mass arrests were made. The crackdown on railroad workers only led to a few fatalities because the press could witness abuses in the urban setting. In rural areas it was easier to use rifles.

The use of force in labor conflicts was nothing new. Closing down a factory to apply pressure on its owners was a socially legitimate practice, although it could lead to episodes of violence, destruction, and clashes with strikebreakers. The government itself had deployed trade union members to attack its counterrevolutionary enemies since the time of Luis Napoleón Morones's leadership of the Confederación Regional Obrera Mexicana (Regional Workers Confederation of Mexico). In the case of the railroad workers, the success of Valentín Campa, Demetrio Vallejo, and other communists in defeating the employer-controlled trade union and starting a transformation in the working relations within an industry that was central for economic development led to an equally surprising response from López Mateos. Thousands were arrested and fired, and Campa and Vallejo were given long sentences for "social dissolution," which criminalized almost any political gathering. From the perspective of subsequent urban guerrilla movements, this was another sign that the proletariat had little choice but to take up arms.

The history of revolutionary guerrilla movements in Mexico began, however, with the attack on the army barracks in Ciudad Madera, Chihuahua, on September 23, 1965. The attackers' goal was to briefly occupy the barracks, seize weapons, steal money from the local bank, and take over control of the local radio station to broadcast a statement. However, not all participants arrived on time and they lacked firepower to make up for their numerical disadvantage (about 125 soldiers versus 13 guerrillas) and the defenders' strategic position. Two leaders of the movement—called the Grupo Popular Guerrillero (People's Guerrilla Group, or GPG), without much ideological flourish—were Pablo Gómez and Arturo Gámiz. Both died in the attack, along with six other guerrillas and five soldiers. Ciudad Madera became an important reference point in the mythology of later guerrilla movements in the country, like a Mexican version of Fidel Castro's famous attack on the Moncada military barracks on July 26, 1953.

Gámiz and Gómez had much in common with Jaramillo: both had participated in agrarian struggles for years, had connections to political parties, and had once attempted to negotiate with the government. For some of their followers, the struggle was a continuation of campaigns fought alongside Pancho Villa. Gómez had held talks with López Mateos and various governors. They enjoyed local support but were well aware that landowners, their private security details, and local authorities could commit assassinations and had other means of countering campesino demands. The conflict in the region had led to land grabs, army interventions, and the use of torture against organizers. Gámiz had killed a landowner in retaliation for brutal acts against ejidatarios. Students joined campesinos at a series of demonstrations, protests, and strikes. As in Morelos, governors' interventions shut off any possibility of a peaceful solution for agrarian disputes that, in the case of Chihuahua, revolved around the control of land and forestry resources. Similar to Jaramillo's escape into the hills in 1946 and 1952, for Gámiz the most pressing need to go into hiding was to keep one step ahead of the reprisals for his social activism. Gámiz's daughter Alma told Padilla that her father bore scars from several such retaliations. For the Chihuahua group, Ciudad Madera was emblematic of their conviction that it was better to die fighting than to be executed. Unlike Jaramillo, they saw guerrilla action as part of a broader struggle, viewing prior organization as the basis for effective and armed intervention not limited to local issues but with the ultimate goal of installing a socialist regime.

Historians have characterized this as the first movement directly inspired by events in Cuba. According to Gámiz, in a text written in 1965 about student participation in the revolutionary movement, "No event had caused such an impact on the peoples of the Americas [. . .], nothing had raised people's awareness as much as the Cuban Revolution." The group that attacked the barracks in Ciudad Madera knew Che Guevara's prescriptions for guerrilla warfare. Gámiz had read them and Gómez had traveled to Mexico City in July along with other members of the group in order to take a "course in Guerrilla Warfare." Preparations included a couple of military assemblies in the Sierra Tarahumara. At the second of these gatherings, the group issued a communiqué stating that armed struggle was the only way to create a vanguard to confront the bourgeois state. This strategy required a series of focos that could trigger a movement that could last for decades. According to this document, the combination of state repression, weak left-wing parties, and intellectuals' failure to engage left no alternative.

The Chihuahua group also noted one of the lessons of Guevara's book and took it a step further, in a strategy that would resurface in Mexico's later guerrilla movements: combatants needed to be educated in the struggle, and the masses needed to be given the reasons why they should support the vanguard and become aware of the true nature of capitalist exploitation. Gámiz and Gómez were teachers, and several trainee teachers and their supervisors (normalistas) took part in the attack. In a text addressed to "students," Gámiz stated that their real education would come from "contact with the masses, in revolutionary activities," instead of through individualistic training at universities that would turn them into employees or members of the "urban petite bourgeoisie." Revolutionary violence served a didactic purpose. It did not require resounding victories but drew its strength from the careful selection of its targets and the heroism of its fighters. By 1966, the Chihuahua movement had been almost completely eliminated. Splits appeared after Ciudad Madera. Eventually some of the groups that emerged from this defeat joined the coalition that formed the Liga Comunista 23 de Septiembre (September 23 Communist League, alternatively LC23S or La Liga).

Despite the inspiration of the Cuban Revolution, Castro's government did not support the GPG, nor did it support Mexican revolutionary groups as it did elsewhere around the world. Good diplomatic relations with Mexico were more valuable to Cuba than the possible appearance of ideologically like-minded guerrilla movements in Mexico (even after the discovery that the Mexican government was helping the Central Intelligence Agency [CIA] spy on the Cubans). By the early 1960s, however, the example set by the Cuban guerrillas and Guevara's texts had already marked the course of Mexico's revolutionary movements. Yet a wide range of historical and ideological positions shaped by local experiences defined their different outcomes.

Here it is worth making a brief digression to consider the theoretical legacy of the Cuban Revolution. The violence of Mexican guerrilla groups was not simply spontaneous, even when delivering justice. In every case, it was a central aspect of a practice built upon theory and analysis. Régis Debray's *Revolution in the Revolution?*, published in Cuba in 1967, assembled ideas already circulating since the early 1960s and put them into a systematic framework. Drawing on his direct access to Fidel Castro and documents relating to the movement that triumphed in 1959, Debray summarized the tactical and strategic lessons learned. He might have been less enthusiastic had he written his book after the failure of Guevara's *foquista* approach in Bolivia, a struggle in which Debray played a marginal role. The failure was unimportant, anyway, because Debray's premise was that the past should not determine present actions, and that there was no reason why the Cuban experience could not be replicated in other countries. Military strategies had to follow a political line. Specifically, this meant that the guerrilla should not be an "armed self-defense" movement or act on behalf of campesino movements. The guerrillas, as a vanguard of the revolution, needed to be isolated from the rural society that protected them, and keep their activities as secret as possible from civilians. Acts of "armed propaganda," like the executions of public enemies, needed to be a military display of the adversary's weakness. Debray also advocated ignoring political parties and other institutions or laws that distracted guerrilla movements from their mission by leading them to think that the political rules of peacetime might benefit them.

An implicit sense of transcendence guided this theory: while the government was always bent on eliminating them, the guerrillas had to plan for the future and wait years for the focos to cause the regime's collapse. The revolutionary had to bear in mind that "life is not the highest good" in that struggle. Valor—and, by implication, masculinity—was something for the youth: "Physical aptitude is the prerequisite for all other aptitudes," asserted Debray. The foquista theory's impact in Mexico was the subject of lengthy internal discussions in the 1970s. In practice, its impact was attenuated by the fact that the most effective rural guerrilla groups, from Ciudad Madera to Guerrero, had deep roots in local politics, ruling out the possibility of Debray's isolationism. A revolutionary vision inspired directly by Leninism and the antifascist Soviet struggles seems to have had a more direct impact on their approach to revolution. Distinguishing between urban and rural settings was not so important that it prevented armed campesino groups from establishing cells in cities such as Acapulco and Aguascalientes. The largest urban revolutionary organization of the 1970s created focos in the northwest, Guerrero, and Oaxaca.

Two of the most important guerrilla groups of this period were established in the state of Guerrero. Despite their eventual defeat, these groups had a strong influence on other revolutionary movements, and their leaders remained legendary figures in later decades. Although the groups led by Genaro Vázquez and Lucio Cabañas appeared at similar moments, had shared origins, and overlapped geographically in their areas of operation in the Costa Chica and Costa Grande regions of the state, they fought the government in parallel. The division exemplified the centrifugal tendencies of the Mexican Left as well as the complex collage described by Alex Aviña as the "revolutionary politics of the imagination" in Guerrero, where the repression of social movements already had a long history. As we will see below, Guerrero also became a laboratory for the military's most brutal methods of repression.

Self-defense was the initial motivation for both movements, whose leaders were forced into hiding to escape government forces. For many years, Vázquez and Cabañas had attempted various types of social protest that invariably met with violent reactions from Guerrero's state authorities. Beginning in the late 1950s, both men gained experience and recognition within movements that eventually brought the downfall of Governor Raúl Caballero Aburto in 1960, after twenty-one protesters were killed in Chilpancingo in a massacre that marked the start of the rebel movement in Guerrero.

The events of December 1960, in which several students were among the victims, overstepped the mark for a national administration willing to tolerate localized violence as long as it went relatively unnoticed. Since 1958, Caballero Aburto had used the time-worn pretext of disarmament campaigns (*despistolización*) in order to commit acts of criminal and summary violence with old-school pistoleros. The objections to the state governor were motivated by his abuse of power, but they had various origins.

Students in Chilpancingo demanded autonomy for the recently created university; small- and medium-sized producers of copra and coffee protested against illegal manipulations of prices and market access imposed by politically connected groups; parents even demonstrated against school authorities. Later, municipal elections were the subject of protests. These were all civic movements involving members of different classes that were eventually met with violent repression. The Zapatista uprising was a source of inspiration in Guerrero, albeit to a lesser extent than in Morelos, and rural workers, ejidatarios, and small landowners who suffered Caballero Aburto's abuses could echo the same nationalist rhetoric used by the PRI in its criticism of a bourgeoisie pulling the strings of state government. The Communist Party, however, had a strong presence. University students and normalistas injected energy that could be felt in urban settings and began to disrupt the traditional forms of protest and co-optation of previous decades. The Asociación Cívica Guerrerense (Guerrero Civic Association, or ACG), an organization whose members included Vázquez and Cabañas, took shape outside the PRI's corporate structure, thus challenging the rules of the game and the control that the caciques and their hired guns exercised over municipal elections and politics. In the years following the overthrow of Caballero Aburto, the cycle of repression and protest began again and became increasingly violent. Starting with the brutal but usually discreet violence of pistoleros and private security forces, often related to electoral conflicts, the 1960s then began to see an increase in mass arrests, excessive brutality, torture, and disappearances at the hands of police officers, state judicial police, and soldiers who were carrying out governors' orders and later direct instructions from the federal government.

The origins of the guerrilla in Guerrero could therefore not be more different from Cuba's foquista model. The guerrilla rebels were not seeking to launch a national movement by lighting a spark in a remote region; they responded organically to regional actors, histories, and factors that acquired their own revolutionary structure.

Vázquez and Cabañas had studied at teacher training colleges (*escuelas normales*). Both had embraced politics with increasing energy since 1960, and both arrived at similar conclusions about the goals of an insurgency. Their differences reveal the difficulty of expecting local leftist movements to embrace unified objectives and methods from outside sources. Both leaders' links to national and state organizations largely explain their differing tactics. In 1965, the two leaders discussed the possibility of joining forces, but this never materialized for ideological and perhaps also personal reasons. When a confused kidnap victim asked Vázquez if he was Lucio Cabañas, the response was quite blunt, as recorded by Laura Castellanos: "What, you think I look like a fag? . . . Don't get us mixed up." Cabañas had past links to the Communist Party, which was distrusted by Vázquez, a former member of PRI-aligned campesino organizations and with a background as a leader of social movements. Cabañas mourned Vázquez's death in 1972, but he had previously referred to their incompatibility because his program called for the construction of a socialist project, whereas Vázquez remained closer to revolutionary nationalism; while Cabañas wanted to act as a "phantom," Vázquez was keen to capture liberated territories.

Genaro Vázquez (1931–72) had been on the DFS watchlist since 1961. During the rebellion against Caballero Aburto he had been a founding member of the ACG, which put up candidates for local and state elections. He had met Rubén Jaramillo and had contacts outside the state with the Movimiento de Liberación Nacional (National Liberation Movement, or MLN), a coalition that included Cardenistas and leftist groups that supported Cuba. After the 1962 state elections, another massacre took place and Vázquez was forced to exchange gunfire with the police. Continued repressive measures forced him to break from the MLN in in 1963, bringing him closer to a Marxist position. In 1967, while in jail, he sent out the "ACG Program," announcing a vanguard party that was essentially Leninist, except for the fact that it emphasized nationalism and called on campesinos to take part in the rebellion. Even before his escape from prison in 1968, the ACG was already training its units in guerrilla tactics and carried out various attacks on caciques. It soon turned into a purely guerrilla force, called the Asociación Cívica Nacional Revolucionaria (Revolutionary National Civic Association). By this time, Vázquez was already recruiting students for the armed rebellion, citing the ineffectiveness of the bourgeois legal system. Toward the end of the decade, the group was funding itself through kidnappings and bank robberies, among other operations. A lack of support in the Costa Grande region forced them to move to the Costa Chica, south of Acapulco. But they still could not withstand the large-scale military operation, and they suffered heavy losses as the government gathered intelligence from captured militants and arrested family members of Vázquez and other leaders. Punishing family members was a consistent government strategy. Despite failing to organize an effective guerrilla operation or to mobilize more than a couple of dozen members, Vázquez's project evolved into a vision of a campesino-based uprising that expanded to other parts of the country and looked for partnerships with other Latin American movements. When Vázquez died, probably murdered after a car accident near Morelia, where he was seeking a safehold outside Guerrero, Régis Debray's book was among those in his possession.

Lucio Cabañas took his guerrilla movement further, and left his own lasting mark on it. He distanced himself from the ACG and collaborated with the Partido Comunista Mexicano in developing campesino organizations in Guerrero. His decision to take up arms—something he was reluctant to do in the early 1960s, when he felt the time was not yet right—took him down a path that was independent to the point of isolation. Like Vázquez, Cabañas had taken part in civil protests at the start of the decade, advising ejidatarios and participating in various local protests, while remaining on the sidelines of electoral politics. In 1967, he narrowly escaped assassination during an operation by state judicial police and pistoleros that led to another massacre, this time in Atoyac de Álvarez. Seeking justice was a key motivation for the guerrillas from the outset. Cabañas's group was called the Brigada Campesina de Ajusticiamiento (Campesino Execution Brigade, or BCA), the armed wing of the Partido de los Pobres (Poor People's Party, or PDLP). It began by targeting the police and caciques who employed pistoleros.

His group started small and grew slowly until it had around 100 members under Cabañas's command. It planned for a protracted war rather than suddenly bursting onto the national scene. Security was a central concern, forcing the group to stay on the move in the mountains in order to avoid detection by the army. Cabañas also preferred learning directly from the people as opposed to adopting sophisticated theories. This gave his movement a special relationship with the communities with which he entered into contact as he constantly traveled from place to place in the Sierra de Atoyac. When the guerrillas arrived in a town, Cabañas gave educational speeches at assemblies, emphasizing democratic decision-making. Despite his success when supported by some communities, Cabañas was unable to prevent tensions from arising between the locals and members of his organization.

The BCA followed the lines of Debray's "armed propaganda." Addressing the locals of El Porvenir with a megaphone, Cabañas told them that "we have to teach them [the people] how to kill, we have to teach them to steal from the rich, to rob the government." Revenge, which the theory warned against because it created too close a connection with the civilian population, continued to be part of the revolutionary lessons of violence in Guerrero. Popular tribunals voted on the executions of caciques. Beginning in 1972, the group set up ambushes and killed dozens of soldiers traveling in trucks on mountain roads. These attacks had no strategic purpose other than to expose the army's weakness and to retaliate against abuses committed against campesinos by other uniformed personnel. Cabañas was probably aware of the reprisals taken against civilian populations as a result of such attacks, which included the full repertoire of counterinsurgency brutality, even against children. In 1972, the army abducted more than ninety men from the town of El Quemado after torturing some of them in front of their families. Not all returned, and some spent long stretches in prison. These abuses probably diminished the propaganda value of the guerrillas' harassment of the government, although in Guevara's theory they demonstrated the moral superiority of guerrillas over soldiers. From a critical perspective like Armando Bartra's, the "apocalyptic discourse and militaristic actions" of Vázquez and Cabañas undermined nonviolent political strategies and left a disastrous legacy for the state of Guerrero.

The code of conduct of Cabañas's group emphasized respect for civilian women but lapsed into gendered conceptions of the struggle that, as we will see, resonated with the government's strategies of punishing fighters' relatives. On one occasion, a guerrilla fighter was executed for raping a local girl. But there were no reprisals when Cabañas's men took a girl from Salto Chiquito, despite her father's protests. When Cabañas fell in love with thirteen-year-old Isabel Ayala, from Santa Rosa, he abducted her despite her family's resistance. The group had to accept Isabel as part of their campaign, despite her complete lack of combat training. Isabel, who later defended the relationship as consensual, gave birth to a daughter two months after Cabañas's death.

The 1974 kidnapping of the senator and candidate for governor Rubén Figueroa Figueroa, triggered a large-scale army operation that put Cabañas on the back foot for the first time. His group had carried out several kidnappings, but this one provoked an unexpectedly strong reaction, perhaps because of the victim's close ties to President Echeverría, and because Figueroa had agreed to put himself into Cabañas's hands to begin negotiations. The guerrilla leader had to order two-thirds of his men to scatter to avoid capture. Cabañas was finally killed in combat in December 1974, near Tecpan de Galeana. Figueroa escaped, and as governor he continued his vendetta against the guerrilla leader's family. After being tortured along with her daughter by Mario Acosta Chaparro in Campo Militar 1, where other members of Cabañas's family spent almost two years, Isabel Ayala was raped by Figueroa in his office and bore him a child who died at four months old. (Ayala was killed in Xaltianguis, Guerrero, in 2011, by attackers who have not yet been identified.)

Lucio Cabañas became a mythical figure for leftist revolutionaries in the following decades, and perhaps could already have been thus described in the early 1970s. Armed and political organizations in urban areas tried to join forces with him on various occasions. But Cabañas did not cultivate relationships with leaders of other left-wing groups, and any collaboration with allies outside Guerrero—which the rebel leader had tentatively sought since the late 1960s, and during a trip out of the state in 1973—had to be on his terms. He wanted weapons and logistical support but nothing else, particularly if it limited his authority. Cabañas viewed any political negotiation as futile and armed combat as the only option. He allowed a small group of delegates from the LC23S to join his group in the mountains for a few months, to give them a taste of the hardships of life there. He constantly rebuked them for being too theoretical, and eventually he expelled them. Some collaborations existed with groups in other states, but these were more personal, and he never formed any coalitions. Cabañas's leadership was criticized internally, and there were divisions. The group's cofounder, Carmelo Cortés, accused him of populism and paternalism, and even tried to oust him as leader when Lucio had left for the cities. Cabañas expelled Cortés from the movement, accusing him of stealing another member's wife. Cortés set up another group, Fuerzas Armadas Revolucionarias (Revolutionary Armed Forces), which operated in Acapulco and in the state of Morelos. He was killed by DFS agents in 1975. Some years after Cabañas's death, the PDLP entered an alliance with Unión del Pueblo (Union of the People, or UP), which started in Oaxaca, to form the Partido Revolucionario Obrero Clandestino Unión del Pueblo (Union of the People Clandestine Workers Revolutionary Party), which joined other organizations to form the Ejército Popular Revolucionario (People's Revolutionary Army, or EPR) in 1996. Although other armed movements existed in rural areas, the Guerrero experience was unique for its deep roots in self-defense against local authoritarianism, the increasingly violent government repression, and the endurance of the armed groups that emerged.

Revolutionary violence was not limited to rural guerrillas. Student mobilizations in the second half of the century had their own history and occasionally overlapped with rebel movements. The guerrilla fighters shared their hard-won experience with student recruits in the urban theater. These collaborations transformed the government's strategies and responses. However, the connection is not so simple as saying that the events of October 2, 1968, or of June 10, 1971—the dates of particularly brutal acts of government repression of students in Mexico City—inspired a whole generation of armed rebels. The armed option already existed, and only some students joined. Since the 1950s, for example, the DFS had been spying on student organizations in Mexico City, and on Vázquez and Cabañas, who had studied teacher training at escuelas normales.

Student movements were frequent and diverse. In many cases, repression was part of a dialectic that could lead to radicalization. In 1956, soldiers forced their way into the Instituto Politécnico Nacional (National Polytechnic Institute, or IPN) to break up a strike. This event was one of dozens of student protests that continued until 1968. The reasons for the protests were often related to education institutions' governance structures, resources for students, as in 1956, and other internal matters. But there were also street protests and sometimes conflicts inspired by solidarity with Cuba or Vietnam. Students could also mobilize as consumers: in 1958, students from the Universidad Nacional Autónoma de México (National Autonomous University of Mexico, or UNAM) vandalized buses to protest transportation costs. They occupied the Ciudad Universitaria campus, and other schools protested in solidarity. The rectors at the universities of Guerrero in 1960 and Puebla in 1961 were pressured by students and their supporters on the streets of the capitals of these states. Union activities at universities and schools tended to be politicized. Student protests frequently met with brutal police clampdowns, which fueled rebellions that became more intense and spread—as happened in Chilpancingo in 1960.

In the mid-1960s, a wide variety of leftist student organizations, both from the old-school PCM as well as heterodox Marxist dissidents, were reflecting on revolution from a theoretical perspective while continuing to focus on activism within their institutions. Taking up arms was not the most obvious option for them. It is a common oversimplification to assert that students' ideological radicalization inevitably led to this choice. Although the unity of theory and praxis was a premise of historical materialism, it was essential to distinguish between the two, and violence was not the only corollary of the doctrine. There were many available points of reference, since a homogenous "communist threat" only existed in the official discourse. Similarly to rural movements, the inspiration for taking up arms could come before the adoption of a revolutionary program, or it could be in response to demands for justice. As Montemayor has noted, the decision was born of frustration and repression, but the conditions differed in each case.

A wide range of ideas about students' class identity affected the various links between student movements and other types of mobilization. According to Ariel Rodríguez Kuri, almost three-quarters of captured guerrillas had at least some years of primary education. Their average age was twenty-three. In a rapidly urbanizing nation with aspirations for social mobility stimulated by broader access to secondary and higher education, we cannot say that students were overrepresented in the armed groups. In a text addressed to students in Chihuahua in 1965, Arturo Gámiz explained that they were not a social class, and that belonging to the professional petite bourgeoisie was merely an illusion. The "pure" student struggles, manipulated by existing university organizations, needed to be replaced by a "vanguard theory"; students had to stand alongside campesinos and other social groups to protest against the common enemy: "imperialism, government authority, and domestic reactionary forces," which used pistoleros, police officers, and undercover agents. The sacrifice was necessary, Gámiz said, and required adherents to abandon their professional education. But it was not all abstract theory: several students died at Gámiz's side during the attack on the Ciudad Madera barracks. For Ignacio Salas Obregón, a founding member of the LC23S, students were nothing more than proletarians who produced goods that benefited the bourgeoisie. That kind of class identity, rather than any ability to fight, meant they could become the revolutionary vanguard from within the "university-factory." From this perspective, the 1968 student movement was a "political strike," the embryo of a future general strike.

The mass movement that culminated in the Tlatelolco massacre of October 2, 1968, is significant in several ways. First, it exemplified, for the whole world to see, the new forms in which violence had become a part of politics. During that summer, in the same year Mexico was to host the Olympic Games, several student protests in the capital grew and became more coordinated. The common denominator was the struggle for the political use of public space. The students, starting with a group of high school pupils who sparked everything with a brawl in the downtown area, were behaving in accordance with a long and almost ritualistic use of violence (gang fighting, bus hijackings). Traditionally, the police had been tolerant of this disorderly behavior as long as it took place in certain designated spaces. However, as the government made law and order a priority in the city in the run-up to the Olympics, on this occasion the police responded violently. They raided UNAM and IPN buildings and physically assaulted a group of students who had nothing to do with the initial brawl. This response, as Rodríguez Kuri has shown, was counterproductive, because the Mexico City police were ill-equipped to control a flare-up on a larger scale, however moderate and legalistic its demands; the army was called in to restore order on the capital's streets. For the students, this simply increased the moral legitimacy of their protest. Giving and taking a beating, charging down streets and across plazas, was all part of a usual form of protest based on a specific understanding of what student life was about. In Puebla, during the same period, as Gema Kloppe-Santamaría has described, students at the local Universidad Autónoma de Puebla (Autonomous University of Puebla) already knew that using guns (which were available in their schools), fighting in the streets, and destroying buses were effective means of challenging the government. In the capital, as in Guadalajara, a tradition of hazing, hooliganism, and other habits of male youth implicitly excluded women's participation. This was reflected in the 1968 movement's leadership structure, which had few women members despite being a major component of the movement in general.

Strikes, building occupations, and demonstrations of solidarity swiftly spread to the capital's largest schools in 1968. In pitched battles, students stood their ground using stones, sticks, Molotov cocktails, and sometimes guns. It was assumed that this was the only language that the government—embodied by its repressive institutions—could understand. Hostility toward the police was a form of propaganda that operated in parallel with the "information squads" that explained the reasons for the protests to people across the capital. As Rodríguez Kuri points out, violence entered public life, though not at the expense of internal democratic procedures. Within the 1968 movement, like many others that came before and afterward, major decisions were taken deliberatively, without a central leadership but instead in assemblies that could last several hours, where the representation of the various schools legitimized the movement as a whole. This ended abruptly on October 2. By presidential order, the government's presidential guard and soldiers—apparently without any coordination—fired shots into the crowd gathered in the Plaza de las Tres Culturas and then arrested more than a thousand people. The precise death toll has never been established, and the responsibility for the repression is still subject to different interpretations. This was due to Díaz Ordaz's strategy of spreading contradictory information and preventing proper news coverage. Sowing confusion was also a tactic used on June 10, 1971, when a paramilitary group formed by the Federal District government, in coordination with federal authorities, attacked the first large-scale student protest since the events of 1968. Employing the same strategy of launching a surprise attack and then hiding its hand, the government used plainclothes thugs known as the Halcones (Falcons) to attack students, killing several of them.

The massacres of October 2, 1968, and June 10, 1971, undoubtedly affected armed movements that already existed or that were organized subsequently. A group of IPN football players and their male cheerleaders, the Lacandones, went underground after the events of Tlatelolco. Many young members of the PCM abandoned the party. They chafed at the cautiousness of the old guard (politically weakened and reluctant to take the path of insurrection), in their conviction that an uprising was the only possible response to the repressive measures of a government that had long since stopped listening to their grievances. Members of the LC23S and the Fuerzas de Liberación Nacional (National Liberation Forces, or FLN), which later played a central role in the development of guerrilla movements, came from the same background. But it should be emphasized that their decision to become professional guerrillas, that is, to dedicate their entire lives to the armed struggle, did not preclude action in schools. The willingness to smash windows, start brawls, and sometimes shoot guns would endure on many campuses after the defeat of the revolutionary movements.

The links between schools and armed movements were particularly strong in Guadalajara in the early 1970s, when the intensity of disputes among student groups caused bitter antagonisms. The conflict between the government-backed Federación de Estudiantes de Guadalajara and the Frente de Estudiantil Revolucionario (Student Revolutionary Front, FER) pitted members of urban gangs (the Vikingos) alongside communist youth against the government forces. Clashes over a building occupied by the FER, in 1970, led to gunfire and fatalities on both sides. This prompted a vicious backlash by the police, soldiers, and DFS agents, and hundreds of people were arrested, tortured, and disappeared. The surviving FER members went underground for the same reason that Vázquez and Cabañas took to the hills: the need for revenge and self-defense. More than any coherent ideology, the Vikingos were remarkable for their ability to carry out their illicit activities unmolested in neighborhoods that protected them from police harassment. Something similar can be said of the powerful Sinaloa student movement. The Enfermos (Sick Ones) were active in the state university of Sinaloa. They forged links with local campesinos and were skilled at attacking the enemy in various ways. This combination of political action with criminal practices earned the Vikingos and the Enfermos the admiration of other urban guerrillas. In 1972, the Enfermos staged violent protests after the deaths of two students, forcing the rector of the Universidad Autónoma de Sinaloa to resign. Subsequently, like the FER members, they joined the LC23S, transferring funds to it and expanding its operational capacity. That same year, in the city of Monterrey, the police responded to school riots by making arrests as well as killing one of the students staging a street protest against the repression. This was a particularly visible point in a process that had begun in that city the previous year and that also contributed to the emergence of the LC23S.

In the early 1970s, a number of urban and rural armed groups shared the belief that the time was ripe for a successful attack on the government. For Sergio Aguayo, this included a misperception of the support they could expect, both within Mexico and abroad. So many opinions existed on how to achieve revolutionary goals that cooperation was virtually impossible. One group that tried to form a unified "revolutionary armed forces" bloc in 1970 was known as the Guajiros, a popular reference to naive rural peasants. No coordination was possible even among the movements within the state of Guerrero, as we have seen, although they eventually helped form the LC23S. Foreign backing even came from different corners: the Movimiento de Acción Revolucionaria (Revolutionary Action Movement, or MAR) was established by a group of Mexican students at the Patrice Lumumba University in Moscow, who sought support from various governments until they eventually received training from the North Korean regime. A Guatemalan leader, Marco Antonio Yon Sosa, was killed in Mexico in 1970, and others took part in the UP training. Little support could be expected from Cuba and its proxies in other countries because of the Mexican government's good relations with Havana.

The isolation did not apply to access to theoretical and practical models. Carlos Marighella's *Mini-Manual of the Urban Guerrilla*, published in Brazil in 1969, circulated among Mexican clandestine movements, particularly within groups that formed in cities in the early 1970s. As in Debray's book, the idea was to provide guerrillas with tactics and strategies without assuming their membership in any specific party. But transferring the revolutionary model to the urban setting created striking differences to the foquista approach. For example, instead of adopting a central political line, Marighella recommended small, decentralized groups willing to act quickly without lengthy consultations or traditional hierarchical relationships. Given the asymmetry of power, urban fighters had to always be on the offensive, catching their enemies off guard, preparing their escape route, and avoiding being forced onto the defensive. Offensive acts included bank robberies, kidnappings, and the killing of adversaries and undercover agents. According to Marighella, this required guerrillas to possess a range of skills: familiarity with "their city"; discretion; good marksmanship at close range; knowledge of weapons; expertise in forging documents, making bombs, and repairing electronic devices; and physical fitness. Marighella, however, was worried about the possibility of "patriots" being confused with bandits or common criminals. This called for propaganda during illegal activities:

leaving leaflets in banks after robberies, distributing publications, making radio broadcasts, and writing letters. In contrast to Debray's indifference to the law, Marighella proposed denouncing human rights abuses as another weapon to attract public support. As we will see, not all Mexican groups followed this advice.

Mexican guerrillas, regardless of their chosen methods, shared the view of Guevara, Debray, and Marighella that the revolutionary struggle had to be structured by political analysis combined with military tactics and strategy. They were also united in the belief that it was a male-dominated enterprise because of men's supposed physical and moral superiority. In the example set by Guevara (whose last words were "You are going to kill a man") and Marighella, courage meant being willing to die in combat, sacrificing one's existence as part of a broader movement that suppressed individualism. Perhaps the most important, albeit less explicit, feature of these models was a concept of historical temporality in which swift action would combine with the slow process of building a collective consciousness among the masses in order to bring about the downfall of the regime and, eventually, capitalism itself.

These manuals reflected a limitation in the political analysis reproduced by Mexican guerrilla fighters. Their reading of Marxism led them to view the "bourgeois state" as merely representing a class, in other words an entity without its own rules or motivations, controlled by the owners of the means of production and imperialism. Hence they thought it would be easy to bring down the system once the masses recognized how constitutional legitimacy hid a corrupt complicity with the bourgeoisie. In a piece of self-criticism written while in jail in 1976, Gustavo Hirales explained the LC23S's isolation as a result of its rejection of democratic and legal avenues: "The state was seen as this wall to prevent class warfare, ruling out any engagement with it." This blindness became particularly dangerous in the Mexican case because, even in the 1970s, the state was still drawing on a revolutionary past that enabled it to adopt less short-sighted redistribution policies than the nascent neoliberalism of some contemporaneous South American dictatorships. Because of their comparatively poor counter-insurgency capabilities, Mexican guerrilla movements did not consider state agents of repression as important tactical targets, contrary to Marighella's advice. For them, it was as though all policemen or soldiers, regardless of rank, were the same as the judicial police or DFS agents: they all served the ruling class and acted without autonomy.

Apart from this shortcoming in their analysis, Mexico's underground armed organizations were as ideologically diverse as other leftist groups across Latin America. They placed so much emphasis on their theorizations and discussions, both in recruitment and training, that what might seem to a modern observer to be tiny gaps were to them yawning gulfs. Abundant reference points were available: core texts by Marx, Lenin, Trotsky, and Mao were widely stocked in bookstores and street kiosks. Apart from Marighella and Cuban foquismo, student or guerrilla groups could choose between a Maoist model of popular struggle, the protracted warfare exemplified by Vietnam in its fight against two empires, or an eclectic combination, like the ideology adopted by Monterrey's FLN. Carlos Illades has studied a paradox that arose in the mid-1970s: Marxist analysis offered a solid, easily accessible theoretical common base for developing an intellectually dynamic and open left-wing movement, but at the same time it exacerbated sectarian divisions that further isolated those who had taken up arms. In his 1974 essay *Política y violencia* (Politics and violence), Marxist philosopher Carlos Pereyra described the outcome of the "lack of political culture" of "ultra-leftism" espoused by "terrorist" groups: "Military factors take precedence over politics, thus erasing the entire political perspective."

The MAR is a particularly illustrative example of the effects of this disconnect from reality. The training in North Korea was tough, and theories based on the country's historical experience seemed largely irrelevant. The lack of discipline began there and continued when fifty-three militants returned to Mexico. According to Verónica Oikión Solano, the group's leadership was arbitrary, tended toward improvisation, and divisions soon appeared among its approximately sixty local members, most of whom were students from Michoacán. They never properly gauged the enemy's strength or produced effective propaganda, despite various attempts to join forces with other groups and to share what they had learned in Korea, even collaborating with Cabañas to lay ambushes for soldiers. Identified in 1971, various MAR members were captured and tortured. The group disbanded in the late 1970s. The history of the MAR also suggests that defining a movement by its military successes or failures is not necessarily helpful in understanding its historical significance. Unlike most guerrilla movements, it was driven not by a search for justice and self-defense but rather by a willingness to fight and make personal sacrifices for a vague and hopeful future.

Other groups briefly crop up in this history as examples of the different possible paths. The Frente Urbano Zapatista (Zapatista Urban Front) became notorious for robbing banks and a bakery in Mexico City's Narvarte and del Valle neighborhoods. In September 1971, members kidnapped Airports Director Julio Hirschfeld Almada, and received a ransom of 3 million pesos. They gave away some of this money to the poor; the rest was recovered by the government after seven of the eight members of the group were arrested a few months later and sentenced to prison. The UP planted several bombs in 1972 and defined its position by its persistent criticism of other "petit bourgeois" movements.

The most successful attempt at ideological and organizational unification was the LC23S, established in Guadalajara in 1973. The organization began with around 250 members drawn from groups associated with student movements (such as the Guajiros, Enfermos, FER, and Lacandones) and from unaffiliated members of various guerrilla groups such as the MAR, which had now merged with other groups. In the words of Rodríguez Kuri, instead of being a compact organization, the LC23S was "a confederation of armed groups." From the outset, it engaged in a twofold struggle: externally, in its armed attacks; and internally, in its efforts to unify its heterogenous components. Its founders gave it a structure that recognized its diverse origins: there were overlapping political and military commands and territorial divisions that included twenty-two states of the country divided into five zones. They would undertake their operations in rural and urban spaces, although the latter ended up taking precedence, despite the organization being named after the date of the attack on the Ciudad Madera barracks. According to Romain Robinet, the LC23S did not adopt the Cuban model and opted instead for a hardline Leninist ideology, enriched by Frantz Fanon and Mao. The recruitment strategy, which allowed the membership to grow to between 445 and 696 members in 1974 (according to DFS figures), emphasized study groups that gave priority to ideological coherence.

From its first operations, the LC23S prioritized attacks on enemies defined in class terms, including the representatives of a state that was the servant of the bourgeoisie. Initial targets were banks and hostages who could be kidnapped for large ransoms. The LC23S viewed such actions as "harassment" rather than frontal attacks, which included "expropriations" and "executions." These initial actions were also defined by the urgent need for funds to supply its groups with weapons and training. These were "subsistence" actions which, according to self-critical former members, only increased their isolation and militaristic approach. The LC23S's costs amounted to some 600,000 pesos a month, according to an estimate by Laura Castellanos. A large chunk of the money went toward buying weapons and renting safe houses.

The LC23S's revolutionary activities were never solely about the use of violence, although that was always the priority. Propaganda and education were parallel goals, in addition to armed activities. One of its first steps was to publish a periodical called *Madera*, for the "working-class masses." The editorial in the first issue, which came out in January 1974, already reflected the contradictions underlying the group's educational purpose: the LC23S had to fight against its internal "errors and deviations"; only then could workers unite under the proper leadership, "merging Marxism-Leninism with the workers' movement, the strength of organized revolutionaries with the destructive force of the masses." *Madera* needed to communicate messages but also be the "organ to exercise revolutionary leadership over the movement as a whole." This may explain why it was not an easy read, brimming as it was with theoretical references and cryptic allusions to internal adversaries criticized as militarist, petit bourgeois, or embodying other kinds of "opportunist deviation." The correct ideology was the result of—and at the same time confirmed the option of—the armed struggle. Ignacio Salas Obregón, one of the LC23S's founders and early leaders, wrote a text defining a belief shared by all the armed groups: normal and democratic politics was impossible because "the effectiveness of the warlike activity of the bourgeoisie could not be beaten with whining and moaning, but only with a well-designed military and political strategy." From this perspective, educational initiatives were boiled down to defining "military tactics based on the understanding that war should be waged according to the rules of war, and that revolution is war."

Writers for *Madera* affirmed the inevitability of a new revolution. But strategically, they agreed that the time was not yet ripe for the final assault. They recognized their weaker position relative to the bourgeoisie in terms of arms and other resources. They needed to use the element of surprise and superior mobility. Harassment, they said, included the assassination of officials and other attacks on police officers and soldiers, with the aim of wearing down the enemy's strength, disarming them, and taking their money. The LC23S no longer viewed the street protests that had inspired so many students as expressive and liberating opportunities but as another component of military tactics. "Peaceful protests in areas where the bourgeois have the advantage" were to be avoided because they forced the organization to protect civilians from repression; sudden, small, and scattered actions were more effective. Repression, a sign of the enemy's weakness, was inevitable and complaining about it was a waste of time. Asserting rights was an illusion and something to be avoided by professional fighters. Sacrifice was a victory in itself, as Salas Obregón personally demonstrated.

Infighting plagued the LC23S from the outset. The risk of infiltration by undercover agents stoked suspicions and internal conflicts. The military leadership was at odds with the movement's political arm; Salas Obregón ordered expulsions and various executions. *Madera* acknowledged that the

LC23S had misunderstood "the activities of the political police" and was overly confident in the integrity of its own members. Other groups also executed their militants to punish undercover operatives or snitches who had passed on information to the government. Napoleón Glockner and Nora Rivera, for example, were tortured by the government to reveal the location of a safe house in Nepantla (in the state of Mexico, southeast of Mexico City), where five other FLN members fell.

During its most active phase, in 1973 and 1974, the LC23S intensified political violence. Although it had more than 800 militants, the group never gained enough traction to absorb other movements, as demonstrated by the failed attempt to recruit Cabañas. Decimated by the late 1970s, the LC23S became just one of many other organizations still active: the Fuerzas Revolucionarias Armadas del Pueblo (Revolutionary Armed Forces of the People), the PDLP, the UP, and the FLN. Gen. Mario Acosta Chaparro estimated that in 1979, around thirty organizations had more than 1,800 members in total, though Adela Cedillo put the first number closer to forty.

The LC23S also exemplified how guerrilla movements struggled to expand their support base beyond the dictates of a masculinist, modernizing ethic marked by paranoia. Many women were in the group's ranks (65 of the 445 total members, according to DFS), but they did not hold leadership positions and could not counteract the organization's internal gender roles. Women's participation in the LC23S and other armed organizations was belatedly recognized, as Lucía Rayas points out, by individual memories of sacrifice and willingness to risk the sexual violence they often suffered at the hands of state forces. Rayas estimates that forty-three women were disappeared between 1971 and 1983. Future research on this issue is likely to unveil a wider and more influential participation. Also, the LC23S did not consider Indigenous groups key players in the revolutionary struggle, although it did deploy units in areas where they were numerous. In most organizations, a Marxist-Leninist-oriented analysis was still making it difficult to move beyond identifying political actors in terms of class or in relation to imperialism from a national perspective. In the 1970s, the FLN began to work with Indigenous groups in Chiapas. The process was slow but eventually led to the creation of the Ejército Zapatista de Liberación Nacional (EZLN) in the 1980s.

Another factor that explains the isolation members of the LC23S and other organizations imposed upon themselves was the decision that all of them had to make as individuals at some point, to go underground and become "professional guerrillas." This meant becoming fully committed to the cause and relying entirely on the organization for economic and emotional support. This decision could respond to a vision of the future, or to a desire for revenge that was more or less personal. In some cases, such as with Napoleón Glockner, leaving the family for good became unavoidable, in order to keep one step ahead of the police. The consequences, as in his case, could always be fatal.

More important than the infighting and isolation in the eventual defeat of the LC23S was the repression unleashed after Monterrey businessmen Eugenio Garza Sada was killed in September 1973 in a botched kidnapping attempt. The business sector accused President Echeverría of having allowed the crime to take place. In response, the Policía Judicial Federal (Federal Judicial Police, or PJF), the DFS, and probably also groups with private sector backers, were given carte blanche to wipe out LC23S members, shunning any remaining pretense of legality. This, in turn, fueled internal rifts. While one faction of the movement, based in Monterrey but present in several regions, focused on political initiatives in trade unions and eventually laid down arms, the Brigada Roja (Red Brigade) in Mexico City persisted with the more aggressive stance of Salas Obregón. But new kidnappings and bank robberies only helped the DFS, criminologists, and progovernment media outlets define the LC23S as a purely criminal organization. In January 1974, the Enfermos organized an uprising in Culiacán, recruiting campesinos in their area for a campaign they called Asalto al Cielo (Storming the Skies). They clashed with the police, secured weapons and vehicles, but were unable to fend off the army and security forces that descended on Sinaloa to finish the destruction of the movement. In the following years, LC23S members who still believed in the propaganda value of violence executed randomly selected police officers in response to the government's repression, as they did after the 1975 killing of two LC23S members in the middle of Mexico City's Ciudad Universitaria campus.

The vague logic of justice behind these actions reflected the myopic understanding of the state by the LC23S and other organizations. Carlos Pereyra had noted its consequences in 1973: incapable of properly acknowledging the class logic of the state as a mediator rather than a mere servant of the bourgeoisie, "the depoliticized radical becomes obsessed with provoking repressive violence, the only surefire means of 'proving' that official policies are against people's interests." The result of rejecting the state's autonomy and negotiating ability was that "ultraleftism . . . was unable to find another interlocutor, another reference point, another framework for action than the one established by its [violent] relationship with the state."

The attitudes Pereyra criticized were common in most clandestine organizations of the time. If we look at some patterns we can understand why the simultaneous obsession with, and misunderstanding of, the state apparatus created what he called "a terrifying dialogue with official violence." The guerrillas' inferior military capabilities forced them to give extra meaning to each action. Long discussions were held to select victims whose fate would convey a precise political message. One of the first such kidnappings was Genaro Vázquez's targeting of the son of the cacique Agustín Bautista Cabrera in 1970. Julio Hirschfeld was kidnapped by the Frente Urbano Zapatista in 1971 because he was a senior public official and connected to the bourgeoisie as an employee of H. Steele. The kidnapping of the US consul in Guadalajara in 1973 by the Fuerzas Revolucionarias Armadas del Pueblo achieved the release and transportation to Cuba of thirty militant detainees, in a double blow to the empire.

On a propaganda level, kidnappings ended up being counterproductive. In the case of Bautista's son, as with Garza Sada and several others, the attack did not go according to plan or the subsequent negotiations failed, and the hostage ended up dead. Media reporting on kidnappings was effective at criminalizing the guerrillas. In cases such as with Figueroa and Garza Sada, when the guerrillas seemed to make the state look weak, the authorities doubled down on their repressive measures, with more troop deployments, attacks on civilians, and disappearances of militants. An exception to these tactics was the FLN, which forbade criminal acts to prevent revolutionaries from being mistaken for common criminals.

Bank robberies, another common practice, were also meant to send a message. Paquita Calvo, who took part in one, told Glockner that "the idea was to symbolize how the armed vanguard was returning money to the people by taking it out of the hands of their worst exploiters: the financial bourgeoisie." These "expropriations" also targeted pharmacies, bakeries, and liquor stores. The assailants sometimes left behind printed messages to explain their attack; but occasionally things went wrong and helped criminalize the guerrilla in the eyes of the public. In one such instance, eleven people were killed during the robbery of the Banco de Comercio in Villa Coapa—a suburb south of Mexico City—an assault attributed to the LC23S in 1975. They also expropriated vehicles when necessary, even when victims had no links to the government or the bourgeoisie.

Other actions, such as the use of explosives, were purely propaganda exercises, although their meaning was not always easy to decipher. The Comité de Lucha Revolucionaria (Revolutionary Struggle Committee) planted five bombs simultaneously in Mexico City in 1969 to announce their arrival on the scene. In Glockner's words, perhaps ironic but certainly an example of how isolation distorted the guerrilla's perspective, the idea was to "let society know it is not alone."

Executions were less common but similarly justified by the quest for justice. This was defined not only in financial terms but also in a penal sense, as a consequence of specific transgressions. Cabañas's BCA killed police officers, soldiers, and caciques in Guerrero. The LC23S's various units were allowed to kill uniformed soldiers and police, trade union leaders, or hostages when they deemed it necessary. The punishment was justified in the context of a history of abuses. These explanations, generally ignored by the press, were spread by study groups, short-lived propaganda campaigns, and pamphleteering. Today, it is hard to gauge their effectiveness beyond the militants' fleeting memories.

To understand Pereyra's description of the "terrifying dialogue with official violence," here we should focus on state violence. As in previous eras, new practices blended with the sediments of older ones. Anticommunism, although exacerbated by the Cold War and the Cuban Revolution, already existed since the 1920s and had been used to justify extralegal violence. The DFS was the most important institution within a security apparatus that remained essential for political control for decades. As Aguayo shows, the DFS's history faithfully documents the vicious circle of secrecy, paranoia, and espionage that was the basis for brutal decisions like those taken by Díaz Ordaz against the students in 1968.

But the official response to guerrilla movements was paradoxical: while quietly ordering the annihilation of rebel factions, the government denied their existence in public communications, or reduced them to the status of criminals. By not acknowledging the existence of hostile guerrilla groups, the authorities could not admit that they had set up repressive squads to combat them. Therefore, it set up paramilitary units such as the Halcones and the Brigada Blanca (White Brigade), and also ordered extrajudicial killings and disappearances of guerrilla members or sympathizers. What we now refer to as the dirty war was a covert modus operandi gradually adopted by the state to circumvent legal restrictions, without formally violating civil rights, but within a militarized approach to the conflict. Changes in the public sphere and Mexico's expectations of international respectability from the mid-twentieth century made it harder for the state to criminalize its enemies and commit spectacular acts of violence, as it had done against the Cristeros, for example.

When revolutionary armed groups committed particularly scandalous attacks, like high-profile kidnappings, the state broke its silence. Echeverría, pressured by business groups but probably also motivated by his own anger, condemned the murder of Garza Sada and ordered a far-reaching campaign of repression that had more than whiff of revenge. The LC23S was decimated. Its members were rounded up and tortured, in a method that increased the number of disappearances rather than the size of prison populations. In August 1976, the LC23S's botched kidnapping of Margarita López Portillo, the president-elect's sister, gave fresh impetus to efforts to wipe out the guerrillas by any means necessary, with the additional support of US-backed antidrug campaigns.

The government's decision to prioritize police or military operations, despite the PRI's long track record of negotiating with or absorbing dissidents, was based on a superficial analysis that overlooked the social roots of the rebels' grievances. According to General Acosta Chaparro, the guerrilla movements were simply the product of Cuban and Soviet manipulation of Mexican students. The evidence for such an analysis was almost nonexistent; Cuba did not want to jeopardize its relations with Mexico. For Miguel Nazar Haro, agent and later director of the DFS, all the armed groups were the same: a bunch of overzealous students with no real ties to workers or campesinos. As a result, negotiations were never part of the counterinsurgency strategy. Social campaigns organized by the army in Guerrero merely complemented the government's repressive measures. Although guerrillas were not recognized as belligerents, fighting them was considered a war.

In 1976, the Brigada Blanca was formed as an unofficial paramilitary group to consolidate the work of various agencies, incorporating dozens of judicial police and military officers, some trained abroad. For six years, this organization—based in Mexico City's Campo Militar 1 and operating nationwide—was involved in executions, disappearances, and the torture of urban guerrillas. Despite the number of victims probably in the hundreds, there were no legal consequences for its members—including Nazar Haro who, like other Brigada operatives, after the most intense period of the dirty war transitioned into illegal businesses, such as car theft, with the same level of impunity.

The Brigada Blanca was the state's most brutal and systematic instrument of extralegal coercion, but its practices date back to the early postrevolutionary decades, when Luis Napoleón Morones, Gonzalo N. Santos, and other politicians ran their own groups of thugs and pistoleros. These experts in violence carried out acts of repression, though in a decentralized way and with a more precise use of force. In the 1970s, a federal structure began to replace the gun-toting pistolero model. Guerrero was the laboratory for new methods: systematic torture was used to extract information; families and communities were punished; disappearances became commonplace. The 1968 student movement was, in Montemayor's words, "a laboratory of large-scale repression" that involved the military, the police, and the judicial authorities. Coordination between the various institutions responsible for mass arrests, killings, kidnappings, and other forms of intimidating social movements became simultaneously more organized and less precise.

October 2, 1968, revealed another important dimension of this new repressive apparatus: the apparent lack of a central command structure. Díaz Ordaz used the Batallón Olimpia (Olympia Battalion), under the command of the Ministry of Defense, to arrest student leaders, while sharpshooters from the government security forces were deployed to ambush protesters and soldiers. This catalyzed violence, spread confusion in the crowd, and eliminated any evidence of the chain of command and the number of victims. The Halcones, who attacked the protesters on June 10, 1971, were set up specifically to carry out extralegal attacks. The group, consisting of hundreds of men trained and paid by the Federal District Department, was created in 1967 without any official acknowledgment of its existence. However, after the June 10 massacre, it had to be dissolved. Its training centers were dismantled and its members ordered to stand down; some were transferred to other police units, others became criminals, none faced punishment.

In parallel to these extraofficial groups, other bodies continued using violence, adhering to legal practices to different degrees. These included the army, the presidential guard, the judicial police, the (already poorly regulated) DFS, the Dirección General de Investigaciones Políticas y Sociales (General Directorate of Political and Social Investigations), the Dirección de Investigaciones para la Prevención de la Delincuencia (Investigative Crime Prevention Directorate), military intelligence services, various police units, and even rural defense forces. In the field, the army could carry out illegal raids and mass arrests, which concluded in disappearances without any legal basis or accountability. Ministerio Público agents, prison authorities, and judges held all these institutions together by strictly applying laws when dealing with suspects but overlooking them when state actors committed acts of violence—effectively continuing the discretional approach that made pistolerismo possible. Everyone acted in ad hoc coordination. The capital's police, for example, could make arrests on the basis of information provided by the DFS; those detained could be tortured at the capital's police headquarters with the participation of members of other branches of the state security apparatus, in Campo Militar 1, or elsewhere. The most fortunate were tried in a court of law. Beginning with the Díaz Ordaz administration, the government invested heavily in arming and modernizing its forces but without setting up a joint command structure.

This type of state violence typically circumvented administrative and legal procedures and reduced the likelihood of the police being held responsible. Presidents did not directly order executions and preferred to turn a blind eye to DFS procedures. The agency's directors, meanwhile, often exaggerated the supposed threat posed by guerrilla movements in order to gain influence and continue their parallel business operations. This deliberate lack of coordination led to schisms and acts of sabotage within the security apparatus, which became clearly apparent during the government's war on drugs in subsequent years. The reemergence of guerrilla movements in the 1990s with the EZLN and EPR provided further proof that repression could still be delegated. In Chiapas, paramilitary groups were used to attack Zapatistas without the government taking any responsibility. In Guerrero, state judicial police officers killed seventeen campesinos in Aguas Blancas in 1995. In this case, the video of the massacre forced the resignation of state governor Rubén Figueroa Alcocer, son of the governor who had been kidnapped by Cabañas and had taken revenge on his family.

The repressive system that developed in the 1960s and 1970s combined public acts of brutality with equally extreme but hidden acts of violence, following both traditional and new methods. Starting in the 1950s, governments of various countries shared with each other a series of counterinsurgency tactics used by France in Algeria, by the United States in Vietnam and elsewhere, and by the armed forces of most Latin American countries against their own peoples. The lessons learned were then disseminated by schools and advisers. Several of those who fought against guerrillas in Mexico received training in the United States, at the School of the Americas and at the International Law Enforcement Academy in Washington, which Nazar Haro attended. Acosta Chaparro studied at Fort Benning and Fort Bragg, also in the United States. Torture was part of this training, and was associated with the doctrine of low-intensity conflict, which combined other kinds of "psychological operations." Although there were fewer Mexicans in these educational institutions compared to the number of trainees from other Central and South American countries, they did establish links: in their testimonies, victims in Mexico refer to the participation of US and South American military officials in their torture sessions.

However, these new developments did not completely supplant former practices. Torture, for example, was already common in the capital's police stations. During antiguerrilla operations, this practice intensified because it was now used not only to extract confessions but also to gather intelligence and spread terror. Guerrillas who fell into the hands of the police were quickly handed over to experts, normally DFS agents, who inflicted pain and fear to collect information in order to arrest other members of their organizations. Speed was of the essence, because the arrest of one guerrilla member raised the alarm among the others and prompted them to leave their safe houses. Guerrillas knew what to expect when captured. Some preferred to fight to the death, others, according to the police, committed suicide, or tried to resist for as long as possible before talking. The latter approach was taken by Napoleón Glockner and Nora Rivera, referred to above, although eventually they revealed the existence of a safe house in Nepantla and were later released. This might have been a ploy by their torturers to give the impression that they had collaborated voluntarily; subsequently their fellow guerrillas executed them after deliberations that simulated trials. Sometimes the intelligence gathered using torture was registered in judicial statements and secret files. Nazar Haro took part in several torture sessions. After inflicting unimaginable physical and psychological abuse, he kept meticulous notes of his victims' words, seeking to connect names and reconstruct groups. He asked them what activities they had participated in, whom they knew, who had introduced them, when, and where. The aim was not to build a legal case but to reconstruct personal networks and detain more people. Arrests led to safe houses where papers would help state agents continue the hunt. Witness statements were not a priority in DFS investigations because all witnesses were suspects. Undercover agents within organizations complemented the intelligence gathered in this way, although their reports often amounted to mere rumors. Planting informants and agents provocateurs could be an effective preparation for making arrests and undoubtedly ramped up the paranoia and isolation of guerrilla groups.

Torture was such a routine element of these operations that there was no problem in presenting the detainees to the press a couple of weeks after their capture, after keeping them in a legal limbo that was in fact a hellish experience. In other cases, bodies were simply dumped, bearing marks of torture. LC23S member Tereso Molina was left on an empty lot, assumed dead after being tortured. He was rescued by the Red Cross and survived. With guaranteed immunity, those responsible did not need to exercise much caution. Although it was simple for the judges to convict individual guerrilla members, sentencing was a lower priority than wiping out organizations and spreading terror among their members.

Torture, therefore, went beyond intelligence gathering and also served as extrajudicial punishment and an expected deterrent. This was another established practice of the Mexican police, only with an extra level of cruelty and the possibility of prisoners being killed. As Gladys McCormick has shown, psychological humiliation was combined with physical pain. In Campo Militar I, police stations, and other unofficial centers of detention, an assortment of ruthless methods were used, including mock executions, solitary confinement, starvation, electric shocks, beatings, prolonged stress positions such as strappado, asphyxia, submersion in sewage, *tehuacanazos* (forcing carbonated water with chili up the nostrils), and the use of rats to gnaw on different parts of the body; some victims had their feet flayed or mutilated, or saw their babies and other family members abused or threatened; sexual attacks were frequently a part of the mutilations and humiliations, and women were raped. The abuse of women kidnapped in Guerrero, in particular, was designed to spread fear among communities that supported the rebels. To prolong the pain, teams of torturers took turns, sometimes assisted by doctors to keep the prisoners alive or conscious. After weeks of such violence, prisoners could be disappeared or otherwise disposed of.

The killing and disappearance of detainees was central to the extralegal tactics used to fight guerrilla groups. Some militants died in clashes with the police or soldiers during these two decades, but probably more died after their detention. An early example was the case of the Asociación Cívica Nacional Revolucionaria's Epifanio Avilés, a participant in the failed hold-up of a cash-in-transit van at the intersection of Xola and 5 de Febrero in Mexico City. He was arrested by the police in Coyuca, Guerrero, and never seen again. Organizations of family members of the disappeared and student protests (like the one in Sinaloa) sometimes forced the authorities to admit that they had people detained or under guard, but in many other cases the authorities never acknowledged those held in their custody. Acosta Chaparro killed detainees on the site of their interrogation, according to the statement of one of his subordinates later published by *Proceso* magazine. The bodies were normally hidden; some are believed to have been cremated in Campo Militar 1. Others were thrown from planes or helicopters into Lake Chapala or the Pacific Ocean, a precursor of the "death flights" organized by the Argentine dictatorship in the Río de la Plata after the 1976 coup. During Rubén Figueroa Figueroa's period as governor of the state of Guerrero (1975–81), people were pushed (alive or dead) out of aircraft that took off from the military base at Pie de la Cuesta, near Acapulco. Acosta Chaparro was accused of ordering thirty such flights but was acquitted by a judge in 2004. Some bodies were left in public places to spread fear.

In hundreds of cases, there was documentary evidence of official responsibility for disappearances showing that victims had been in official custody prior to their probable execution. Salas Obregón, the LC23S leader, was captured during a clash in Tlalnepantla on April 25, 1974, and kept in extralegal custody at Campo Militar 1. He was never seen again. Years later, a photograph surfaced together with a long statement taken on June 10, 1974, after his detention by DFS agents.

Aside from a few well-documented individual cases, the history of the Mexican state's dirty war is still obscured by the subsequent criminal careers of its agents and the reluctance of recent administrations to fully open the archives. The DFS's success on the front lines of this dirty war brought about its eventual downfall. The numbers of agents on its payroll increased from 120 in 1965 to 3,000 in 1981. Directors such as Nazar Haro became untouchable, and others, like Fernando Gutiérrez Barrios, continued to rise through the ranks of government. As drug traffickers began to replace rebel movements as governments' main security concern, the DFS continued using the same methods, only now they faced individuals and groups with plenty of financial resources, as we will see in the next chapter. The independence and impunity enjoyed by police chiefs and agents in their extralegal use of violence became a privilege that paid dividends with the sale of protection. The same thing happened with other government agencies, although there is less evidence. We know about the DFS's leading role in fighting the guerrillas as a result of the documentation that has been made public in the past two decades thanks to pressure exerted by human rights organizations, academics, and journalists.

Less evidence exists about the army's role due to restricted access to military archives, although testimonies suggest that it bore as much, if not more, responsibility, for illegal abuses as the police and intelligence services. According to José Sotelo Marbán, researcher and later critic of a 2001 special prosecuting commission (the Fiscalía Especial para Movimientos Sociales y Políticos del Pasado [Special Prosecutor for Past Social and Political Movements], or FEMOSPP), the archive of the Secretaría de la Defensa Nacional (National Defense Secretariat, or SEDENA) showed that the army was implicated in 80 percent of the disappearances. As Thomas Rath has pointed out, since the first half of the century, the Mexican armed forces had been the government's most reliable instrument in a system in which many state or parastate actors used violence, with none monopolizing the legitimacy of its use.

The dirty war was also aptly named because of the inherent messiness of its administration. Army officers such as Acosta Chaparro were not immune to the lure of drug trafficking. Federal and state judicial police officers—who had increased their firepower during the internal armed conflict—were also tempted by its fruits. As repression became a higher priority for the state, the army and federal agencies such as the DFS enjoyed newfound prestige, although violent state actors continued to be scattered, as they had been in the first half of the century, with police officers and pistoleros acting at the municipal level.

This is one reason why it remains difficult to talk about numbers. FEMOSPP, set up during the Vicente Fox presidency (the first not controlled by the PRI or its predecessors), investigated and officially confirmed more than 480 disappearances out of 788 reported cases until the late 1970s. The Comisión Nacional de Derechos Humanos (National Human Rights Commission) acknowledges the disappearance of 532 people during the 1970s and the early 1980s. Other sources, including FEMOSPP, human rights organizations, and archives, compiled by Adela Cedillo and Fernando Calderón, suggest as a high estimate a total of 3,000 disappeared people, a similar number of detainees, and some 7,000 torture victims. There is still no definitive count, but further research may reveal higher numbers. A 1978 amnesty benefited more than 1,500 prisoners who had been tried after their detention, a less common outcome according to anecdotal evidence.

The problem is partly due to the lack of an end date: extrajudicial executions and disappearances by government forces have never stopped, although now they are also committed against those suspected of common crimes. The Asociación de Familiares de Detenidos Desaparecidos y Víctimas de Violaciones a los Derechos Humanos en México (Association of Family Members of Disappeared Detainees and Victims of Human Rights Violations in Mexico) registered more than 1,300 forced disappearances between the mid-1960s and 2001. The numbers we know today increased dramatically in the second decade of the twenty-first century, although many of the disappearances are now perpetrated by criminal groups. No definitive numbers exist for deaths caused by guerrilla operations, but it is reasonable to assume that they were much lower. The government did not consider it necessary to quantify fatalities in order to justify its counterinsurgency operations, probably because doing so would have acknowledged the existence of its adversaries. The lack of a more or less definitive number to emblematize the human cost of the armed conflict indicates the monumental task required in order to reconstruct the history of violence during this period. It also means that the state's strategy of eliminating chains of command and using extralegal methods achieved its objective of preserving impunity at both the individual and political levels.

It would be a mistake to think that civil society's silence did not reflect the support of some sectors of the population. As Rodríguez Kuri points out in reference to the events of 1968, and as Aguayo confirms with regard to acts of repression in subsequent years, the government's strategy of using violence was based on a conservative consensus that accepted extrajudicial violence. This position was imposed on public opinion through national newspapers and television, and was rooted in right-wing authoritarian ideas in Mexico and abroad. Since the 1960s, as Luis Herrán has shown, Catholics and anticommunists saw violence against the Left as a legitimate form of political action. The ease with which the governments responsible for the repression avoided almost all legal ramifications cannot be explained without acknowledging this consensus. The lack of investigations into the hundreds of accomplices in extralegal practices also speaks to the social acceptance and silence surrounding these abuses—a silence only briefly interrupted by dissent from the Left and human rights organizations.

Numbers were not the only aspect of this history that have been hard to pin down. Dates and the names of those involved are also difficult to identify. The period tends to be called the dirty war or counterinsurgency, but this terminology poses some difficulties. As McCormick suggests, rather than a constant state of war, we could talk about a low-intensity conflict that waxed and waned. But even to talk about a war or a conflict to describe those years is to accept a metaphor used by the guerrillas and the government that is more revealing of their symbiotic relationship rather than of a genuinely widespread conflict. The war created the enemies, not the other way around. From the government's perspective, it could be better described, following Montemayor, as a joint counterinsurgency initiative from the Díaz Ordaz to the López Portillo administrations. As we have seen, however, the coordination had its limits and, at least in public, the guerrillas could not be acknowledged as a political movement with social bases, let alone an enemy force. Guerrilla groups also thought they were waging a war, because they no longer viewed politics as an option. The "dirty war" label implies that the state's actions had hegemonic weight, whereas, as we have seen, this was instead a period in which two conceptions of the legitimate use of violence came into play. This emphasis on the state's leading role can be seen as a result of the number of victims but also derives from the fact that, since the 1980s, human rights organizations and later the official investigations have adopted this perspective in order to reconstruct and punish the crimes committed during this period.

In the 1960s and 1970s, it remained difficult to put a name to what was happening. Many contemporary observers recall that, despite the evidence of government abuse, their experience as members of the guerrilla and victims of abuse seemed to be shrouded in silence. Even the South American exiles who had arrived in Mexico in the 1970s found it hard to comprehend that guerrillas existed in Mexico, let alone a mass campaign of torture and disappearances similar to the ones that forced them to leave their countries, but that was committed by the same government that received them and offered them asylum. The Mexican government's ambiguous relationship with Cuba, its control of the media, and its constitutional stability was at odds with the experience of South American countries of that time. The scale of repression in those nations seemed incomparable to Mexico, although the most recent research indicates this is not necessarily the case. As we have pointed out, the silence was the consequence of the difficulty in reconstructing events in Mexico. However, the comparison with South American dictatorships remains valid: torture and disappearances were the instruments used by the Mexican state to control the situation, and violence had a profound social impact, particularly in certain regions such as Guerrero, and among some social groups, such as students and campesinos. The disbanding of armed groups toward the end of the López Portillo administration was as comprehensive as in South American countries.

The lack of popular support and the internal divisions within the leadership of most groups in Mexico meant that their defeat was enveloped in the kind of silence that Elena Poniatowska described in the 1980s. Many guerrilla members found it difficult to admit that the revolution was not imminent, that the masses probably did not want it, and that it was still possible to negotiate strategically with the government from the left, at least in regions where the PRI's dominance was not based on the stubbornness and the use of force that still characterized states such as Guerrero. It is possible to talk about a rupture within the Left (reformists versus revolutionaries), but it may be more accurate to talk about a gradual process of self-criticism that eventually led to taking advantage of the opening of the electoral system begun by López Portillo's government. As Rodríguez Kuri and others have pointed out, an unplanned consequence of the guerrilla movements was precisely to speed up that process. In any case, the criticism of the path of armed rebellion in Mexico began at an early stage. Intellectuals such as José Revueltas and Carlos Pereyra were the leading critics, but they were joined also by militants who had been on the front lines, such as Gustavo Hirales and Paquita Calvo Zapata. This self-criticism helped maintain the validity of Marxist thought in the social sciences and political analysis, taking it outside the secretive and sometimes narrow-minded study groups where the LC23S recruited its members.

The process of rescuing and recounting the experience of those years and giving it politically significant historical meaning—in other words, the memory-building process—was initiated by the most unlikely of actors: the mothers, other family members, and friends of the victims of repression. Most of these victims appear before us in a blurry outline: names and photographs from school IDs, a piece of information containing their last known whereabouts, the name of the organization they had chosen to join, and little else. Revolutionary groups themselves commemorated some events and heroic names, such as the attack on the Ciudad Madera barracks or Lucio Cabañas, but they did not cultivate the same devotion for the memory of lesser-known rebels, especially if they were women. Thanks to the efforts of their families, however, the memory of the dead and the disappeared—regardless of their participation in the guerrilla—inspired demands for truth and justice. The victims were defined not by their militancy but by their disappearance.

It was not easy to condemn the government's illegal abuses. More than eighty political prisoners in Lecumberri since 1968, including Revueltas, were forced to stage a hunger strike the following year to protest against the delays in their trial proceedings—they had no other way to complain about their conditions of detention or the irregularities in the charges against them. The authorities used common prisoners to attack the strikers. Some prisoners belonging to revolutionary organizations refused to add their names to complaints, and some even refused to benefit from official pardons. They were motivated by Salas Obregón's rationale since he founded the LC23S: only wimps appealed to the law, claiming that their rights had been violated. Despite being rebuffed by the very men they were trying to protect, sisters and mothers persisted in knocking on doors to seek answers from the government and to make their voice heard in public. In the mid-1970s, families who dared to take these actions got harassed, abused, and sometimes even kidnapped; they had few lawyers willing to work with them and the media ignored them. Even compiling a list of detainees was difficult. It was not until 1977 that such a list was published; it contained the names of 244 political prisoners. By this time, Rosario Ibarra de Piedra from Monterrey had become a visible leader. To exert moral pressure on Echeverría and López Portillo, she organized a hunger strike in the metropolitan cathedral in 1978. Her efforts led López Portillo to issue an amnesty that year. Ibarra de Piedra's public profile grew over time, thanks to her tireless quest to unearth the truth. She ran for president in 1982 and 1988 and was elected a national congresswoman in 1994.

Lodging complaints and building memory is an ongoing process. The information that began to be compiled in the 1970s remains a key element in the continuing search for the truth. While the PRI remained in power, there was no acknowledgement of past repression. In 2001, under the PAN government, the archives of the Ministries of the Interior and National Defense began to be slowly opened. Although they were subsequently partially placed off limits, and despite FEMOSPP (closed down in 2006) leading to the prosecution of only four people, including Echeverría, with no significant convictions, the investigations and resulting reports have been useful in continuing to reconstruct what happened during those two decades. The story told in this chapter is therefore still one of delayed justice.

CHAPTER SIX

VIOLENCE AND ILLEGAL BUSINESSES

—

THE VIOLENCE ASSOCIATED with organized crime is very close to us, and it has not yet completed its most destructive cycle. At the same time, it already has a long history, stretching back almost half a century. The narrative in this chapter will not describe a chain of cause and effect or a succession of father-and-son drug traffickers. Personal styles are misleading ways of classifying violence. We cannot even talk about generations, because some names are long-lasting (like that of Ismael Zambada García, a.k.a. "El Mayo") or very short-lived (like the leaders of the Familia Michoacana). Nor will this chapter be a history of drug trafficking. As we will see, this industry has always been mixed with other legal and illegal businesses, and its close ties to the use of violence have only developed in recent decades.

This history had no precise location, origin, or epicenter; instead, it was a combination of locations, regions, national strategies, and international connections. (I use the past tense in this chapter because, although many situations sound familiar, we cannot assume their indefinite continuity.)

In the fifty or so years covered by this chapter, the space itself changed, shortening the distances between cities and countries by road, air, and sea. Therefore, we should proceed chronologically but also jump from one place to another in an attempt to reflect as far as possible the wide range of actors and practices involved.

From the outset, readers must be aware that the available information on these issues is unreliable and that historians have not yet been able to separate the wheat from the chaff. Many journalistic reports on criminal groups and leaders are based on testimonies, confessions, and official documents. Together with television series, corridos or ballads, and other realist narratives, these versions of events all claim to explain important episodes and figures, but not all accounts are equally objective or rigorous. When contemporary narratives do not contradict other sources, they tend to impose a perspective that emphasizes the personality of major players. It is true that many bosses consumed drugs and alcohol, with paranoid and impulsive tendencies; very few had a formal education. But we cannot reduce this history to a chain of acts of revenge and outbursts of rage. Apart from neglecting the broader processes that I will try to outline in this chapter, such an explanation tends to deny these same narcos the ability to assess the changes taking place within the state apparatus and in their business activities. Another explanation, which sometimes appears in those same reports and in academic studies, reduces the causes of today's drug trafficking to the criminalization of drugs and social marginalization. Although these processes were already underway since the first half of the twentieth century, they are not sufficient to explain the growth and sophistication of the drug industry in recent decades. In the 1960s, US demand for drugs exploded, increasing drug exports from Mexico to the United States and the import of guns in the other direction.

This chapter shows how the use of violence changed from being a cost of the drug business, during its expansion in the 1970s and 1980s, to becoming an asset, a resource that is central to explaining the explosion of homicides and other crimes against people in recent years. During this transition, the industry itself changed. It was no longer limited to the production and export of drugs to the United States but included other lucrative and illegal activities—kidnapping, extorsion, human trafficking—in which coercion was the common denominator.

A key factor in the change was the role of the state and its agents. Until the 1980s, as Benjamin Smith points out, judicial and drug enforcement agents and officers from other police units not only provided protection for drug traffickers but also extorted them with the threat of violence. These state agents stole the traffickers' money and their product, tortured them to extract confessions, and even killed those who disobeyed. Drug traffickers were not initially experts in violence, but they paid money to those who were, and who wore a badge. This allowed them to continue a business that, despite the rhetoric, very few in Mexico considered to be criminal in the same way that it was viewed by the US government. Drugs were banned in both countries in the first half of the twentieth century without their prohibition triggering a wave of violence. What changed in the last decades of the century was the amount of money at stake.

Beginning in the 1980s, narco kingpins began to reassess their relationship with the state officials. While continuing to send money to the most senior federal government officials, they turned local and federal police into their employees. In exchange for regular bribes, these law enforcement agents offered security in their operations (for example, by protecting the landing and unloading of aircraft from the south) and harassed rival groups. Several police officers became capos, such as Juan José Esparragoza Moreno, a.k.a. "El Azul" (Blue) (Badiraguato, Sinaloa, 1949–2014?), who became a DFS agent despite having been linked to the business since his youth in Sinaloa. For the most aggressive bosses, it was a logical step to move from buying off police to creating their own security details, recruited from the same ranks as the police or the armed forces. In turn, this transformed the use of violence. In the twenty-first century, turf wars broke out between groups fighting over the control of cities or border crossings. This led to levels of brutality that would have shocked mid-century pistoleros.

Today, we are feeling the effects of these changes. The number of homicides in Mexico is comparable to numbers of victims of violence in countries experiencing civil wars. We could also equate present-day Mexico to the Revolution or the Cristero War in terms of violent deaths, although this cannot be done very accurately because the quantitative sources are so different: the deaths calculated for those civil conflicts are estimates, whereas the crime of homicide is now more carefully tallied. Violence today is more predictable and more localized in its effects on the general population than in the 1910s. It is not a civil war, although many of its victims are unarmed civilians.

Another process that defines the changes in this more recent period is the transformation of the national space. Confrontations, assassinations, and massacres took place throughout the country, not just in a handful of border towns. Attackers could travel hundreds of kilometers to carry out an attack, while their bosses enjoyed their wealth in modern and relatively safe cities. More regions became pathways for trafficking goods by road, air, sea, and even through tunnels. Links to South American cocaine producers proved decisive in the growth of the industry and the consolidation of some leaderships. Methamphetamine production and trafficking opened links to Asia, exploited also to produce fentanyl. Working with distributors in the United States became a key resource for the most successful groups. As profits soared, bosses could invest more in experts in the use of force, purchase more weapons, and gather intelligence. Violence changed from being local, defensive, and artisanal—as inherited from the era of the pistoleros—to reaching an almost industrial scale and level of complexity.

In the old days, the business was not completely free of violence, but there were rules that reduced the need to use it. Since the 1930s, local and state police interest in the drug trade could lead to deaths. Evidence exists that homicide was a resource used to neutralize threats from the government or competitors. The most famous example is the 1944 assassination of Sinaloa state governor Rodolfo Loaiza by pistolero Rodolfo "El Gitano" (The Gypsy) Valdés. Sinaloa offers multiple early examples of methods to come. The nota roja on Francisco Contreras's death in 1977 reported that "he was shot fifty times, Culiacán-style." His father had been assassinated the previous year in a similar fashion. The list of guns used by the twelve-man posse who arrived in two pickup trucks sounds familiar today: AK-47 assault rifles, R15s (a.k.a. M16s, used by the US Army), and .45- and .38-caliber pistols. Policía Judicial Federal agents were also killed, as in the case of Jorge Rosete Carrillo in Ensenada in 1980. The reports of these homicides, from Loaiza to Rosete Carrillo, did not highlight the drug-trafficking connections although they did reveal the increase in violence as part of the business. Hiding one's hand was still possible and beneficial.

In the 1970s, a system existed in which bribes for officials worked their way up the state apparatus; drugs did not stay in Mexico, and the business remained on a manageable scale, without affecting third parties or becoming a part of other types of illegal activities. The army, the PJF, and the DFS were in charge of law and order, but their officers and agents systematically exploited or protected the narcos. PJF agents, for example, took advantage of trafficking activities in their *plaza*, the city assigned to them, and did not confuse their role with that of their clients. What these agents did was increase the level of danger in the business, because protection could suddenly change for political reasons or trigger conflicts between state representatives at various levels and in different institutions.

Sinaloa's reputation as the "birthplace of drug trafficking" does not mean that the business began there—it had already existed in different forms and in various places since the early twentieth century. Rather, the idea refers to a bucolic mythology about the early narcos and the rise of some groups with roots in the state. Poppies, and later marijuana, were crops that had supported an illegal agricultural economy at least since the 1930s. Opium and heroin had weak domestic demand; the main customer was the United States, where consumption skyrocketed in the 1970s. Two generations of future drug traffickers, from Ernesto "Don Neto" Fonseca (b. 1930) to Joaquín "El Chapo" (Shorty) Guzmán (b. 1957)—both from the Badiraguato municipality—started out with the hard work of growing, packaging, and then transporting these drugs. Many of the men and women in the business were related to one another as uncles and aunts, cousins, siblings, brothers and sisters-in-law, parents-in-law, and—most commonly of all—compadres (godfathers). These connections sealed close and frequent social interactions, work alliances, and pacts of loyalty.

These "family" values reflected the vulnerability of the business activity that connected the actors. More than the government's destruction of crops, something done primarily for show, drug traffickers were mainly concerned about the theft of their product. Thieves of packages of marijuana or opium paste counted on the belief that the victims would not report it, and police would not investigate. Anyone who did press charges would be arrested for trafficking. The loot was easily converted into cash. As a result, robberies were often committed by competitors within the same business, or by police officers who could in turn sell the drug to other traffickers. In Jesús Malverde's shrine in Culiacán, devotees thank the mythical bandit for his protection in shifting their product. But the most effective way to prevent such robberies was through direct punishment. Such was the fate of Juan Manuel Salcido Uzeta, a.k.a. "El Cochiloco" (The Crazy Pig), who was mown down by machine gun in Guadalajara for allegedly stealing several tons of cocaine. In the mythological narco origin stories, violence was only used for self-defense or fair punishment.

The use of weapons and the association with government agents became an inevitable part of the drug trade beginning in the 1970s. The US government's eagerness to criminalize the consumption and production of certain drugs had already become a problem some years earlier. The Mexican government had successfully hoodwinked the gringos and kept up an appearance of control, but the deception became harder to pull off when Richard Nixon's government found fighting drugs to be a politically profitable way to crystallize the social conservatism of voters worried about new trends in popular culture, protests against the Vietnam War, and African Americans' struggles for their civil rights. The Mexican government was pressured in various ways, including the temporary closure of border crossings in 1969 with "Operation Intercept," an initiative designed to prevent marijuana from entering the country. The US Drug Enforcement Agency (DEA) was set up in 1973 and soon opened offices in Mexico, although the Federal Bureau of Narcotics already had agents in the country and influenced drug legislation and policing. Pressure increased in the 1970s. Operation Condor, which targeted Sinaloa producers in 1976, was a binational cooperation that mobilized thousands of Mexican soldiers and led to hundreds of arrests and the destruction of crops. US military assistance was provided in exchange for arrests and seized drug shipments.

It would be a mistake, however, to suggest that the Mexican government simply acted as Washington's puppet. Operation Condor complemented the concerns of Díaz Ordaz and Echeverría about leftist revolutionary groups in places like the Universidad Autónoma de Sinaloa and in the mountains of Guerrero. Counterinsurgency techniques shaped operations, such as the use of torture to obtain information and the execution and disappearance of prisoners. As we saw in chapter 5, federal agents had significant leeway to combine counterinsurgency roles with anti-drug trafficking activities.

Operation Condor did not have a long-term impact on illegal crops grown in Sinaloa and on the borders of Sinaloa, Chihuahua, and Durango— Mexico's Golden Triangle. Crops were still cultivated in states further south. The destruction of plantations was not new and would be repeated in sub-sequent years, as if to prove its ineffectiveness. In the short term, Operation Condor displaced activities to other regions. The main players in the busi-ness moved to Guadalajara, more suitable surroundings for their increas-ing wealth and political and social connections. And, without abandoning their links in the northwest, they consolidated national and international business. By 1981, for example, Rafael Caro Quintero had ramped up mari-juana production to unprecedented levels at El Búfalo ranch in Chihuahua. Joining forces with Colombian producers and traffickers from other Latin American countries, the Guadalajara group's bosses strengthened transna-tional relationships that would prove decisive in years to come, ensuring a steady supply of marijuana and cocaine for the US market. The value of Mexican exports grew in the early 1970s and enjoyed a boom in the second half of the 1980s. This led to the diversification of smuggling routes and the multiplication of crop-growing areas, including in the state of Tamaulipas for a period, and more intensively in Guerrero, where poppies were also grown.

Cocaine—already trafficked through Mexico in the 1970s—became the central product in the relationship with the Colombians in the 1980s as US demand for this alkaloid grew. Initially it was consumed by the wealthy and later more broadly in the adulterated form of crack cocaine. The Reagan administration had made it slightly more difficult to transport the prod-uct through the Caribbean into Florida. The Guadalajara group organized safer routes to transport tons of the drug into the United States across the more porous borders in southern and northern Mexico, where chances of detection were low. By the 1990s, more than half the cocaine consumed in the United States entered through Mexico, and at a lower cost for consumers. The production and trafficking of cocaine became a more complex operation, but nothing made it inherently more violent than any other illegal business. However, in the United States the government stoked a moral panic and increased police violence by criminalizing the Black and Hispanic populations. This led to high levels of incarceration, unprecedented anywhere in the world, and a parallel escalation of urban violence. More resources were also allocated to the DEA and its Mexican operations.

The move of some bosses to Guadalajara responded to a new type of coordination with government agents. The DFS protected Caro Quintero's operations in El Búfalo in exchange for payments received by its director, Miguel Nazar Haro. Federal, state, and other local agents worked directly for the major traffickers, allowing their product to pass through airports, checkpoints, and customs, and by providing security for shipments and leading members of the criminal organizations. As the merchandise became more valuable and easier to sell (a kilo of cocaine was worth far more than the equivalent weight of marijuana, and was less bulky), the risk of its theft or confiscation became greater. By making protection essential, these police agents began to inject into the business the brutality and impunity that had characterized pistolerismo since the middle of the century.

Miguel Ángel Félix Gallardo (Culiacán, b. 1946) was a key figure in this transformation for several reasons. First, he was able to establish mutually beneficial relationships with key government agents at both state and national levels. Félix Gallardo had been a judicial police officer in Sinaloa in the 1960s, and a bodyguard and later compadre of Governor Leopoldo Sánchez Celis. The line that once separated narcos from the police was already beginning to blur. Félix Gallardo was able to establish relationships with the federal government through figures such as Rubén Zuno Arce, the brother-in-law of former President Echeverría and son of former governor and founder of the Universidad de Guadalajara, José Guadalupe Zuno. An agreement was reached with the CIA to use the aircraft that brought in cocaine from South America to transfer money and weapons to the Nicaraguan Contra rebels in exchange for access to US markets. Félix Gallardo worked with the various parties who profited from drug trafficking. These beneficiaries included a wide range of actors, from campesinos in isolated regions to the local bourgeoisie that invested newly available capital in legal businesses; for the government, this was a manageable risk that enabled Mexico to remain in Washington's good books by appearing to go after traffickers while officials at different levels were amassing fortunes.

The second explanation for Félix Gallardo's importance was his access to Colombian narcos. Cocaine multiplied the Guadalajara group's profits, so its leaders gave it priority over the production of heroin and marijuana. International links provided a certain legitimacy. Félix Gallardo evoked the type of businessman who could foster productive cross-border relationships, at a time when neoliberal ideas about the benefits of free trade and open markets were taking hold. Among the drug-trafficking capos, he was the one who came closest to social respectability. Before his arrest, photographs showed him in discreet attire, surrounded by expensive cars and motorcycles. He projected an urbaneness that contrasted with other traffickers; he was better educated and had contacts among high-ranking politicians. His personal style may have helped, but cocaine itself was the key to his achievement of a certain acceptance in Mexico. Drug trafficking was not yet tainted by unrestrained violence. And while marijuana and opium were associated with social marginalization, cocaine was a product for the upper classes, and the business provided in influx of dollars during an economic slump and at a time when the Mexican middle class's consumer appetite was growing.

The third reason why Félix Gallardo was important in this history was because he was a bridge between the narcos' old modus operandi and the needs of a business that required more complex structures, divisions of labor, and new ways of reaching agreements. According to Ricardo Ravelo, a transition took place from organizations characterized by cacicazgos based on personal leadership styles and regional strongmen such as Pablo Acosta (Chihuahua, 1937–87) in Ojinaga, to "business corporations" that prioritized profits, expansion, and collective decision-making. In prison, Félix Gallardo showed Diego Enrique Osorno his writings, proving that he cultivated this reputation as a man of peace. In his own telling, one day he read in the local nota roja tabloid that an entire family had been killed, including their cat. Outraged, he gathered local police officers and told them that "the people of Mazatlán do not deserve this." Thanks to his participation in the investigations, those responsible for the crime were soon discovered.

The history of the following decades shows that the distinction between old and new methods was never clear. While Félix Gallardo represented the desire for a certain respectability and invested money in legal assets, he employed pistoleros and worked with police officers, such as Guillermo González Calderoni, who kept alive the tradition of siphoning off the profits of drug trafficking. González Calderoni became a linchpin for collaborations with capos. He created a stream of income for prominent figures in national politics during the administrations of Miguel de la Madrid and

Carlos Salinas. In 2003, he was assassinated in McAllen, Texas. The idea of "modernization" can be a misleading concept for understanding this transformation, and it is certainly useless as a way of classifying the different actors. The use of force never ceased being an integral part of the business.

The narco-businessman's vulnerability to this habit of violence became abundantly clear after the torture and murder of DEA agent Enrique "Kiki" Camarena in Guadalajara in February 1985. Caro Quintero blamed him for the destruction of El Búfalo by federal forces. DFS agents kidnapped Camarena and he was tortured and killed by Caro Quintero, abetted by Ernesto Fonseca and Félix Gallardo, in a house that had belonged to Zuno Arce. This act of punishment broke the basic rule of not stirring up trouble with gringo agents. The US government's response led to tensions between the two governments, including the kidnapping and transfer of a Mexican citizen to the United States without an extradition order. The same calculation applied to previous and future collaborations between the governments: one US citizen's death outweighed the hundreds of Mexican law enforcement fatalities. In Mexico, Camarena's murder focused public attention on the extravagant conduct and dangerous impulses of people such as Caro Quintero, and led the Mexican state to double down on its strategy of prioritizing the capture of the most notorious crime bosses. Camarena's death made no tangible difference to the development of the business, although it did contribute to the disintegration of the Guadalajara group. Caro Quintero and Fonseca were arrested months later and Félix Gallardo continued to operate as "the Boss of Bosses" until he was arrested by González Calderoni in 1989.

Organized crime groups continued to want smooth business operations for maximum profitability. That year, a meeting was held in Acapulco to divide up the different routes and territories among the members of the Guadalajara group. It is likely that this effort at coordination, allegedly originated by Félix Gallardo while in jail, was actually an order from the highest echelons of federal government. According to information not substantiated by the courts, Carlos Salinas's government, acting through the president's brother, Raúl, played a central role in protecting drug trafficking at a national level. Camarena's murder had destabilized relations with Washington, but nothing prevented the continuation of a business that generated fabulous profits and generous kickbacks, and which was still relatively discreet when it came to settling internal scores. However, the rampant growth and violence of the industry in the 1990s thwarted the development of any master plan. An unplanned series of alliances and splits in different regions, during successive cycles of conflict, caused the business to move away from the structure imagined by Félix Gallardo and the federal government. But the episode of the Acapulco meeting illustrated a new reality: state actors were not passive recipients of bribes; they tried to shape the business.

This has led to the suggestion, for example, that the Salinas brothers favored the Gulf Cartel, which controlled the routes through the state of Tamaulipas to the eastern United States. The agreement between the Sinaloans, who operated in the west and in Chihuahua, and the Gulf group, was in any case a pillar of the business's national organization during those years. Matamoros-based cacique Juan Nepomuceno Guerra controlled the region's illegal businesses beginning in the 1930s. His authority came from a long history as a smuggler who had incorporated drugs into his business after trafficking alcohol, prostitutes, automobiles, and other items, although always from his region. His nephew Juan García Ábrego succeeded him in the 1980s and entered the cocaine business.

Despite their roots and traditional approach to business, the bosses of the Gulf criminal groups were not averse to using violence. Nepomuceno Guerra killed his wife in a fit of jealousy over her perceived infidelity with comedian Resortes (Adalberto Martínez Chávez); García Ábrego avenged his brother's death, on July 17, 1982, with several subsequent murders committed on the seventeenth of each month. After García Ábrego's arrest in 1996, infighting broke out. Osiel Cárdenas, who eventually took control, saw the use of violence as being central to the business, but also as a personal privilege. He had a friend killed to take his wife and had a photograph of the body sent to him to certify that Hilda Flores González was now "only mine." Cárdenas had started out in the business as a PJF madrina, robbing and extorting traffickers who wanted to take product through his plaza in Miguel Alemán, Tamaulipas. As a boss, he expanded those predatory methods throughout the state, using torture and assassination to mark his control over the most profitable routes. Cárdenas expanded his tools beyond the use of brute force, by recruiting soldiers and informants, using communications systems and manipulating press coverage.

Amado Carrillo Fuentes, a.k.a. "El Senor de los Cielos" (The Lord of the Skies), was another new boss who exemplified the difficulties of establishing the kind of business leadership that Félix Gallardo hoped to achieve. Carrillo Fuentes started out as a junior member of the Guadalajara group, which he had to leave in the early 1980s because Caro Quintero could not tolerate the fact that he was favored by Sara Cosío, a daughter of an upper-class family from the city. Although Carrillo Fuentes was not assigned Ciudad Juárez during the 1989 meeting in Acapulco, he eventually took control of that plaza (a term that began to be used for areas controlled by narcos, not only judicial police) thanks to his ability to manage a fleet of aircraft (hence his

nickname). After Rafael Aguilar Guajardo's death in 1993, Carrillo Fuentes
became one of the most powerful crime bosses of the decade. In addition
to aircraft, he was skilled in cutting-edge communication technologies,
which he used for his own security and to protect his shipments. His group,
which was beginning to be called the "Juárez Cartel," divided tasks between
different groups according to their functions: security, trafficking, storage,
paying off government officials, money laundering, information management. Similarly to Félix Gallardo, the key to power continued to be the
connections with Colombian providers, who found Carrillo Fuentes to be
more reliable for transporting cocaine than other bosses. After Pablo Escobar died in 1993, Carrillo Fuentes struck deals with the Cali Cartel and the
Rodríguez Orejuela brothers to guarantee continued supplies. "Cartel" is a
misnomer for these organizations, but the term was eventually adopted by
the narcos themselves. The industry was increasingly defined by a franchise
model rather than a centrally controlled structure.

Carrillo Fuentes differed from the old, cacique-style capos in his mobility: he was constantly moving around Mexico, making trips abroad. He
ordered hits (probably including Aguilar Guajardo's murder) in places as
far away from Chihuahua as Cancún. Other leaders were also constantly
on the move. Vicentillo, El Mayo Zambada's son, lived in Culiacán, Mexico
City, and also spent periods in Brazil, Canada, Spain, and the United States.
His father preferred to stay in the mountains of Sinaloa, constantly moving
from ranch to ranch. No one wanted to end up like Pablo Acosta, who was
too attached to Ojinaga, where he was eventually cornered by González
Calderoni. The agility to move from one ranch, city, or country to another
was necessary because there was always the risk of being attacked by rivals
or arrested. By the same token, mobility was possible thanks to protection
from high-ranking state officials. Carrillo Fuentes was shielded because he
paid off police officers and soldiers around the country, including Ernesto
Zedillo's antidrug czar, Gen. Jesús Gutiérrez Rebollo. Carrillo Fuentes's de-
mise was the result of those dangers and the violence that he was prepared
to commit on his own body in his quest to leave behind his peripatetic
lifestyle and "retire" from the business. He died in 1997 after undergoing
plastic surgery and liposuction at a Mexico City clinic. Several of the doctors
involved in the operation were killed shortly afterward.

Carrillo Fuentes's disappearance unleashed centrifugal tendencies that
had been barely contained during the hegemony of the Juárez Cartel. That
year, Esparragoza proposed that Vicente Carrillo Fuentes, Amado's brother,
be put in charge of the Juárez plaza. A member of the Guadalajara group but
formerly a DFS agent, El Azul Esparragoza did not have a route or plaza of

his own and relied on making deals with other bosses to move his product. He did have connections with the police and members of the political class, enabling him to stay in business despite being jailed after Kiki Camarena's death. Esparragoza's proposal to restore the peace imagined by Félix Gallardo was doomed to failure. Any alliance was precarious, especially because there had already been a costly dispute between factions in Tijuana and Sinaloa, and soon a conflict would break out between the Pacific and Gulf groups over the control of Ciudad Juárez. Clashes and killings had their internal logic, even though the business was flourishing and continued to enjoy significant official protection. Collaboration between the offshoots of the Guadalajara group began to weaken in the 1990s and gave way to a territorial fragmentation characterized by outbreaks of violence that mixed personal and strategic issues.

The territorial organization proposed in 1989 and 1997 involved agreements for the smuggling of products over the main border crossings. The purpose was in part to solve the problem that Tijuana posed for the Sinaloa traffickers. That city, one of the key border crossings in terms of volume of human and commercial traffic, was under the control of the Arellano Félix brothers. Ramón Arellano Félix, considered too reckless even by his own brothers, killed a compadre of El Chapo Guzmán at Ismael Zambada's birthday party in 1988. Attempts were made at various meetings to stem the violence (a compadre's blood was worth less than the continuity of the business), but Ramón's impulsive behavior was hard to control, even though the various parties concerned had worked together for years. In 1991, Vicente, the favorite son of El Mayo, was targeted in an attack and recalls that "a very vicious war" broke out at that time, forcing his family to seek refuge in Culiacán. The Arellano Félixes tried to kill El Mayo in 1992, because he owed them money for transporting drugs through Tijuana, but failed in their attempt.

El Mayo Zambada (b. 1948) offered a stark contrast to the Arellano Félix clan. At a very young age, he had started trafficking heroin and forging connections in the United States and later in Colombia. He had a reputation for discretion and seeking peaceful partnerships, such as the one he had with El Chapo, instead of aggressively expanding his business. This good temper was relative, of course. El Chapo and Héctor "El Güero" (Blondie) Palma, another Sinaloan, ordered a hit on members of the Arellano Félix family at the Christine discotheque in Puerto Vallarta in late 1992. It was a carefully planned operation but, like many incidents throughout this history, incompetently executed. Six people died but Ramón and Francisco Javier escaped. In other acts of revenge, Ramón himself fired at El Chapo on a street corner in Guadalajara, and his men tried to kill Amado Carrillo Fuentes at a Mexico City restaurant in 1993.

Many of these attacks were designed as ambushes to prevent open battles between rivals with evenly matched firepower. Things seldom went according to plan. Several trucks would be used to block the victim's vehicle, for example, with gunmen firing from all angles. This was the tactic used by the Arellano Félix brothers to kill Tijuana journalist Jesús Blancornelas in 1997, but the hit played out with typical messiness. Blancornelas survived, but his driver was not so fortunate. A stray bullet by the attackers also killed David Barrón Corona, a.k.a. "Popeye" or "El C. H.," the Arellano Félix group's principal *sicario* (hit man). Barrón Corona had been responsible for another failed operation, which led to the death of Cardinal Juan Jesús Posadas Ocampo in Guadalajara in 1993. El Chapo was imprisoned shortly thereafter for the cardinal's death, although the official version of the event was that the priest was killed accidentally. Reasonable doubts exist about this explanation, but the fact is that mutual attacks were generally chaotic, excessive, and without any concern for collateral damage.

The clash between the successors of Félix Gallardo and Arellano Félix was not simply a personal quarrel. Ultimately, it was about the cost of taking drugs through Tijuana. Although this was not the only area where violence was used, the conflict there lasted longer than most and indicated a shifting logic in the use of violence, in which the public message was as important as the tactical result. Ramón liked using weapons himself when attacking his enemies, as if to show he was serious. This is how he died, in Mazatlán in 2002, exchanging gunfire at close range with a police officer who also died. He had fallen into a trap laid by El Mayo, whom Ramón was looking for in the port city in order to kill him. Ramón should have delegated the job. Even before these events, the Arellano Félix family and its rivals began using the services of experts in assassination and in manipulating the public perception of their power. The Arellano Félix brothers, for example, used California sicarios hired by El Popeye in San Diego and recruited "narco-juniors"—children of the moneyed classes of Tijuana. They also cultivated a reputation for frenzied brutality, exemplified by Ramón himself. When financial incentives failed, they used violence against journalists such as Blancornelas, whose work had the potential to reveal connections with state officials, a source of embarrassment for the government and crime bosses, or simply to create the impression of a lack of control over the plaza. The concern about public perceptions was widespread and expressed through different practices. Amado Carrillo used people to spread information in support of his cause. To maximize the public impact of their actions, in more recent years some organizations even employed cameramen as part of their units to record their raids and post them on YouTube.

El Mayo, meanwhile, cultivated the image of someone who preferred to avoid violence. He sought the government's assistance to ensure armed superiority, and for the arrest or elimination of his enemies. As El Mayo told his lawyer, "The government will always have more bullets, there's no point fighting them." This use of the police to do the dirty work was not the exclusive strategy of any group and could lead to clashes between state forces. In some cases, agents from the Procuraduría General de la República and the PJF, or army officers, fought alongside one group of traffickers against another, or even against each other. The clashes involving government units were the counterpart of unholy collaborations. In Tlaxicoyan, Veracruz, in 1991, seven police officers died and one soldier was wounded after a clash between soldiers and judicial agents. Alcides "El Metro" Ramón Magaña was both the head of a PJF antinarcotics group and the chief bodyguard for Amado Carrillo Fuentes. The Sinaloans attacked the Arellano Félixes by killing local police officers in Tijuana. One PJF agent, Rodolfo "El Chipilón" (Sad One) García Gaxiola, who had also killed other police officers, was executed in 1998 by members of Carrillo Fuentes's group because he was working for both the Juárez and Tijuana Cartels at the same time. Documenting stable alliances between state agents and drug traffickers is difficult: bribe recipients changed constantly and federal strategies of favoring one criminal group over another are hard to define clearly. As research by Anabel Hernández and other journalists has shown, narcos not only paid for police protection but also invested money to ensure that their men were placed in positions where they could be more useful to them.

One effect of this violence—which was personal but increasingly important as part of the business—was that coalitions were not only designed to carve up territories but also to attack common adversaries. El Chapo escaped the high-security prison of Puente Grande in early 2001. While in prison he continued to be in charge of resources and people, and left behind him a wake of accusations that he had raped female inmates and prison staff. Once out, and after a large party in Badiraguato, he wasted no time in pushing for the creation of "The Federation" with El Mayo, which brought together bosses from Sinaloa and Juárez (El Mayo, El Azul, El Chapo, Arturo Beltrán Leyva, Ignacio Coronel, Vicente Carrillo Fuentes). The immediate objective, as proposed at an initial meeting in Cuernavaca, was to "exterminate" the Arellano Félix clan. Their task was made easier by the fact that Vicente Fox's government had made the Arellano Félixes public enemy number one, and because the United States insisted on their capture after they tortured to death a Mexican police officer who had collaborated with the DEA. In 2002, Benjamín Arellano Félix was arrested in Puebla, and Ramón died in Mazatlán, as described above. However, the extermination was not complete. Despite further arrests, the family remained active in organized crime: Enedina Arellano Félix kept the business going, focusing on money laundering through companies that, despite being reported to the Mexican government by the DEA, could carry on unhindered. The organization also regained control of Tijuana and developed a presence in other regions, though now avoiding Ramón's brand of extravagant brutality.

The Federation project shows that the Sinaloans were no longer limited to a regional perspective on the industry. The volume of traffic was so great that it could no longer be reduced to a plaza or stretch of border. Attacking rivals was unavoidable in order to open up spaces at a national level but also in the urban drug-trafficking microcosm. Since the 1990s, some of the violence in Tijuana was caused by fighting over the control of drug dealing on the streets. This trend could also be seen elsewhere, especially when the bigger traffickers paid their subalterns in kind, forcing them to sell the product even though they did not have distribution networks in the United States. This caused deaths over street dealing sites. On the national scale, the fighting was equally fierce and somewhat better documented. Fighting between members of the Tijuana and Sinaloa groups could break out almost anywhere in Mexico.

Unlike the peace imagined by Félix Gallardo, El Chapo and El Mayo's proposed Federation sought to combine their collective influence on government and their solid connections with Colombian producers to establish new financing models. The business was so huge that the agreement included sharing routes, armed groups, and money launderers. Apart from limiting internal clashes, the organization helped bring together groups of investors to fund major operations, especially in view of the diminishing demand and price for cocaine in the United States in the 1990s. These partnerships, which could be formed for a single cocaine shipment, spread risk and rewarded collaboration. Although the Federation soon fell apart, the Sinaloans continued being able to conduct these operations and also to offer funding and services for other actors. This included distribution through channels in the United States and, of course, security. Sinaloa capos could sell drugs to small-time drug dealers in Mexico, pay their investors with drugs or money, and offer them to transport it to the United States if they accepted the former option. Their networks had expanded and they now had a foothold in New York, which had previously been under Colombian control. Although the Federation's capos tried to present themselves as businessmen interested in broadening their reach and handling a wide variety of assets, like in any legitimate enterprise, they could not reverse the trend that made the specialized (though not always competent) use of weapons the key to the criminal activity.

The confrontation between the Sinaloa and Gulf Cartels, which had been prevented by high-level agreements since the 1980s, broke out into open warfare, first in the border region and then in states further south. The process that led to this conflict involved a degradation of the command structures that began, in western Mexico, with the breakdown of relations between the Sinaloans and the group in control of Ciudad Juárez after Amado Carrillo's death in 1997 and, in the east, with the organizational upheaval that came with the collapse of García Ábrego's well-established hegemony in 1996. The creation of the Federation and Osiel Cárdenas's arrest in 2003 intensified a conflict that was unprecedented in its death toll and duration. The Sinaloans wanted easier access to the eastern US routes; the Gulf's groups viewed their fight as a defense of their legitimate territorial rights. Both fought through proxies and their own armed units, such as the Zetas.

Today it seems inevitable to make a link between this new kind of conflict and the emergence of the Zetas. This connection certainly helps to signal the change, but such a conclusion would be an oversimplification. However, the idea that the group introduced a new modality in the use of violence persists because the government, the Sinaloa Cartel, and other organized crime groups promoted the idea, and because the Zetas themselves used it as propaganda. The Zetas appeared as a consequence of the Gulf Cartel's operations, both in its predatory methods in the territories under its control and in its acceptance of the logic of territorial expansion that the Sinaloa and Tijuana groups had already adopted. Osiel Cárdenas was a newcomer to the business when he took over power in Tamaulipas. His signature style, from his beginnings in the town of Miguel Alemán, was to use coercion (a practice sanctioned by his informal association with the PJF) to exploit traffickers. One of his nicknames was "El Mata Amigos" (Friend Killer). He murdered Rolando Gómez Garza to stay with his wife, as pointed out earlier; and he also ordered the killing of Salvador Gómez Herrera, who had been his righthand man during the fight against rival leaders also hoping to take over from García Ábrego. Instead of a succession, Cárdenas saw his victory in this fight as a rupture. According to Ricardo Ravelo, after killing Gómez Herrera in 1999, he told other traffickers, "You need to know that the Gulf Cartel is fucked. It's my organization now." Cárdenas's control over some of the country's most profitable routes was marked by a constant use of violence and an extreme concern for his personal safety. Killing could be useful in business and to get lovers, or for entertainment, but it added a new department to the "business."

Cárdenas used Arturo Guzmán Decena, a.k.a. "Z1," to kill Gómez Herrera. Guzmán Decena suggested a "personal guard" consisting of soldiers like him. However, the proposal was not for state agents to act as bodyguards while maintaining their official positions, as was now routine, but to hire them on a full-time basis, with salaries starting at US$800 a month. The recruits came from the army's special forces with the highest levels of training, sometimes even received in the United States. The group was expert in the use of the most advanced weapons and operational intelligence. They also replicated the military's vertical hierarchy and willingness to sacrifice themselves when following orders. Their duties included protecting shipments and fighting off the groups that El Chapo deployed in disputed areas. When the Zetas began offensive operations, their tactic was to overwhelm their targets with superior firepower, to completely eliminate the enemy, and to achieve the greatest psychological impact. They recruited Kaibiles, a group from the Guatemalan armed forces trained in the use of counterinsurgency techniques, including torture, dismemberment, and decapitation, in order to spread terror among civilians. They set up training camps. These new methods forced the sicarios already in the service of the Gulf Cartel, and then their adversaries, to kill "as brutally as possible." Their professional training, however, gave the Zetas a certain authority. In a 2010 message to Tamaulipas state officials and journalists, they declared, "We don't need to tell people to support us, or to recruit secondary school kids like they do. We're trained for combat and we don't need people who don't know how to use a gun."

The Zetas' specialized use of violence increased their autonomy, especially after Osiel Cárdenas's arrest. Apart from their military ethic, they boasted of their heroic bravery in resisting the Sinaloans, as they claimed to be fighting not only the invaders but also the state itself. The Calderón administration's support for Sinaloa, through the president's most powerful lieutenant, Genaro García Luna—director of the Agencia Federal de Investigación (Federal Agency of Investigation, or AFI) under President Fox and minister of public security during Calderón's presidency—was an open secret that was ultimately confirmed by García Luna's 2023 conviction in US courts on charges related to drug trafficking.

In the messages left beside victims' bodies or on sheets hung in prominent places in urban areas, the Zetas claimed to follow a code of honor that prevented them from harming the innocent—though, as we will see below, they had little concern for collateral damage. One such note, left beside the body of a storekeeper in Xalapa, read, "This is for the government, weren't you going to protect me? This shows what happens to anyone who lacks respect. Sincerely, the Gulf Cartel / Zetas. Respect the letter [Z]." They punished their adversaries for violating the same code. In Chilpancingo in 2008, Heriberto Lazcano, the group's leader after Guzmán Decena's death in 2002, ordered the beheading of eight soldiers in retaliation for the army's support of the Sinaloa Cartel and for arresting and raping an accountant of their group. There are too many examples of excessive violence to be contained in any single book. Over time, these messages became less clear because other groups could also commit atrocities to send a message.

A military structure was hard to maintain on the basis of an economy limited to drug trafficking. Therefore, the Zetas' tactics became their strategy. Brutality became the group's main asset, at the expense of Z1's original purpose. The Zetas' membership grew from a few dozen to several hundred. The new recruits were not necessarily soldiers, but they had to undergo weapons training and harsh initiation rituals. After breaking away from the Gulf Cartel, the Zetas began to profit from their own illegal activities and offered franchises to other groups. The Zeta founders' origins were geographically diverse, which partly explains their willingness to operate outside the Gulf Cartel's territory. Since they had not started out as drug traffickers, it was also easier for them to diversify their predatory activities. Trafficking immigrants, kidnapping, and extorting civilians eventually erased the (always rather theoretical) distinction between the "respectable" drug business and regular criminal activities. Small groups could claim to be Zetas almost anywhere in the country to instill fear. The Zetas tried to extort money in all kinds of situations.

Brutality was more easily justified as a defensive need. From its beginnings, the Zetas were the product of the kinds of attacks faced by the Gulf Cartel. El Chapo understood the predatory threat of Osiel Cárdenas's hegemony. Therefore, to attack him he issued orders to "heat up" his plazas—to commit spectacular acts of violence that would attract government and media attention, creating the impression that Cárdenas was losing his grip on power. The Tamaulipas group then raised the temperature even higher, increasing the perception of chaos in formerly uncontested territories.

To lead the offensive, El Chapo assigned Arturo Beltrán Leyva, also born in Badiraguato, a relative and collaborator of the heirs of the Guadalajara group. His brother Héctor was the boss of the plaza in the state of Guerrero and laundered money. Arturo tried to carry out his duty as aggressively as the Zetas, though without the military structure. Edgar "La Barbie" Valdés

Villarreal was given the job of attacking the various plazas and recruiting gang members from the United States (where he was born) and Central America. They also had the support of García Luna. Hostilities could be said to have started when, after Osiel Cárdenas's detention, La Barbie told Lazcano to withdraw from the plazas from Reynosa to Nuevo Laredo—in other words, leaving the Gulf Cartel only in control of the Matamoros border crossing. In another version, given by Anabel Hernández, La Barbie killed one of Lazcano's brothers in 2002 and then hid out with Arturo Beltrán Leyva in Mexico City. Beltrán Leyva refused to hand him over to the Zetas, and then the war started. Personal issues were impossible to distinguish from strategic considerations. In August 2003, a battle was fought in Nuevo Laredo that resolved nothing but marked the beginning of hostilities in the plaza. The number of deaths in this municipality tripled between 2004 and 2005.

Ioan Grillo has described how new tactics began to be used: paramilitary groups, open attacks on the police, mass kidnappings. These practices spread around the country. The Zetas and the Federation agreed to a truce in 2007. At a meeting near Matamoros, Lazcano received El Chapo, El Azul, El Mayo, Nacho Coronel, and even Vicente Carrillo Fuentes. The war was costing too much. The different groups agreed on a division of states, as well as states that would remain neutral. The cease-fire was short-lived because the tactical genie was already out of the bottle. Unlike in the 1989 Acapulco agreement, this time the federal government's intervention destabilized the situation.

The 2007 meeting is surprising because by that stage Vicente Carrillo Fuentes and El Chapo were enemies. When Amado Carrillo Fuentes died in 1997, the Arellano Félixes tried to take control of Ciudad Juárez. This sparked an initial wave of violence in the city. In 2004, the alliance between the Sinaloans and the Juárez Cartel within the Federation had collapsed, triggering a parallel series of confrontations that turned Ciudad Juárez into one of the bloodiest battlegrounds of the decade. The men deployed from Sinaloa were now fighting the Tijuana group in a new combat zone, Chihuahua. El Chapo, with El Mayo's approval, ordered the murder of a brother of Vicente Carrillo Fuentes, Rodolfo, because he in turn had given instructions for the elimination of various men close to El Chapo, and was doing business with the Zetas. El Chapo explained that ignoring the problem could prove costly to him because "his people were being harassed and killed and his own people were saying that he wasn't defending them." The Juárez Cartel took revenge by killing El Chapo's brother Arturo, who was in prison in Almoloya. Vicente Carrillo Fuentes, who had become a leader after

a particularly fierce internal dispute, employed an expert in the use of violence named Arturo González Hernández, a.k.a. "El Chaky," who tortured,
buried, and burned his victims. While in some situations corpses could be
used as propaganda, the defenders of a besieged and divided plaza such as
Juárez preferred to hide them to prevent too much negative news coverage
and the appearance of chaos.

The battle in Ciudad Juárez was an example of the complexity of forces
at play in the first decade of the twenty-first century. The Juárez Cartel
organized its own defense group, La Línea (The Line). This force included
local and federal police officers and army members, as well as the cartel's
own mercenary hitmen. By the end of the decade, the cartel had joined
forces with the Beltrán Leyvas, now the Sinaloans' enemies, and the Zetas.
For the attack on Juárez, the Sinaloans began to use local gang members, the
AFI, and later the Federal Police. The Juárez Cartel was able to withstand
the onslaught, but all hell broke out in the city.

Ciudad Juárez was an extreme example of what was happening in other
cities. The death toll rose dramatically: in 2007, there were 318 "executions,"
homicides committed by organized crime with assault rifles; the following
year, this figure had climbed to 1,653, a third of the national total. Miguel
Ángel Chávez Díaz de León writes about how foreign journalists, who came
to report on "the world's most violent city," could barely understand the
daily experience of the locals. People were vulnerable to attacks as they
went about their daily lives. Nightclubs, part of a tradition celebrated by
Juan Gabriel in his song "El Noa Noa," were victims of extortion and indiscriminate attacks. The payment of protection money affected large and
small companies alike. Motels, used for all manner of illegitimate but mostly
peaceful activities, became the scene of violence. The municipal police were
perpetrators and victims. It was well known that they were in the pocket of
the Juárez Cartel. Their firepower, however, was no match for their rivals.
Therefore, in 2008, local police officers were the initial target of an attack on
the municipal government institutions. The parties involved in the fighting,
starting with the Juárez Cartel, could force the resignation of officials they
deemed unfavorable, threatening the family of a local councilor or killing
a police officer every forty-eight hours in order to force the replacement of
a police chief.

The enemies saw the conflict as one of total annihilation, and so the
definition of legitimate targets expanded to include, for example, small-
time drug dealers, their clients, and common criminals. They could all be
"executed" even if just suspected of belonging to a rival group. The killing
of women in the city, a problem that had already been making international

headlines for a decade, now reflected how violence had undermined daily life on every level. The "dead women of Juárez"—a common label that falsely suggested the anonymity of the victims—were discovered with marks of sexual violence and mutilations. The same areas of the city where young women workers had been kidnapped since the 1990s, outside assembly plants and in central areas, continued to lack street lighting, and femicides went uninvestigated. This also happened in the case of most "executions," but unlike them, femicides could not be dismissed as collateral damage of the conflict. The federal government's deployment of troops to the city did not help: complaints increased about human rights violations, referring to torture, illegal searches, kidnappings, and the deaths of innocent victims when simply stopping at a checkpoint.

Beyond Ciudad Juárez, in 2008, Anabel Hernández describes how the Beltrán Leyva brothers' break from El Chapo and El Mayo sparked "the worst narco conflict in the history of Mexico. Worse than the one with the Arellano Félix. Worse than the Federation's confrontation with the Zetas." On a personal level, El Mayo and El Chapo disliked Arturo's emotional ups and downs and exhibitionism. It was said that drugs, alcohol, and certain occultist beliefs made him even more unpredictable and dangerous than usual. But probably there were strategic reasons too. The role of the Beltrán Leyva group in the fight against the Zetas had given it the muscle it needed for autonomy, in a similar way that led to the Zetas' split from the Gulf Cartel. The AFI, supposedly controlled by the Sinaloans, captured Alfredo Beltrán Leyva, a betrayal among cousins. One of El Chapo's sons was killed. The brothers made a pact with the Zetas and Vicente Carrillo Fuentes, as mentioned above, and Sinaloa, Chihuahua, and Baja California became more violent. The tactics tried out in Tamaulipas and Ciudad Juárez were now being used in various parts of the country, causing the death toll among fighters, police officers, and civilians to increase in various cities and in total numbers. Arturo sent groups to Culiacán to carry out operations to destabilize El Chapo and El Mayo's fiefdom. He had a wide network of public officials and police officers whom he had bribed, and by 2008 he was no longer dependent on El Chapo. His links with Vicente Castaño, boss of the Colombian paramilitary, gave him direct access to South American cocaine production. In 2009, Arturo was killed in Cuernavaca, leaving a trail of death in his wake. The government released humiliating images of his corpse, perhaps reasoning that it would be good propaganda and send the message, in the criminal organizations' same code, that no quarter would be given to them. What it undoubtedly achieved was the death of four family members of Melquisedet Angulo Córdova, a marine killed in action in the

Cuernavaca operation. They were machine-gunned while they slept, the night after Angulo Córdova's funeral, in Paraíso, Tabasco, 500 miles from Cuernavaca. The violence survived the famous names associated with it, and reached every corner of the country. Although President Calderón spoke of a "war" to justify discretionary military operations, in many people's experience this was not a conventional war but a decade-long period of fratricidal violence with no clear boundaries between combatants and noncombatants. The moral dimension of the enterprise was also in question.

At the same time, the Zetas resisted the offensive in the northeast and expanded their area of operations to other regions of the country. They sent men to Culiacán, where people's supposed loyalty to El Chapo and El Mayo did not prevent the Zetas from carrying out operations to heat up the plaza. It was a similar procedure in Michoacán, Guerrero, and other places: arrive with a reconnaissance group, gather intelligence, and then attack the enemy's key assets and actors. These targets generally included local police officers, nightclubs, and small drug-dealing premises or *tienditas*. Civilian fatalities were no longer collateral damage but part of the strategy. In Michoacán, as we will see below, the Zetas faced a moralistic but no less brutal group called the Familia Michoacana. In Chiapas, they stole ephedrine from the Zambadas. In Mexico City, they killed high-ranking security officials under García Luna's command. The Zetas also sought to seize territories from the Federation in Guerrero, where the drug trade complicated a long history of confrontations between guerrillas and the army. El Chapo ordered attacks on the remaining guerrillas in order to maintain the support of the armed forces in their fight against the Beltrán Leyvas and the Zetas.

In the second decade of the twenty-first century, violence increased and continued to spread. Militarized tactics and collateral damage continued. Therefore, for example, the Zetas' massacre of seventy-two immigrants in San Fernando, Tamaulipas, in August 2010, cannot be explained simply in terms of their fighting against the Gulf Cartel. Rather, it was the result of an illegal economy drastically transformed by the use of force. Once an element of an operation, violence had become the key resource of organized crime.

The past ten years have seen significant ruptures but also continuities. This means it will take time to grasp all the consequences. At first glance, it has been a period of "disorganized crime." Armed groups proliferated, capitalizing on their firepower and impunity; their increasing mobility redrew the map of Mexico. The type of combat that began with the break between the Sinaloa, Gulf, and Juárez groups in 2003 worsened with the arrival onto the scene of the Zetas and the Beltrán Leyvas.

In 2020, some of the old groups, such as the Sinaloans, were still operating. The Gulf Cartel reincarnated in a group now known as the CDG (for "Cartel del Golfo") and formed an alliance with Sinaloa and the Familia Michoacana to fight the Zetas—an alliance that experienced its own schism, leading to the creation of the Cartel del Noreste. Another new organization was the Cartel de Jalisco Nueva Generación (New Generation Jalisco Cartel, or CJNG), which emerged out of the Milenio Cartel in Michoacán, and has associations with the Sinaloa group. Led by Nemesio Oseguera Cervantes, a.k.a. "El Mencho," the CJNG started out by fighting the Caballeros Templarios (Knights Templar), the group that succeeded La Familia, and also against the latter's adversaries, the Zetas. Later, it inevitably turned against the Sinaloans. The CJNG's connections in South America, Asia, and the West Coast of the United States and Canada meant it could rapidly expand and accumulate capital. The group proved capable of openly challenging the armed forces and preventing the capture of its high-ranking members. In this sense, guerrilla groups such as the Fuerzas Armadas Revolucionarias de Colombia (Revolutionary Armed Forces of Colombia, or FARC), which gave training to the CJNG, served as a model. In 2015, it brought down a military helicopter and soon afterward dozens of its own fighters were killed, though this probably did not make a dent in its total number of combatants. It is too early to know whether this group will achieve dominance in this complex landscape and reverse the centrifugal forces of disorganized crime.

A common explanation for this "organizational headache" was the third arrest of El Chapo in 2016 and his extradition to the United States the following year. His absence created coordination problems that exploded in 2024 after El Mayo was betrayed and flown north across the border, triggering a bloody confrontation in Culiacán between his people and El Chapo's children, Los Chapitos. A deeper reason for the disorganization lies in the levels of violence that have marked recent years. Since the mid-2000s, Mexico's homicide statistics have been persistently high, reaching their worst level in 2018 and again in 2019: the Instituto Nacional de Estadísticas y Geografía (National Institute of Statistics and Geography, or INEGI) indicated a rate of 27.3 per 100,000 inhabitants in 2018, comparable to Brazil and Colombia. According to the Sistema Nacional de Seguridad Pública (National Public Safety System), 2019 saw a peak of 34,720 murders, of which 24,446 were committed with a firearm. Of these, a high proportion—between 20 and 60 percent, according to different models—were carried out by criminal groups. The number of intentional homicides in 2023 was 13 percent lower than in 2019, although a large number of disappearances could obscure the precise trend.

This classification of homicides is a somewhat speculative exercise. As Adèle Blazquez writes, even in people's experience in places such as Badiraguato, supposedly close to the capos, it was difficult to explain a homicide or give it meaning, beyond the certainty that one death foretold more deaths. Therefore, as Diego Enrique Osorno has pointed out, in Tamaulipas people do not refer to victims as "dead" but rather as "riddled with bullets, thrown into a car's trunk, wrapped in a blanket, mown down, stuffed into a steel drum, and above all executed." Most homicides went uninvestigated and approximately 10 percent were punished in 2018. Sometimes Ministerio Público agents told victims' family members that if they wanted to find out what happened they would have to do the investigations themselves. This lack of follow-up blurred the lines between the dead, who were "fighters," civilian victims of confrontations between criminal groups, and victims of other kinds of interpersonal violence.

The lack of information is a result of the militarized strategies of recent federal administrations. The implicit idea was that those killed in "confrontations" with the armed forces or after "executions" by criminal groups were themselves criminals, hence it was unnecessary to investigate the crime. On the one hand, this implied that those guilty of homicide always used violence with great precision and avoided unnecessary deaths—a fantasy whose falsehood was already clearly evident in the 1990s with the events at the Christine discotheque in Mazatlán and the killing of Cardinal Posadas Ocampo in Guadalajara. Furthermore, this idea implied that the armed forces only killed in combat situations. Many reports rebutting this were supported in the investigations following the June 2014 massacre in Tlatlaya, in the state of Mexico, when soldiers executed twenty-two people in their custody.

The Mexican public was not completely inured to the dehumanization of the "executed." The San Fernando massacres in 2010 and the disappearance of forty-three students in Iguala in 2014 sparked protests that forced the administrations of Felipe Calderón and Enrique Peña Nieto to mitigate the bad press. The number of disappearances also reflected this situation. Both the criminal groups and the armed forces had learned that the press was less interested when there were no bodies. Such furtive homicides only became known when the victims' families protested or found clandestine mass graves. In 2020, the government itself estimated that 60,000 people had disappeared since 2006. The result of adding up the numbers of those killed in executions, fighting, and disappearances contradicted the idea that "criminals" were a pathological minority in society who did not deserve the same rights as the rest of the population. Reality brought this falsehood crashing down under its own weight.

Maps of municipalities with high levels of violence, produced by David Shirk and the Justice in Mexico team at the University of San Diego, show that violence has increased, spread across the national territory, and become concentrated in a few key cities in recent years. The ten most violent municipalities in the country accounted for a third of the homicides in 2018. These included old hot spots (Ciudad Juárez, Tijuana, Acapulco, Culiacán) but also cities not previously considered dangerous, such as Cancún, Irapuato, and León. There were new conflicts in old places. Levels of violence escalated in some parts and diminished in others. Clashes between the CJNG and the Sinaloa Cartel—combined with disputes between lower-level groups over local drug distribution points—reignited violence in Tijuana. Veracruz became a more dangerous state after the Zetas took extortion and human trafficking to new depths of brutality. Guanajuato, more recently, became a disputed territory where oil theft from Pemex pipelines financed old and new groups, such as the Santa Rosa de Lima Cartel. Michoacán and several coastal regions of the Pacific also saw higher homicide rates. While the border areas of the north and the Golden Triangle have also suffered high levels of violence, the most recent maps show that it has now spread to central, southern, and southeastern parts of Mexico that previously had few cases. The number of people internally displaced by insecurity suggests a fluid, large-scale problem: according to estimates from the Encuesta Nacional de Victimización y Percepción sobre Seguridad Pública (National Survey on Victimization and Perception of Public Security), 8,726,375 people changed their place of residence in Mexico between 2011 and 2017 to protect themselves from violence.

Michoacán was an example of the new geographical distribution of violence and an important case in its own right. In this state, the business of illegality was connected with the extraction of resources from legitimate sectors and from the infrastructure that made this possible. The groups that emerged from that mixed economy were based on a byzantine combination of family links, local rootedness, alliances, and rivalries with organizations from the north. Since the 1970s, the Valencia clan from Aguililla, Michoacán, had produced opium paste, marijuana, and then methamphetamines. They collaborated with larger groups to take their product to the United States. Other investments included legitimate export businesses, such as avocados. This variety of activities was emblematic of the diversification of organized crime in the twenty-first century: the extraction of resources from export sectors, especially avocados, limes, and mining, alongside comprehensive control over key municipal districts for drug production and trafficking. Maritime trade at the ports of Lázaro Cárdenas, Michoacán, and

Manzanillo, Colima, enabled the Valencias and then other groups to import the raw materials for methamphetamine production from Asia, and then ship it westward and northward. The Gulf Cartel and then the Sinaloans allowed the Valencias access to the US markets.

In 2006, the Familia Michoacana announced its arrival by rolling five heads on the floor of a disco in Uruapan. The group, whose members originally had connections with the Valencia family but had become its adversaries, claimed to be fighting the Zetas, who had to strengthen the connections between the Gulf Cartel and Michoacán but were eventually ousted. In another ironic aspect of this history of alliances and betrayals, the Zetas had originally come to the state on the orders of Osiel Cárdenas to support Carlos "El Tísico" (The Consumptive) Rosales Mendoza. This group, called La Empresa (The Business), was at the origins of the Familia. Meanwhile, Juan José Farías, a.k.a. "El Abuelo" (Grandpa), from Tepalcatepec, who had been associated with the Valencias, formed a group called the Matazetas, whose origins can be traced back to the early days of the CJNG and the self-defense groups that began to spring up around 2013 to displace the heirs of the Familia Michoacana, the Caballeros Templarios. This genealogy is as complicated as it sounds. In addition to the number of actors, the recent history of violence in Michoacán reflects different rhythms of change: the duration and adaptability of leaderships such as the Farías and Valencia families contrasts with the rapid changes and short lifespans of other actors and groups.

The Familia Michoacana and the Caballeros Templarios distinguished themselves from other criminal groups by adopting a localist rhetoric. In contrast, the Zetas were not defined by a shared origin, and they could be seen everywhere as an invading force. In the Sinaloa and Tamaulipas Cartels, the leaders' origins were an important source of authority. But in the propaganda spread by the Familia (through newspapers, messages left in visible public places, videos), defending the home turf was a central issue, along with a pseudo-Christian and businesslike ideology formulated by its leader Nazario Moreno González, a.k.a. "El Más Loco" (The Craziest). The integration of licit and illicit economic activities in Michoacán explained why the group could see the state as a self-sufficient entity and emphasize territorial control.

A gap soon opened up between what was practiced and what was preached. The display of five heads in 2006 was, according to La Familia, an act of "divine justice" against those who had invaded the state and raped women. However, La Familia developed a reputation for its predatory practices and abusive control over the local population. This only worsened under the Caballeros Templarios, who replaced La Familia after a series of arrests and the supposed death of its founder. Moreno González was officially killed during a gunfight in Apatzingán in 2010, but he died again in 2014, in Tumbiscatío, during a clash with the army. In the meantime, he had led the Caballeros Templarios, although the organization's public face was Servando Gómez Martínez, a.k.a. "La Tuta." Between 2011 and 2014, approximately, the Caballeros took control over municipalities, offering "security" to their inhabitants while in fact imposing a repressive regime that was not about upholding rights or delivering justice but about preventing the area from "heating up." While using physical punishment against those caught disrupting the peace, they sold drugs outside schools. They justified their control by claiming they were "protecting" women, a common theme in the regionalism of organized crime—as if outsiders were the only ones who ever committed rape.

Salvador Maldonado Aranda and Romain Le Cour Grandmaison have described how the Caballeros Templarios exercised a more invasive control over municipalities than other organizations. In order to establish a local presence, they threatened or killed municipal government officials and police officers. They demanded a percentage of the local budget and exclusivity in construction contracts. They taxed local businesses, raising prices of basic products such as tortillas.

Unsurprisingly, around 2013, a self-defense movement emerged that drove the Caballeros Templarios out from key cities such as Apatzingán. These groups, partly funded by local farmers as well as leaders of lesser criminal organizations such as El Abuelo Farías, had no legal basis but claimed to be the legitimate defenders of local communities. The Peña Nieto government swiftly intervened to disarm them but soon came around to their way of thinking. Deploying soldiers to local areas did not solve the problem of how to distinguish "legitimate" armed citizens from their "criminal" counterparts. By neglecting to tell them apart, deciding who should or should not be prosecuted, the federal government acknowledged that it lacked the monopoly on the legitimate use of force. Community police and self-defense outfits, which also appeared in Guerrero, demonstrated that, on the contrary, the use of weapons was a widely available political resource.

This use of coercion, by both criminals and "legitimate" groups, affected public life. In 2018, a total of thirty-seven mayors (including candidates and former officeholders) and sixteen journalists were killed. This indicates the continued interest of criminal groups in controlling government administrations and influencing public opinion at a local level. These figures do not mean that organized crime only targeted uncooperative public officials;

in some cases, Anabel Hernández suggests, the attacks were the result of criminals' belief that politicians had betrayed them by supporting other groups too instead of showing them complete loyalty. In Michoacán, this threat coincided with the electoral transfer of several municipal districts from the PRI to the Partido de la Revolución Democrática (Democratic Revolution Party) since the start of the century. Unlike the older groups, such as the Sinaloa, Juárez, Gulf, and Arellano Félix Cartels, the more recently established organizations, such as the CJNG and Caballeros Templarios, tended to work on the basis of fear rather than bribery in their relationships with local officials. When they considered it necessary, they also engaged in open combat with the armed forces. They seemed less dependent on protection from the highest echelons of federal government. This is a tentative conclusion, based solely on the absence of incriminating evidence of the kind revealed during the Calderón administration with the US trials of El Chapo, Vicente Zambada, Genaro García Luna, and others. However, the trend toward the use of guns to impact politics is clear, as shown by the killing of candidates during the 2021 and 2024 campaigns. The latter was unprecedented, with at least twenty-nine candidates assassinated.

These changes helped to gradually erode the myth of drug traffickers as the people's champions who simply wanted to make a living without bothering anyone. Skepticism has also grown over the idea that local communities and whole regions viewed them with admiration and gratitude. The image was cultivated by the criminal organizations themselves. It overlooks the role of violence and accepts as true the hypotheses that narcos redistribute wealth or that people were ever consulted about the entry of an organized criminal group into their towns. Le Cour Grandmaison's perspective seems more helpful: the entrenchment of illegality and violence in a certain locality could not be understood according to binary ideas about the state fighting crime, or lawfulness versus illegality, and applied equally throughout the country. The relationship between state agents and criminal organizations existed on a spectrum ranging from confrontation to collaboration, and varied according to specific local histories.

In Michoacán, as in other regions, organized crime depended on the use of violence to extract rent from different parts of the economy. Self-defense movements also needed local support to sustain their activities, though without relying mainly on illicit businesses. Both patterns can be found in places where the state apparatus has weakened to the point that certain functions, such as security, have been ceded to armed groups. However, it is important to maintain the distinction between these places and others, even those such as Sinaloa or Baja California, where drug trafficking was a long-established business and the state did not disintegrate to the same extent, while the illegal economy survived in the same niches where it had prospered for decades. In the second decade of the century, the connection between legal and illegal sectors here subsisted through bribery and money laundering rather than levying "taxes." Drug trafficking continued to be central for organized crime groups' larger operations; this activity still required the collaboration of public officials, coordination between multiple investors, and international contacts. Some well-funded groups subcontracted services (deliveries, production, hits) and surrogates who themselves committed other crimes to make more money. In most cases, these organizations were interested not in replacing the state but in using its resources and negotiating a status quo that would allow them to avoid war. Even in the case of Michoacán with the Caballeros Templarios, local bosses established their control without completely eliminating the cronyist mechanisms and reciprocity that were formally managed by the municipal authorities.

Violence spread, but it did not reduce the amount of drugs produced and transported. The routes may have become more complicated but the demand remained. The most irksome thing for El Mayo, according to his son Vicente, was that he now had to pay more money to the government because competing groups were also paying off the generals. While other illegal activities paid for the war and brought new players into the business, cocaine, heroin, marijuana, and methamphetamines continued to be the most lucrative. Large quantities of weapons flowed freely into the country from the United States. In July 2007, customs agents in Hidalgo, Texas, stopped an old Chevrolet that was taking into Mexico a badly hidden consignment of two AK-47s (complete with bayonets), more than 10,000 rounds of ammunition, and four magazines. This incident is notable as a small example of a trafficking operation that the authorities in both countries were doing little to stop. Some years later, news broke of the Fast and Furious operation, in which involved US authorities deliberately allowed weapons to enter Mexico. The aim was to gather evidence against criminals, but its real effect was to provide weapons for hundreds of crimes, including some committed in the United States.

The diversification of illegal activities did not alter one basic fact: clashes between organized crime groups were centered on the control of space. What began as a fight over areas of production and crossing points into the United States became, in the new century, a broader dispute over access to strategic areas that included regions, cities, and routes. The result was a reorganization of the national territory. Collaboration was less valuable than force, which was often aimed not at reducing the power of rivals but at eliminating them.

The fighting that spread to various regions in the twenty-first century could not be described as a war between two well-defined groups. It was less like a game of chess than one of checkers, in which the pieces could change color in the middle of the game. For example, after fighting each other, the Zetas teamed up with the Beltrán Leyvas, and the Sinaloans allied with the Gulf Cartel, which had become enemies of the Zetas. Meanwhile, the Juárez and Sinaloa Cartels, direct descendants of the Guadalajara group, became bitter adversaries. Michoacán was even messier. Beneath these top-level divisions, there was another board where the pieces moved even faster. Mid-level operatives such as Héctor "El Negro" Saldaña in Monterrey could work for two groups and have his own markets and connections with the authorities. The actors' origins no longer mattered, if they ever had, in explaining their loyalties and enmities.

To equate the twenty-first-century conflicts with a war would be dangerously misleading. As we have seen, the analogy has been used to justify militarization and to describe the struggles between criminal groups. The "battles" in Ciudad Juárez, Nuevo Laredo, Sinaloa, and Michoacán brought to mind conflicts between small states asserting their claims to sovereignty over their territories. Some aspects of these conflicts resembled a conventional war: the protagonism of experts trained in the use of weapons, discipline, and logistics; the aim of total destruction of the enemy forces; the mobility of fighting units across the "borders" between their territories, and the arrangement of "cease-fires."

However, the analogy can only be taken so far. First, because these were obviously not true states involved in conflict, or revolutionary movements agitating to overthrow the state. Nor was there any real professionalization of these "armies." Their value systems, whether the military honor of the Zetas or the traditionalism of the Familia Michoacana, were simply fictional constructs for public consumption and recruitment purposes. Small and large groups alike, from the Zetas to the gangs controlled by the Beltrán Leyvas and the Juárez Cartel, constantly broke the chain of command. They always reverted to the logic of financial profit—if indeed they had ever abandoned this as a priority. Given the expansion of contested territories, the distances between them, the number of combatants and caliber of the weapons used, the groups had to finance their campaigns by any means necessary. Apart from fighting, they also engaged in extortion, kidnapping, human trafficking, theft or taxing of public resources, renting space for drug trafficking, and even smaller-scale drug dealing. More than political sovereignty, they wanted to extract resources.

These groups like to portray themselves as being skilled with weapons. In fact, as we have seen, they constantly demonstrated their ineptitude, missing targets and causing unnecessary collateral damage. Their specialty was not calculated precision. The new weapons—.50-caliber rifles, grenades, "cop-killer" pistols—increased firepower but made accuracy unnecessary. Some operatives, such as the former members of the Grupo Aeromóvil de Fuerzas Especiales (Airborne Special Forces Group, also known as GAFES), were better trained in their use, but they constituted a minority compared to the more or less improvised civilian gunmen.

The central role of violence accelerated the rhythm of the mutations. The Guadalajara group under Félix Gallardo lasted more than a decade; García Ábrego led the Gulf Cartel from the 1980s until his arrest in 1996. Such longevity became increasingly rare. The longest-standing bosses, such as El Mayo, El Chapo, and El Azul, survived because they were able to adapt to political and business changes, while maintaining some autonomy from their allies. Government intervention was a factor in the instability, since strategies varied with the administrations and between one level and another in the state apparatus. We know, however, that, since the 1970s, the collaboration of various bosses with the CIA, DEA, DFS, PJF, the army, and state and municipal security forces only exacerbated the general paranoia.

Even when hostilities ceased, after an agreement was reached between bosses, fighting continued between troops when conflicts were personal and therefore hard to manage. Truces were fleeting and punctuated by "betrayals," often committed by players vying for better positions within their respective hierarchies. The idea of betrayal was a way of justifying homicides, but it also referred to an imaginary order in which there were clear hierarchies, with each boss at the top of an organization chart with lines indicating subordination and discipline. This was how the Mexican and US investigative agencies conceived the situation. The DEA and FBI saw the "cartels" like the Italian American Mafia: rigidly vertical hierarchies, secretive, disciplined, and traditionalist. Félix Gallardo and others were called "El Padrino" (The Godfather), as if they were characters in a Francis Ford Coppola movie. Journalists also used the term "mafia." But reality was far too fluid, chaotic, and visually shocking—more like a Quentin Tarantino movie.

This fiction explains not only the strategy of "decapitating" the cartels, which the DEA and its partners in Mexican government have implemented with great fanfare since the 1980s, but also its failure. The mistake began with the notion that capturing the capos was an event external to the life of criminal groups, something delivered from on high, like a fatality that no one really deserved. In fact, since federal police officers entered the business fully in the 1970s, arrests were manipulated by the criminals themselves and could include homicides. This happened even after Kiki Camarena's death, where the arrest of Rafael Caro Quintero and Ernesto Fonseca allowed Félix Gallardo to continue operating for a few more years. The arrest of El Chapo in 1993 benefited Amado Carrillo Fuentes. Often the "decapitation" of one group was in fact the government's intervention in favor of another. The ensuing conflicts could weaken the group through infighting among junior figures who wanted to occupy the empty throne. Such an explanation, however, implied the existence of a system of well-organized ranks in which everyone had the same rights as someone else at the same hierarchical level. The organizations' structures were not enduring or rational. The fall of a boss into government hands was the result of intergroup rivalry, but it also led to a new internal configuration.

Just as interesting as knowing why one capo fell is knowing why more did not suffer the same fate. The answer could be inferred in the armed resistance unleashed in Culiacán after the brief detention of Ovidio Guzmán, El Chapo's son, in October 2019. President López Obrador ordered his release hours later in order to prevent greater bloodshed. The state once again admitted its inability to defeat organized crime, the weakness of its security forces, and the uselessness of applying the DEA's strategies. This was too embarrassing, even for a president who constantly ignored or deflected blame for the deterioration of security in the country over six years. Ovidio was recaptured in 2023 and extradited to the United States. The informal extradition of El Mayo in 2024 illustrated the reasons why decapitation could usefully be avoided, as it started a period of violence in Sinaloa that has benefited few outside US courtrooms.

To attribute all failures in law enforcement and military campaigns to corruption is misleading because it implies a purely moral and therefore anachronistic vision of politics. Alexander Dawson argues that the changes in the Mexican and global economy, inequality, and new attitudes toward consumption have all prepared the ground for organized crime groups to become influential in society. The complicity between drug trafficking and other illegal businesses was also found in civil society. This tolerance explains the lack of a judicial counterpart to police investigations, as flawed and scarce as they are: the problem is easier to frame as a war than as one of justice. Attributing everything to official dishonesty leads to an understanding of this complex history as the result of conspiracies that suggest narcos and police forces were puppets of the powerful. Many experts divide this history into six-year presidential administrations, assuming that each president had his preferred methods of corruption and favored organizations. In reality, top-down agreements tended to be fragile; President

Calderón's militarization of the conflict was motivated by the idea that the state needed to regain its integrity. But, as we have seen, the strategy imposed in 2006 had no impact on conflicts already underway and failed in its main objectives, whether they were to win a "war" or reduce the level of illegality.

The fact is that presidents come and go, but the violence remains, imposing its inevitable and unpredictable logic. Criminal organizations seem to have lost respect for the government. However, it is too soon to say whether this is an irreversible trend toward a war of everyone against everyone. Much still depends on the response by the state and the public as a whole. The evidence from the last decade suggests that violence is so entrenched within society that it would be impossible to eliminate it rapidly, and that attempts to combat it exclusively through military means will only make matters worse. Based on the available evidence, we cannot go further without descending into prophecy.

CHAPTER SEVEN

ALL VIOLENCE IS GENDER VIOLENCE

G ENDER-BASED VIOLENCE has been central to Mexicans' experiences in the twentieth and twenty-first centuries. This violence exists when the relationship between aggressor and victim follows social patterns in which gender difference is conceived as a hierarchy. What characterizes gender-based violence is not the difference between men's and women's bodies but the specific way society construes this difference as male superiority. In other words, men do not hit women because they are stronger but because most people accept that a muscular difference justifies their use of violence. A husband's beating of a wife should not be seen as an episode of family life contained within the four walls of the home but as an interaction connected to other social relationships that transcend the division between public and private space.

There are a number of different forms of gender-based violence. It is important to distinguish homicide—the category of first-degree murder that comprises all premeditated acts causing the death of a person—from femicide, which is violence committed against women because they are women. Femicidal violence is not a simple act (killing someone) but also includes a series of actions that have physical or emotional effects (such as rape, abuse, insults, beatings, or abandonment) and are connected like links in a chain that can lead to homicide. Like other forms of violence, it sends a message. A single ideology runs through all these acts, from the most trivial to the most harmful: the use of violence is an expression of the hierarchical system we call patriarchy.

But ideology alone is not enough to explain violence. We need to consider the actors involved. As Marcela Lagarde and other writers have pointed out, femicide involves the state's failure to protect victims who are vulnerable because of their social status. It is often claimed that feminism is an attempt to politicize an aspect of daily life that pertains to the private sphere. But it is more persuasive to turn this argument on its head and say that it is the patriarchy that politicizes violence by giving a legal seal of approval to men's greater physical strength and to the separation of the public from the private space. A patriarchal system endures because it benefits men of different classes while juxtaposing the belief in women's supposed inferiority with other social hierarchies. The belief in that gendered order justifies the use of violence as a punishment for women who do not accept "their place," but it also permeates other forms of violence, such as those explored in previous chapters. It is not simply about a confrontation between men and women. Men, as victims, can be negatively feminized—in other words, seen as merely passive. Women can also contribute to the perpetuation of the patriarchal order. Gloria González-López has shown how adult women in families where there has been incest or sexual violence "have been socialized to internalize the same sexist beliefs that have oppressed them as women throughout their lives."

Despite patriarchy's resilience, gender-based violence has a history insofar as society itself changes over time. This history cannot be told in the same way as the history of other forms of violence. Gender relations do not change from one day to the next because of political events or new laws. They change more slowly because they are based on attitudes or prejudices that, at least until recently, were not open to public debate. This does not mean that social or political upheavals, such as those set in motion by the Revolution, are unimportant, but that their impact is registered on a series of norms and expectations that have their own momentum. It would be an erroneous simplification to say that twentieth-century gender relations were the same as those of previous eras. If men beat women in the colonial era, then what made the twentieth century any different? But history is not about saying that what is happening today had already happened yesterday; instead, it is about looking for solid reasons to criticize the notion that things must be accepted because that's the way they are, and that nothing can be done about it. In this chapter, I will describe various forms of gender-based violence. It is important to keep in mind the above definition of femicide because it connects impunity with different types of violence, from apparently harmless catcalls to more serious attacks such as rape and murder.

The violence against women, minors, and homosexuals referred to in this chapter is harder to describe than the aggression of pistoleros or soldiers or criminal gangs because the evidence is more slippery. Nor is it a type of violence that can be limited by precise time periods or geographical boundaries. The previous chapters give examples of sexual violence at different points of the twentieth century as a part of other practices. In this chapter, we will take a broader chronological perspective and consider gender-based violence as a common thread.

If we had to indicate a relevant transformation for the entire period in question, a decisive moment could have been the acknowledgement in recent decades of the high cost of gender-based violence to society as a whole. Previously, it was not easy to conceptualize femicide in terms of action and effect, as the law defines crimes. Therefore, it is only in recent years that it has been quantified like other crimes; some penal codes have now begun to categorize it as a specific crime. Impunity remains the common denominator of femicide, which in turn reinforces the silence surrounding gender-based violence. Therefore, it is still difficult to know the result of new attitudes. We can observe, also in recent years, an apparent increase in the rate of femicide. This social acknowledgement of the cost of gender-based violence gives us a fresh perspective and permits the optimistic use of the past tense. Such a perspective, which we might call feminist, is also useful for tying together in this chapter some of the loose threads in this book, revealing connections between different forms of violence.

The core problem in discussing the history of gender-based violence is its invisibility. Long considered a "private" matter, marital violence was something people preferred not to hear about, especially from the victims. The same was true of sexual abuse within families, where victims often stayed quiet because of threats or the belief that sexual intercourse between a father or uncle with a daughter or niece was somehow normal. This enforced silence extended beyond the domestic sphere. Verbal and physical harassment on the street was part of the same "sexual terrorism" that took place in the home because, among other things, it implied that women had no right to their own space or to respond to their aggressors. We should also remember that, as we saw in chapter 3, the Catholic Church actively protected a hierarchy in the family and religious practices that included, albeit implicitly, the husband's ability to "punish" other members of the family unit. The predatory sexual behavior within the Catholic Church, exposed in recent decades, was a less defensible but still complementary part of such hierarchies. The same institutions responsible for prosecuting these crimes are silent: police women who have been sexually abused in their workplace prefer not to speak out to avoid possible reprisals and because it rarely leads to changes that could protect them.

The legal process, however, gives us enough evidence to begin to tackle the silence surrounding rape, an offense clearly defined in criminal legislation. We can take a typical example of rape in the early twentieth century where the perpetrator was known to the victim (as a neighbor, family member, employer) and was in a position of authority because of his age or other reasons. The attack often included physical aggression and other actions, from the deceit of "seduction" to the promise of marriage, which devalued the victim in others' eyes and in her own self-esteem. Since the definition of rape required physical violence in addition to penetration, cases were often reclassified as abduction, statutory rape, or indecent assault. Victims had to press charges for such crimes, but in the case of abduction or statutory rape, proceedings were suspended if the accused subsequently agreed to marry the victim. Within court statistics, these crimes were the clearest indicator of violence against women, and even so the numbers concealed more than they revealed.

Rape statistics registered by judicial authorities during the twentieth century represented only a small fraction of the total number of such crimes, and their incidence did not seem to follow the trends of other violent crimes. Whereas the relative incidence of homicide declined and then increased throughout the country, rape followed a different trajectory. The rate of people prosecuted for rape was steady since the second decade of the century, and showed an increase from 1980 to the present day; the rate of convictions among the accused rose from less than 1 to more than 4 per 100,000 inhabitants from the 1920s to the first decade of the twenty-first century. The evidence from court records, which have been studied more closely for the first half of the twentieth century, justifies skepticism of official statistics because it offers many examples of cases in which violence was not reported by victims, the authorities did not believe them, or the witnesses or victims refused to appear before a judge, leaving the case incomplete. The increasing number of accusations and convictions recorded in the last four decades might reflect a greater willingness to report crimes and give punishments rather than a genuine increase in the frequency of such assaults. Another hypothesis, backed by qualitative evidence, is that violence against women is indeed on the rise.

More recent data indicate a very high number of rapes not recorded in court files, and this number is even higher if rapes committed within the family setting are included. Often a part of other forms of domestic violence, sexual abuse by a friend of relative is even harder for the victim to report. To give us an idea of the prevalence of such rapes, we can quote a 2006 INEGI report (*Panorama de violencia contra las mujeres* [Overview of violence against women]). Of the women aged fifteen and over taking part in the survey, 6.6 percent had been "physically forced to have sexual relations" with their partner. A gulf exists between this percentage, based on the survey of a sample of the population, and official numbers: the same percentage (6.6) of the total population of women aged fifteen and over in 2005 would mean that 2,377,304 women had been raped by their partner at some point. In contrast, between 1927 and 2006, only 120,297 people had been convicted for any kind of rape in Mexican courts. And we should remember that this number represents only a fraction of the actual rape victims: it was only in 2005 that the Supreme Court ruled that marital rape was actually a crime. If we define rape more broadly than the sexual aspect of the attack (anal or vaginal penetration, in the usual legal definition), and include any use of the victim's body against their will and damaging their sexual well-being, as proposed by contemporary feminist critics, the situation is even bleaker and the available figures even less reliable.

For the victims who reported such abuse, the actual process of filing a complaint and appearing before the authorities and the accused was an ordeal. The procedure included an examination of the victim's genitalia, not regularly performed by a doctor, and was conducted publicly in the police station. The purpose of these examinations was to determine whether the victim had had sexual intercourse recently or some time before, on the assumption that it would be easier for a sexually active woman to lie about what had happened. The mandate to include physical evidence in the examination reinforced the implicit guilt of the victim, who had somehow provoked the abuser's "natural" instincts. These examinations could determine that rape had not been committed if there were no signs of violence, such as bruising, on other parts of the body, even if there were abrasions or cuts in the vaginal or anal area. Even when physical evidence existed, most cases were based on the conflicting statements made by the victim or the accused, which were evaluated in accordance with considerations of the moral character of both parties.

The Federal District Penal Code of 1871 included rape as a crime against honor. Although this changed in the twentieth century, the implicit premise remained that the issue was not only the psychological and physical integrity of the rape victim but the reputation of the man (husband or father) who was supposed to protect "their" women from abuse by other men. Similar to other honor crimes, such as defamation or slander, the authorities only prosecuted cases of sexual violence if the aggrieved party had made an accusation. It was assumed that both parties had equal recourse to negotiating a solution to the problem. What had become a brutal attack often ended up as a transaction in which the victim accepted some of the blame and the attacker avoided any criminal punishment or even shaming.

As with other crimes against honor, such as defamation, the basic difficulty was establishing who was telling the truth. Faced with the high cost of showing physical evidence, victims had to present their case convincingly in front of men who judged or contradicted them. But it was difficult to use the "correct" language to describe the sexual act. Juana Espinosa was ten years old in 1921, so perhaps she did not know how to use euphemisms. When her mother accused her son-in-law of raping her, Juana clearly described to the judge how the accused had raped her and "made her cry." Because the medical examiner found no injuries on the rest of Juana's body, the judge and jury agreed that there had been no violence, and convicted Manuel Alvarado of statutory rape instead of rape. As shown in this case, the accused tended to claim that if there had been any sexual contact, then it was voluntary for both parties. To make matters even worse for the victim, the process required a *careo*, or face-to-face confrontation, with the accused. This procedure was designed to give both parties a chance to give their version of events and to answer questions from the authorities or the person they were facing. It is not hard to imagine the victim's fear when brought face to face with their attacker. For this reason, careos have not been used in rape cases since 2005.

Since marriage could end the case, the authorities started out by assuming that victims had an incentive to lie. Apart from traditional ideas about women using strategies to seduce men, victims in the twentieth century were confronted with social attitudes that were supported since the end of the nineteenth century by positivist criminology, according to which women were naturally deceitful. For Cesare Lombroso, the criminologist with the greatest influence in Mexico since the late nineteenth century, women had a natural ability to resist penetration and the cause of most rapes was men's lack of access to prostitutes. In contrast, an objective and irrefutable piece of information for Mexican authorities was a medical examiner's observation of whether the victim had recently consumed alcohol, which would undermine her credibility still further. The premise, in short, was that women were liars and had complete control of their sex lives.

Unlike homicide, rape was hardly mentioned in the press or in other public sources of information; such violence was not perceived as a serious problem and publicity was damaging to everyone, victims included. Until recently, as González-López points out, in some states rapists were treated more leniently than cattle rustlers. The regular practices of nota roja publications in the middle of the century continue to this day: rape is a news story if accompanied by homicide, and the reporting tends to make victims responsible for their own fate.

Few victims came forward because punishment was not the best solution. Recent studies of violence against women show the ambiguity of relationships that combine affection with abuse, in which emotional mistreatment is part of a continuum that leads to physical abuse. Reporting to the authorities can be a costly strategy socially, economically, and emotionally. A 1996 study in Cuetzalan revealed that less than half of abused women filed charges against their physically abusive husbands. Accusing or leaving the abuser was even more difficult for pregnant women, who had to endure the mistreatment and take the blame for it in order to avoid losing financial support. As Marta Torres Falcón shows, this led women to use other strategies to resist and counter violence.

We must not assume from this evidence that society did not regard rape as a serious transgression. There are indications that victims' families or the authorities could carry out some form of extrajudicial punishment. In his memoirs, Gonzalo N. Santos writes that when he was governor of San Luis Potosí during the 1940s, he issued orders—publicly and without needing to overcome any major procedural obstacles—for the execution of four soldiers accused of rape by campesinos from Mezquitic. In Puebla and elsewhere, as Gema Kloppe-Santamaría shows, rape could lead to lynching. However, these extreme punishments for rape did not extend to other types of sexual abuse; instead, with their uncommon brutality, they seemed to define rape as a strange or pathological act.

Santos's summary justice also obscures the fact that violence against women, particularly rape, was part of the revolutionary legacy that led to his own rise to power, and to the careers of many caciques like him. Although the revolutionary mythology tends to forget it, sexual violence was a factor in troop-civilian relations. In chapter 1, I mentioned the infamous, though perhaps apocryphal, episode in which Pancho Villa ordered the execution of women who formed a military unit, as well as the rape of the women of Namiquipa. Other armies, including the Zapatistas, were accused of rape, although it is hard to tell such accusations apart from the propaganda that portrayed the rebels as barbaric. Real or expected abuse of civilians led many families to seek refuge in cities; however, revolutionary mythology offers us the image of the soldadera as a prototypical brave woman joining the cause, accompanying her man, whom she fed and healed. Some women certainly did follow the armies and even commanded troops with weapons in hand. However, the folklore did not entertain the possibility that the decision to join the cause was in itself a way to avoid being abducted or suffering other kinds of abuse. A striking contrast exists between episodes of revolutionary violence against women, on the one hand, and official mythology, on the other, in which sexual abuse by hacendados became one of the reasons for joining the revolt and seeking justice. When the Revolution cloaked itself in the legitimate defense of honor, it used women to justify violence between men.

The problem of the invisibility of violence against women becomes even more complex when we examine other types of use of force that, although linked to rape, were not seen as crimes. Domestic violence was widespread in the twentieth century. It included a variety of coercive, physical, emotional, and sexual behaviors committed within nuclear or extended families. The statistics available for most of the 1900s do not distinguish between the crimes of homicide, bodily harm, battery, or threats committed within the domestic space, although new attitudes toward gender-based violence reveal the possible magnitude of the problem.

From the late nineteenth century, newspaper articles unwittingly proved this invisibility. The language used by journalists to describe domestic violence reflected an ambivalence about the criminal nature of these acts. The perpetrators of violence were criticized in the press, but the habits of the female victims were also mentioned, as if they justified the attack. The tabloid *La Prensa* reported a double homicide in 1941 as the result of a divorce, and the independence of the victim and her mother: "Yesterday's tragedy was gruesome but it holds some lessons for many Mexican mothers who let modernity take over their morals and disrupt normal life at home." In these cases, the crime was one of "passion." This expression harks back to nineteenth-century theories about regular menfolk, who could not be called "born" criminals, succumbing to fits of jealousy and attacking their women in acts of violence that the press and authors of fiction characterized as "tragedies" rather than crimes. This implied that the assailant was essentially a noble figure forced by circumstances (such as "modernity") to use force. To call something a crime of passion was to justify it, and often meant letting the perpetrator go unpunished.

When domestic violence resulted in bodily harm, rape, or even homicide, the law and informal norms tended to keep the authorities on the sidelines, or to mitigate the aggressor's criminal responsibility if he was defending his honor. Article 310 of the Federal District's 1931 Penal Code, in force until the legislation's reform in 1994, specified that "anyone catching his or her spouse in the act of sexual intercourse or on the point of engaging in such an act, and who kills or wounds one or both of the guilty parties," would receive a sentence from three days to three years of prison, in other words, a shorter sentence than given for homicide, which carried a sentence of eight to thirteen years. Beyond the letter of the law, it was common knowledge that police and court procedures were generally lenient toward violent husbands. Patricio Cárdenas, who killed his wife in 1957 for insulting his honor, told journalists that he was confident he would escape punishment (the final adjudication is unknown). Many acts of violence were simply ignored by the police and the courts. Although we cannot know how often this tolerance benefited husbands or other male aggressors, recent evidence indicates that this attitude persisted even among government officials. In Guanajuato, according to a study by María Aidé Hernández García, only 10 percent of raped women pressed charges. Those who did received no emotional support, and Ministerio Público agents urged them not to continue with their accusation. This negligence formed part of the femicide chain. In 2013, in Guanajuato, Laura Patricia Aguilar sought protection from domestic violence. She was ignored and her husband killed her.

Defending honor justified the disregard shown by government or third parties for preserving the division between the public sphere (courts, newsrooms, gossip) and the domestic space: the four walls that ideally surrounded the home where conflicts could be resolved discreetly but also, if necessary, brutally. This public-private dichotomy was a fiction for most people because many homes literally lacked the physical walls needed to keep family disputes private. The family was generally not only a couple and their children but also included grandparents, cousins, uncles, compadres, and others who might be involved in a row. Neighbors' intervention in the liminal space between the public and private realms could be a form of punishment, by spreading rumors about people with unsavory habits, or could prevent violence by keeping an eye on things. The defense of privacy often meant expanding the space in which domestic abuse could go unpunished.

The problem of domestic violence became visible when feminist organizations drew attention to it in the 1970s. In the early 1980s, as Rosario Valdez Santiago notes, new organizations began offering services to battered women, and rape victims could go to shelters. In the 1990s, partly as a result of pressure from feminist groups, the various levels of government started to complement civil society initiatives and take action through specialist agencies and prosecutors' offices, shelters, and other services for women suffering abuse. In more recent years, the strong links between feminist movements in different countries of the Americas have increased the importance of this work.

As a result of those efforts, we have data to evaluate the prevalence and social costs of family violence. According to a 2013 INEGI survey, 63 percent of women aged fifteen and older had suffered some kind of violent abuse. Another very comprehensive INEGI household survey (*Encuesta nacional sobre la dinámica de las relaciones en los hogares* [National survey on the dynamics of relationships in the home]) showed an increase in the percentage of women respondents who reported being victims of different types of violence: from 66.1 percent of respondents in 2016 to 70.1 percent in 2021. For sexual violence specifically, the results showed a similar trend, from 41.3 to 49.7 percent. In both surveys, the percentage of women who suffered violence at the hands of their partner and chose not to press charges or seek any kind of support was 78 percent. A study in Chiapas found that domestic violence was a factor in the death of women during childbirth, and another registered a weight difference of more than one and a half kilos between babies born to women who are abused and to those who are not. An analysis of women admitted to hospitals in Mexico City in 2001 for the treatment of intentional injuries showed that most had been attacked by a partner. Most women hospitalized after attempted suicides had been victims of family violence. Femicide rates increased in the first decades of this century.

Women attacked men less frequently, but such incidents help us understand the patriarchal logic. Since the early postrevolutionary years, some cases caught the public attention and became examples of disorder in gender roles. This happened, for example, when a female aggressor used a firearm, inverting the balance of power in domestic and sexual relationships. The public was drawn to these cases because they opened up discussions about the behavior of men and women in general and the effects of modern mores. In media narratives, the cast of characters seemed to have clear moral attributes: the abusive husband, the bigamist, the long-suffering wife, the proud lady. These stereotypes gave some of the accused women the chance to explain their actions in public through jury trials and in the press. Paradoxically, while these anomalous cases were fascinating for people, they also covered up the more ordinary domestic violence. The fact that a few women may have stood up to some abusive men did not mean that most cases of gender-based violence were legally or informally punished; the visibility of the protagonists in these melodramas complemented the silence surrounding most female victims.

There were several famous cases in the 1920s, such as when Nydia Camargo killed a man who betrayed her trust and affection in 1925. The famous lawyer Querido Moheno was her defense attorney during her jury trial. His arguments for Camargo's acquittal were partly based on patriotism—the victim was Chilean. María Teresa de Landa, the first-ever Miss Mexico, was also pardoned after killing her husband in 1929, after it transpired that he was married to another woman; in 1927, María Teresa Morfín killed her man because he said he was going to leave her. In these cases, studied by Elisa Speckman and Víctor Macías González, the evidence against these women was incontrovertible, but the jury members were persuaded by eloquent defense attorneys and by the accused women, who were able to give their own account and portray themselves as deserving of compassion. Juries put their consciences above the letter of the law, assuming that the women standing in the dock had defended their feminine virtue by using violence. If duels—a well-known but increasingly rare custom—allowed men to use force to defend their honor, then the cases involving these women suggested that they had the same right, at least in the case of those who displayed decent morals and had the cultural and economic resources to mount a public defense of their reputations. But if we pay close attention to their defense arguments, this right to use force was construed as a defense of traditional femininity, which the victims (bigamists, brutal politicians, treacherous foreigners) had attacked beforehand. Therefore, we cannot interpret these cases as part of an early feminist movement to push for equal rights and an end to gender-based violence. Rather, in the long term, these famous murders (as in all uses of violence) had an effect different or contrary to their immediate goal.

When jury trials were abolished in 1929, women like Camargo, de Landa, and Morfín lost the platform where their voice could be heard. The press continued to report on other cases of women killing men, but the possibility of an acquittal through an appeal to public opinion diminished. The nota roja published these stories but tended to do so in a way that no longer showed the accused woman defending her threatened femininity. On the contrary, such incidents embodied the danger of ambitious, hedonistic, or rebellious women associated with "modernity." These negative portrayals, combined with the elimination of jury trials, meant that women who were victims of domestic abuse and used violence defensively became dependent on the compassion of judges who now presided over closed-door proceedings. Despite their audiences' prejudices, as Martha Santillán Esqueda observed in 1940s court files, accused women continued to use a range of resources to avoid punishment.

Reality was less melodramatic and its characters less glamorous. Prostitutes were the prototypical victims of gender-based violence because they were morally degraded (calling a woman a *puta* was the worst insult possible). Their work forced them to deal with clients who, simply by taking part in the transaction, saw law-breaking as a lesser problem. As a result, these clients sometimes did not pay for the service and on occasion also committed physical abuse. Because prostitutes worked in places and at times that made them less visible, except to their clients and the police, they could be swiftly forgotten if they disappeared.

The power that pimps and others had over sex workers of both sexes gave them tight control of their movements and their time, whether they worked on the street or in brothels. While they would make better money than in other jobs, prostitutes were exposed to various types of exploitation, including drug and alcohol consumption and physical abuse. The most visible personification of this exploitation were called *cinturitas*, a type of pimp who beat women, cut their faces, or threatened them as a means of control. But they were really just another element in a concentric structure of gender-based violence that was used to limit prostitutes' autonomy and earnings: pimps, police officers, brothel owners, and even regular clients provided security against the threats of the night. As we saw in chapter 4, the force used by these actors seemed closer and therefore more controllable than the dark threat of abusive clients and anonymous attackers.

The first mass murderers of women in Mexico gave the threat a name. Francisco Guerrero Pérez, a.k.a. "El Chalequero," who murdered various prostitutes in the wastelands of Peralvillo (a Mexico City neighborhood) in the 1880s, was only arrested when he killed a woman who was not a prostitute. As in the contemporaneous case of London's Jack the Ripper, El Chalequero's crimes implied a lesson for all women who moved in dangerous spaces. Prostitution in Mexico City at that time was beginning to consolidate as a business structured by the collaboration between brothel owners and police officers. This came at the expense of the prostitutes who, like El Chalequero's victims, tried to work independently in peripheral areas frequented by travelers.

In the twentieth century, reforms supported by early feminists led to regulatory changes that had the unexpected effect of increasing the danger for sex workers and giving greater power to the men who exploited them. The law regulating prostitution and permitting brothels, which were generally managed by madams, was repealed in 1940 as a means of combating exploitation. However, prostitutes continued to face the threat of extortion by the police, who could accuse them of "offenses against decency." This led to the industry fragmenting into illegal and officially protected brothels (such as the one run by Graciela "La Bandida" Olmos, a favorite of politicians), cabarets of varying quality, and street prostitutes. As Santillán Esqueda and Fabiola Bailón Vásquez show, these female workers ended up being even more vulnerable to extortion and common crime. The men who exploited them now did so outside any formal framework but with the same old complicity of the police and the threat of violence. Although regulations in later decades added a reference to the crime of exploitation, criminalizing the activities of pimps, the tendency toward third-party control over the work of prostitutes remained. Nightlife, at least in the capital, was growing rapidly from the 1940s, both in terms of the number of cabarets and their cultural influence through popular music and movies. Prostitution was at the center of a thriving sector of the informal economy. Violence was an important variable in this business, and various actors, including those connected to the state, could make a profit or become emotionally invested—as in the triangular affair involving a prostitute, a pimp, and a policeman in Emilio Fernández's *Salón México* (1949).

El Chalequero continued to cast a shadow into the twentieth century but there were other names. The most famous case of a killer of women was Gregorio "El Goyo" Cárdenas. As mentioned in chapter 4, Cárdenas killed three prostitutes in 1942, and buried them in his house's backyard. But he was arrested only after strangling his young, middle-class girlfriend. El Goyo became the subject of collective fascination, partly because, as the well-educated son of a family with some money, he pretended to be a lunatic and thus avoided prison. Multiple psychological examinations, in which he was talkative, made him famous for the sexual nature of his crimes, which probably included rape and necrophilia, and for his eloquence when discussing them. His crimes enabled the public to associate violence and sex in the framework of a scientific approach used to study some exceptional cases.

The sadism that Cárdenas embodied became common currency in the press and works of literature, even though Marquis de Sade's books were still not available in Spanish. It is unnecessary to go back to the roots of the term, or even to read the criminologists or psychiatrists who began to use it, to understand the key idea: sexual pleasure could be aroused if it was accompanied by pain in the person who was the object of desire. If this were true, de Sade and El Goyo were only doing what other men might also enjoy if there were no social constraints. In the mid-1940s, the public was obsessed with Cárdenas's crimes: people consumed books, magazines, and even films in which the implicit fantasy in his crimes was that sexual pleasure derived from cruelty. We cannot say that this fascination increased gender-based violence, but we can say that El Goyo Cárdenas updated the threat of violence facing prostitutes, making women on the streets at night fair game for anonymous male predators.

From that time on, there was an interest in femicides committed by men who acted as lone killers and used violence to satisfy their erotic desires, although the term "serial killer" was not coined until some decades later in the United States. Films like Juan Bustillo Oro's 1950 *El hombre sin rostro* (The man without a face) were examples of the Mexican public's interest in this issue. Starring Arturo de Córdova, the film explored the idea that serial killers of women were intelligent, psychologically complex men. The reality was more prosaic. Since El Chalequero, the common denominator of serial killers had been their victims' low position in the gender hierarchies: women with less visibility or social capital, whose work or isolation made them less identifiable and their absence less noticeable. In 1962, a policeman was arrested for strangling twelve prostitutes in hotel rooms. His crimes were not solved until the murderer, Macario Alcalá Canchola, left a note challenging the chief of police to discover his identity. The only job for the detectives, who only bothered to carry out their duty after the note was published, was to force the hotel management to disclose the suspect's name. The case of "La Mataviejitas" (The Little Old Lady Killer), studied by Susana Vargas Cervantes, took some of the shine off the serial killers' masculine sophistication but confirmed that the victims were defined by their vulnerability. Juana Barraza, a former lucha libre wrestler, was captured in Mexico City in 2006 and convicted of murdering sixteen elderly women. She may have killed as many as thirty-two women by entering their homes pretending to be a nurse. The simple and basic fact is that what defines serial killers is not any psychological complexity or astuteness but the availability of easily forgettable victims whose murder could go unpunished.

No tally exists for violence against prostitutes because, as with other crimes, statistics tend to focus on the accused rather than the victims. Several well-publicized cases show that sex workers' lives were of little value. In one particularly famous example, in 1964 three sisters, Delfina, María del Carmen, and Eva González Valenzuela, known as "Las Poquianchis" after the name of one of their first brothels, were sentenced to forty years in prison for murdering dozens of prostitutes enslaved for years in their brothels in the state of Guanajuato. The press, movies, and books took full advantage of the case—a special issue of *Alarma!* on Las Poquianchis allegedly sold a million copies. However, the atrocities committed by the González Valenzuela sisters were merely taking the business of sexual exploitation to its logical extreme. For more than ten years, the sisters ran brothels and bars in various parts of Jalisco and Guanajuato. They kidnapped, tricked, and bought adolescents, generally from remote rural locations. Once they had their victims in their establishments, they prevented them from leaving, beat and starved them, made them take drugs, and force them to have abortions if they got pregnant. They were also accused of ordering their staff to get rid of the captive girls once their age made them unprofitable. The police found a mass grave on a ranch owned by the González Valenzuelas containing many human remains, mostly of women but also some babies. The sisters were captured because one of their prisoners escaped and reported them to police agents who did not belong to the network of public officials, facilitators, drivers, and others who participated in or protected the business. Otherwise, the sisters might have continued with their practices, even though they were not particularly powerful. Their business was hugely profitable and was based on their (largely accurate) calculation that the abuse and eventual death of sex workers would go unreported.

The obsession of experts, journalists, and readers with famous cases such as Las Poquianchis or the few serial murders that were identified as such had the effect of obscuring the daily violence experienced by prostitutes. It also created the impression that the victims were completely passive when faced with danger and therefore depended on men's protection. In the context of the concentric violence surrounding them, however, it is unsurprising to see how night workers—including waitresses, cabaret dancers, and prostitutes—could use violence to defend themselves, settle quarrels with each other and with clients, and reclaim a measure of dignity in a context that generally made women's supposed passivity a pretext for their exploitation.

Notorious cases like those mentioned above pose a narrative trap: the problem, like in the movies and television series, lay in solving the crime, finding the culprit, but without questioning the normalization of femicide. Therefore, the women killed in Ciudad Juárez since 1993 were presented as anonymous, both in their physical traits and in their social vulnerability. Many were tortured and mutilated, yet hundreds of these murders were never satisfactorily investigated. Their common elements have prompted many hypotheses, generally linking them to organized crime, the cause of the high level of violence in the city since the 1990s. What we do know for certain is that the victims were young and poor, that their bodies were dumped in wasteland outside the city, some of them showing signs of extreme violence, and that the local police were inept or complicit. In the state of Mexico, which has had the highest homicide rates of women in recent years, most of the victims worked in the informal economy and often in places where organized crime controlled the streets. Although it is tempting to speculate about a link between femicide and drug trafficking in these two locations, this explanation falls short: these patterns did not exist wherever there were organized criminal groups, and gender-based violence does not need organized crime to be prevalent and go unpunished.

The Ciudad Juárez cases drew international attention to the high rates and excesses of violence against women in Mexico. The flip side of these gruesome crimes was the invisibility of a phenomenon that seemed to be expanding in recent decades: the trafficking of women and girls for prostitution through networks that begin locally, sometimes at the family level, and eventually reach other countries. In parallel with these networks, migration from Central America and other regions of the world to the United States through Mexico was often accompanied by sexual violence. At a migrant shelter in Iztapalapa, investigators found that twenty-three out of ninety women had been raped. Reporting such crimes when the victims were in transit and legally vulnerable was even less useful than normal. Lack of protection in dangerous places was a common problem for prostitutes, assembly line workers, and migrants.

Gender-based violence also affected many other groups whose rights were denied by normative ideas about gender roles—in other words, what a "real" man or woman should be. This included, for example, privations and punishments for minors, independently of their sex, as if they were adults. Parental violence against children is rarely reported since it is seen as a patriarchal prerogative. Other kinds of violence justified by the difference of age, including incest, were extensions of the beatings and other types of domestic violence against women.

The experience of people whose gender identity and sexual preferences fail to conform to the gender binary has also been strongly marked by gender-based violence. Homosexuality was already persecuted in colonial-era Mexico, but it was not until the twentieth century that this oppression became more closely associated with types of brutality and coercion that did not necessarily come from the state. It was not classified as a crime in the Federal District's 1871 and 1931 penal codes, which did refer, however, to indecent acts. In the twentieth century, as gay sociabilities became more visible, the obsession with maintaining normative divisions led to symbolic and physical assaults, even including homicides. The most famous such case was the notorious "Dance of the 41" in 1901, when a group of men were arrested in the capital for dressing up as women during a party. The police and the press publicly humiliated those without the money to get themselves out of trouble. Since homosexuality was still largely a taboo, the number 41 became synonymous with gay identity. Although the men were not accused of committing "unnatural" sexual acts, the extensive news coverage of their arrests officially stigmatized anyone who looked or behaved differently from what was expected for their gender.

As Carlos Monsiváis has pointed out, homophobia had been an entirely conventional attitude ever since the revolutionary years. This became clear, for example, in a purge of intellectuals working in government in 1934. In this context, it is unsurprising that same-sex relationships and social interactions developed in relatively private settings. Even so, campaigns to promote "decency" in the 1950s and 1960s, as Víctor Macías-González observes, led to dragnets, detentions, and public humiliation. They raised the risk of more serious forms of violence.

Prejudices began to worsen once nota roja publications identified male homosexuality with the underworld of prisons, prostitution, and nightclubs. From the 1970s, *Alarma!* magazine began publishing images of *mujercitos* (lady boys) picked up during raids. These photographs, studied by Susana Vargas Cervantes, were a vehicle for spreading ideas about homosexuality as an endemic pathology in some parts of the city. Homophobia was also part of the magazine's language: "Two men were married! A love-triangle of sissies . . . Yuk!" This kind of representation enabled the continuity between verbal and physical violence. Various derogatory words for homosexual men like *puto* or *maricón* were the preamble to physical aggression.

As victims and suspects, homosexuals—particularly those without much money—faced a dual threat of police extortion and common crime in the places where they socialized. The same media that celebrated prejudice give us one of the few records of attacks on male homosexuals. In 1970, *Alarma!* reported on how same-sex couples who went to the police in Poza Rica seeking protection ended up being arrested. The risks do not appear to have diminished in recent years. A male rape victim in Ciudad Juárez chose not to tell the judge that he was gay because his lawyer advised him that the justice would assume there had been no coercion. It does not require a great leap of logic to understand how this erosion of rights translated into violence. As with prostitutes, attacks on transexual women or gay men were rarely reported because the police did not consider victims to be worthy of state protection, and perpetrators of violence normally went unpunished. As with femicide, these acts of aggression were part of a continuum that ranged from insults to beatings, arbitrary arrests, rape. and even murder.

It is impossible to gauge the extent of this problem from court records. Evidence from other sources is varied and anecdotal but shows very clear patterns. In the 1970s, there was a series of murders of gay men in Mexico City and Veracruz. Although a couple of arrests were made, the crimes against at least eighteen men, committed over the course of several months in hotel rooms, were never completely resolved. A police detective named Ángel Godínez Guillén, quoted in *Alarma!*, revealed the prejudices that enabled impunity: "Crimes against deviants are never, or almost never, solved." Detectives were therefore unable to solve crimes involving "problems between perverts." When investigations were carried out, they frequently focused on looking for suspects in gay hangouts. Police referred to these incidents as "crimes of passion"; they sought explanations in the victims' sexuality, extorted or intimidated families, and in general hardly bothered to investigate cases properly. Abducting or kidnapping homosexuals was a low-risk activity for murderers such as Antonio Contreras Monroy. Some of his victims were never even identified. The nota roja normalized such unsolved homicides: "Another victim strangled," read the terse headline in *La Prensa*, also in 1970.

The situation did not seem to have improved as the century drew to a close. Fernando del Collado and other researchers have compiled stories of murders of homosexuals, which they categorize as hate crimes. The victims were attacked in spaces associated with prostitution and nightlife, and the use of force was excessive. Of the 387 homicides he counted between 1995 and 2005, del Collado found that 56 men had been strangled and 113 stabbed; in some cases, gang rape had been committed before the murder; in others, the bodies were mutilated and dumped in public spaces. Robbery and extortion were part of cases that ended in manslaughter. A former soldier found guilty of four homicides, Raúl Osiel Marroquín Reyes, began by kidnapping his victims to extort money.

These were hate crimes not only because of how they were carried out but also because they represented the most violent extreme of a dehumanizing discourse. After his arrest, Marroquín Reyes claimed that his violent acts were not purely instrumental: he killed "for the good of society." The message was the same, albeit in a different medium, as that expressed in a poster left beside a viciously mutilated body in the state of Mexico: "We don't want gays." These crimes were not pathological but a logical extension of statements that frequently came from voices associated to religion, government, and the sensationalist press: the bishop of Querétaro, Mario de Gasperín Gasperín, for example, stated in 2006 that homosexuality was a perversion; others viewed homosexuals as a threat to childhood. Homophobic violence was therefore fulfilling a social mandate, a moral obligation for aggressors who believed they were protecting masculinity.

Gender-based violence is part of broader social relations and too entrenched in daily life to be changed drastically through legislation or political measures. However, it is possible to detect developments over the course of the century that correspond to new ideas about gender relations. In the late twentieth century, moves were made toward accepting homosexuals and increasing their safety after so many years of moral censure, supervision, and hostility. Women's organizations, which had been fighting for equality since the 1970s, soon began advocating for women's right to safety and protection from abuse by men in the home. Mexican governments, since the Echeverría administration, responded with gestures of support for the demand for equality in the workplace and in politics but without making safety a priority. Although these initiatives may seem superficial, the demands that they responded to gained momentum as they were embraced by human rights organizations and movements.

At first glance, it seems ironic that the defense of women's rights could become more visible at a time when Mexican governments were using dirty tactics in their counterinsurgency campaigns. But there was a connection between this defense and the early campaigns against torture and disappearances. Rosario Ibarra de Piedra was the mother of one person who disappeared, and she soon set up an organization along with other women. As happened in Argentina in 1976 with the Madres de la Plaza de Mayo, public protests against human rights abuses gained eloquence when coming from voices that showed that the impact of political repression was gendered. Rape was part of the repertoire of torture used during campaigns against guerrilla fighters. Its use became more blatant in subsequent decades. The army and the police were accused of gang-raping nineteen women in Mexico City in 1989; thirty-two women in Acteal, Chiapas, in 1997; and twenty-six women in Atenco, state of Mexico, in 2006. Punishment has not been straightforward, but the accusations themselves suggest that it is no longer possible to normalize this kind of act as a residue of other coercive practices.

More recently, accusations against sex trafficking and pedophile networks gained unprecedented importance thanks to investigations by Lydia Cacho and other journalists. The Puebla police kidnapped Cacho. She also suffered threats and attacks coordinated by the governor of the state of Puebla, Mario Marín, along with his business associates, who had been accused by Cacho of raping minors. Sex trafficking, which, as we have seen, was already recorded in the middle of the century, has become a high-profile issue in recent years as part of accusations of human rights violations of minors and migrants. International pressure and failed attempts to silence Cacho helped reduce the implicit tolerance that allowed such practices to continue. Something similar could be said about the more recent development of groups supporting the rights of people who refuse to accept binary gender identities. Taking to the streets and reporting homophobic violence has helped open the eyes of a generally apathetic public.

The official response to these pressures has ranged from cautious preventive measures to more ambitious legislation. The creation of women-only areas on public transport and new victim-protection measures within the

Ministerios Públicos constituted a tacit recognition by state and municipal governments of their own failings. In 2006, Congress passed antiviolence legislation for women's benefit (Ley General de Acceso de las Mujeres a Una Vida Libre de Violencia), which had been drafted by Marcela Lagarde and other women legislators and activists. Based on a view of violence that connected it to other types of inequality and perceptions that normalized it, the law sought to reduce impunity and to force state and federal governments to play a more active role in investigating and preventing crimes. The law defined femicidal violence as the "extreme form of violence against women, the result of the violation of their human rights in the public and private spheres, caused by the set of misogynistic behaviors that can lead to social and official impunity, and can result in women becoming victims of homicide and other types of violent death." Apart from physical abuse, this wide-ranging law also included physical, psychological, patrimonial, economic, and sexual violence. Another significant moment came with the 2009 ruling of the Inter-American Court of Human Rights on some of the Ciudad Juárez cases, which used the term "femicide" and urged the Mexican authorities to be more proactive. In the following years, the penal codes of some states began to include femicide as a category of crime, with Morelos, Veracruz, and the Federal District defining it as the act of someone who "takes a woman's life for gender-based reasons." Among other things, this has made it possible to count these cases in a way that indisputably reflects the broad reality of gender-based violence.

Despite the above, gender-based violence did not seem to diminish; some indicators even suggested it was increasing. Some right-wing and religious sectors saw feminism and equality as attacks on Christian morals. Violence against women in public transport remained an everyday reality. There was—and remains—a long way to go for women to be able to enjoy the city and the night in the same way as men.

In recent years, resistance to gender-based violence has become more visible and aggressive in movements involving new types of protest. Inherent in these collective actions has been a skepticism about the ability of institutions to resolve matters. Reporting sexual abuse in the workplace and especially in universities used publicity and building occupations to raise the cost of abusive behaviors that in the past were not considered problematic and that internal protocols could not solve. As Susana Vargas Cervantes wrote in an email to the author,

> Much of the gender-based violence is reported on social networks, and many women have found this method to be very effective because

there is no legal process, which means that the state cannot revictim-
ize the women and they can be publicly supported by their friends.
. . . Women have achieved a lot collectively: organizing together,
reading books together, and developing women's support groups,
"If you mess with one of us, you mess with us all," raising awareness
widely. And a community of women has come together, supporting
each other against violence, in a very powerful way that does not
require the state's involvement.

These same frustrations prompted mobilizations in support of legalizing
abortion. Protests following some particularly heinous femicides showed
how individual stories raised awareness and brought thousands onto the
streets. The names and faces of Ingrid Escamilla, Mara Castilla, and Lesvy
Berlín acquired unexpected power. Protesters used their own form of violence, more performative than physically dangerous, against police barriers,
buildings, and monuments in Mexico City. Some considered these protests
excessive. It would be wrong, however, to assume that the violence in the
marches was of the same order as the punitive and brutal summary executions of rapists or the lynchings mentioned above. For the victims of sexual
abuse, the conviction of their attacker was significant (and potentially heal-
ing) not as revenge but as an acknowledgment of their experience. When
placed in the context of the history of the violence suffered by women,
the rage expressed in these protests can be better understood: the routine,
threatening, and enormously costly abuse of women and people of non-
normative sexualities was part of a continuum of violence that, in extreme
cases, led to death. In other words, women's protests opened up discussions
about violence as a problem for all, not only from the perspective of victims.

The demands of those mobilizations, but also of many women's organizations since the 1970s, have been that the state invest in protecting
vulnerable groups, as the top priority, and then tackle aggressors. This was
not only about introducing stronger punishments or improving the cat-
egorization of gender-based crimes; it also required a joint effort by civil
society and state to alter the conceptions of gender and the attitudes that
have permitted this violence to continue for so many years. Simply put, the
problem of violence could only be tackled on several fronts.

Examining gender-based violence is the best way to conclude this book,
because it is in public, academic, and political discussions about this issue
that we can find a new approach to violence in general. Feminist critique

is not simply a fad or a response to an immediate situation. Instead, it is a systematic effort to show how different types of violence make sense from a perspective that considers the social construction of difference and its real effects. One premise of this critical vision is that violence must be understood within the framework of other social relations, particularly those that mean a hierarchy based on the differences of people's bodies. The link between the social construct of masculinity and violence is not a mere hypothesis. Digging just a little deeper into how violent men describe their own acts unveils rationalizations based on the premise that the inferiority of women and resentment of homosexuals is a requirement for masculine superiority. The ultimate target of all kinds of violence is the body, and women's bodies have been at the intersection of power and prestige, and the ideas that divide life into private and public spheres. Although violence is based on these dichotomies, in reality it cuts across them and, if we look carefully, actually undermines them. It reveals the fragility of such binary visions of sexual identity and, by extension, of masculinity itself. Viewing women as natural victims helps translate these hierarchies into violence. The feminist critique of gender violence has been the one that has best expressed not only the intersection of ideas about gender and class but also the fundamental artificiality of the patriarchal ideology.

Feminist efforts to understand violence in modern-day Mexico show in abundant detail how its most extreme forms, such as homicide and rape, are part of a continuum of coercive practices that begin with seemingly innocuous gestures, such as a catcall or a negative comment, but which form a chain that enables physical violence. This chain also helps us to understand the social tolerance for the different forms of violence considered in this book. Misogyny is the best-examined manifestation of a reasoning that we can also find if we look at attitudes toward political, religious, agrarian, or criminal violence: the victims bear some of the blame for their fate, and the aggressors are supported by moral norms shared with those who do not directly perpetrate the violence but tolerate it.

Feminism's critical perspective helps us to understand violence as not a temporary pathology or an instrumental resource but an act of horizontal communication, aimed not exclusively at taking control but also at forging connections between aggressors and their publics. As Rita Segato has shown, by treating women violently, men expect peer approval. Obviously, this approval is not universal, and relatively few men actually commit violent acts (otherwise, life in society would be impossible). However, the reality of this normalization of gender-based violence cannot be denied, and we all participate in it in some way. Like other forms of violence, femicide and sexual violence also convey a message that is received by other actors in society and understood in specific contexts, giving an ideological, religious, or moral ideological value to the use of force. We can therefore accept, taking Segato's view, that all violence is gender violence.

Another contribution of this feminist perspective on violence in Mexico is to offer a model for addressing the problem in a practical way. For Segato, understanding all violence as an expression of the patriarchal ideology requires "rethinking solutions and redirecting policies of pacification to the realm of people's intimate relationships." This proposal sounds paradoxical, since the struggle against gender-based violence implies going beyond the public-private dichotomy that has enabled its normalization. However, it works well because it reflects the superiority of a nonpatriarchal perspective to understand not only the cost of violence but also the best ways to challenge it. This would enable us to understand aggressors and victims as closely related instead of anonymous, located in a shared field of communication that has in the use of force one way, among others, of strengthening dominant ideologies. Thanks to this critical vision of gender relations we know that various kinds of coercion are connected and that resolving the most extreme examples is only one aspect of the work. We must also confront aspects of daily life in which violence is not yet a physical action but desensitizes people to the pain of others.

Recalling the moral justifications, practices, and perpetrators of violence discussed in previous chapters confirms this formulation. By acknowledging that all violence is gender-based, we also correct the initial hypothesis that we took from Hannah Arendt. Violence does in fact have one predictable long-term effect: it strengthens the patriarchy. Violence as a form of communication therefore transmits a lasting message, as Segato notes. We can finish this history with another quote from her, in a passage that evokes her ideas about humans' creative capacity:

> History is and must be unforeseeable. Since it is unforeseeable, we can hope for freedom. And as something unforeseeable, it is the signal and guarantee of freedom, in the sense that the future responds to such a vast number of vectors, and to the interplay of so many and so diverse intentions, that it cannot be calculated despite all our efforts to do so.

FOR FURTHER READING

———

T HE FOLLOWING IS NOT a comprehensive bibliography of the issues covered in this book. I have included authors mentioned in the
text as well as others who were important for this brief history. The
comments are not critiques but recommendations for readers wishing to
delve deeper into a particular subject. I have also used newspapers and some
archival documents, and I would be pleased to help interested researchers
access them. For the sake of practicality, this section follows the same structure as the book itself.

INTRODUCTION

Hannah Arendt's ideas can be found in On Violence (New York: Harcourt,
Brace, 1970). It is also worth reflecting on Walter Benjamin, "Critique of
Violence," in *Reflections: Essays, Aphorisms, Autobiographical Writings* (New
York: Schocken, 1978); Frantz Fanon, *The Wretched of the Earth* (New York:
Group West, 2004); and Norbert Elias, *The Civilizing Process: The History of*

Manners, trans. Edmund Jephcott (Oxford, UK: Blackwell, 1978). A useful synthesis is provided by Richard J. Bernstein, *Violence: Thinking without Banisters* (Cambridge, UK: Polity, 2013). For this chapter and throughout the book, Rita Laura Segato, *Las estructuras elementales de la violencia* (Buenos Aires: Prometeo, 2003); and Rita Laura Segato, *La guerra contra las mujeres* (Buenos Aires: Prometeo, 2018), were both important. For a more detailed analysis of the relationship between gender and violence, Pierre Bourdieu, *Masculine Domination* (Cambridge, UK: Polity, 2001), is very useful, although in this book I do not use his definition of symbolic violence and I do not dwell on the problem of domination. Readers interested in comparisons can start with Robert Muchembled, *A History of Violence* (Cambridge, UK: Polity, 2012); Pieter Spierenburg, ed., *Men and Violence* (Columbus: Ohio State University Press, 1998); Eric A. Johnson, Ricardo Salvatore, and Pieter Spierenburg, *Murder and Violence in Modern Latin America*, Bulletin of Latin American Research (Hoboken, NJ: Wiley-Blackwell, 2013); Eric A. Johnson and Eric H. Monkkonen, *The Civilization of Crime* (Urbana: University of Illinois Press, 1996); and Eric H. Monkkonen, *Murder in New York City* (Berkeley: University of California Press, 2001). I should note, however, that several of these works are generally based on a European model that does not apply so well to the case of Mexico. For a critical perspective on what we know and do not know about crime today, see Fernando Escalante Gonzalbo, *El crimen como realidad y representación* (Mexico City: Colegio de México, 2012).

REVOLUTIONARY VIOLENCE

The historiography on the Revolutionary period is so vast that any recommendation will be arbitrary. Here is my attempt. A series of reflections for an introduction to revolutionary violence can be found in Jorge Aguilar Mora, *Una muerte sencilla, justa, eterna . . . Cultura y guerra durante la Revolución Mexicana* (Mexico City: Era, 1990). See also Claudio Lomnitz-Adler, *Death and the Idea of Mexico* (Brooklyn, NY: Zone, 2005). For a general overview of the Revolution that can help in considering the different types of fighting, see Alan Knight, *The Mexican Revolution* (Lincoln: University of Nebraska Press, 1990); Friedrich Katz, *The Life and Times of Pancho Villa* (Stanford, CA: Stanford University Press, 1998), and "El papel de la violencia y el terror en las Revoluciones mexicana y rusa," in Friedrich Katz, *Nuevos ensayos mexicanos* (Mexico City: Era, 2006); John Womack Jr., *Zapata and the Mexican Revolution* (New York: Knopf, 1969). Regional details can be found in Frans J. Schryer, *The Rancheros of Pisaflores: The History of a Peasant Bourgeoisie in Twentieth-Century Mexico* (Toronto: University of Toronto Press, 1980);

and Daniel Nugent, *Spent Cartridges of Revolution* (Chicago: University of Chicago Press, 1994). Insightful testimonies of everyday life are found in *Mi pueblo durante la Revolución* (Mexico City: Museo Nacional de Culturas Populares and Instituto Nacional de Antropología e Historia, 1985); Lidia E. Gómez García, "Vida cotidiana en tiempo de guerra: Las mujeres cholultecas durante la Revolución mexicana," in Evelyne Sánchez et al., *Revolucionarias fueron todas* (Puebla: Benemérita Universidad Autónoma de Puebla, 2013); and Francisco Ramírez Plancarte, *La Ciudad de México durante la revolución constitucionalista* (Mexico City: Botas, 1941). Another worthwhile analysis of the period is found in José Luis Trueba Lara, *La vida y la muerte en tiempos de la Revolución* (Mexico City: Taurus, 2010). Literary accounts are essential: Mariano Azuela, *Los de abajo*, in *La novela de la Revolución Mexicana*, ed. Antonio Castro Leal (Mexico City: Aguilar–Secretaría de Educación Pública, 1988); Nellie Campobello, *Cartucho*, and Rafael F. Muñoz, *Vámonos con Pancho Villa*, in the same anthology; Martín Luis Guzmán, *El águila y la serpiente* (Mexico City: Fondo de Cultura Económica, 1984). The film version of Muñoz's book is *Vámonos con Pancho Villa* (dir. Fernando de Fuentes, 1935). A memoir that is essential for understanding the uses of violence not only during these years but over subsequent decades is Gonzalo N. Santos, *Memorias* (Mexico City: Grijalbo, 1984). On the demographic cost, see Robert McCaa, "Missing Millions: The Demographic Costs of the Mexican Revolution," *Mexican Studies / Estudios Mexicanos* 19, no. 2 (Summer 2003): 367–400. For gender perspectives, see Mary K. Vaughan, Gabriela Cano, and Jocelyn Olcott, eds., *Sex in Revolution: Gender, Politics, and Power in Modern Mexico* (Durham, NC: Duke University Press, 2006); and Ana Lau and Carmen Ramos, *Mujeres y Revolución, 1900–1917* (Mexico City: Instituto Nacional de Estudios Históricos de la Revolución Mexicana, 1993). On new attitudes, see Jorge García-Robles, *La bala perdida: William S. Burroughs en México, 1949–1952* (Mexico City: Milenio, 1995).

AGRARIAN VIOLENCE

On this topic there is also a trove of historical, sociological, anthropological, and economic studies, and the period in question is longer. Recommended reading includes Héctor Aguilar Camín, *La frontera nómada: Sonora y la Revolución Mexicana* (Mexico City: Siglo XXI, 1977); Christopher R. Boyer, *Becoming Campesinos: Politics, Identity, and Agrarian Struggle in Post-revolutionary Michoacán, 1920–1935* (Stanford, CA: Stanford University Press, 2003); Keith Brewster, *Militarism, Ethnicity, and Politics in the Sierra Norte de Puebla, 1917–1930* (Tucson: University of Arizona Press, 2003); Romana Falcón, *Revolución y caciquismo, San Luís Potosí, 1910–1938* (Mexico City: Colegio de México, 1984), and *El agrarismo en Veracruz: La etapa radical* (Mexico City: Colegio de México, 1977); Paul Gillingham, "Who Killed Crispín Aguilar?," in *Violence, Insecurity, and the State in Mexico,* ed. Wil G. Pansters (Stanford, CA: Stanford University Press, 2012); Alan Knight, "Habitus and Homicide: Political Culture in Revolutionary Mexico," in *Citizens of the Pyramid: Essays on Mexican Political Culture,* ed. Wil G. Pansters (Amsterdam: Thela, 1997); the chapters by Salvador Maldonado Aranda, Alan Knight, Wil G. Pansters, and Stephen Lewis in *Caciquismo in Twentieth-Century Mexico,* ed. Wil G. Pansters (London: Institute for the Study of the Americas, 2005); Antonio Santoyo, *La Mano Negra, poder regional y Estado en México: Veracruz, 1928–1943* (Mexico City: Consejo Nacional para la Cultura y las Artes, 1995); Elisa Servín, *La oposición política* (Mexico City: Fondo de Cultura Económica, 2006); Benjamin T. Smith, *Pistoleros and Popular Movements: The Politics of State Formation in Postrevolutionary Oaxaca* (Lincoln: University of Nebraska Press, 2009); John Tutino, *From Insurrection to Revolution: Social Bases of Agrarian Violence, 1750–1940* (Princeton, NJ: Princeton University Press, 1988); and the chapters in Ben Fallaw and Terry Rugeley, eds., *Forced Marches: Soldiers and Military Caciques in Modern Mexico* (Tucson: University of Arizona Press, 2012). An essential work is Armando Bartra, *Los herederos de Zapata* (Mexico City: Era, 1995). A microhistory that is a model for other works and a comprehensive account is Luis González y González, *San José de Gracia: Mexican Village in Transition* (Austin: University of Texas Press, 1974). Literary works include Juan Rulfo, *Pedro Páramo* (Mexico City: Fondo de Cultura Económica, 1955), and *El llano en llamas* (Mexico City: Fondo de Cultura Económica, 1953). Notable films are *Rebozo de soledad* (dir. Roberto Gavaldón, 1952) and *Río Escondido* (dir. Emilio Fernández, 1948). Contemporary studies include Veronique Flanet, *Viviré, si dios quiere: Un estudio de la violencia en la Mixteca de la costa* (Mexico City: Instituto Nacional Indigenista, 1977); James Greenberg, *Blood Ties: Life and Violence in Rural Mexico* (Tucson: University of Arizona Press, 1989). On caciques, readers can begin with Paul Friedrich, *The Princes of Naranja: An Essay in Anthro-historical Method* (Austin: University of Texas Press, 1986), and *Agrarian Revolt in a Mexican Village* (Englewood Cliffs, NJ: Prentice-Hall, 1970); and Jeffrey Rubin, *Decentering the Regime: Ethnicity, Radicalism, and Democracy in Juchitan, Mexico* (Durham, NC: Duke University Press, 1997).

RELIGIOUS VIOLENCE

The historiography on this subject is comprehensive and evolving in a very interesting way. See Jean Meyer, *The Cristero Rebellion: The Mexican People between Church and State, 1926–1929* (New York: Cambridge University

Press, 1976), and subsequent critical works. On the subject of Cristeros and campesinos, I suggest Adrian Bantjes, *As If Jesus Walked on Earth: Cardenismo, Sonora, and the Mexican Revolution* (Wilmington, DE: SR, 1998); Matthew Butler, *Popular Piety and Political Identity in Mexico's Cristero Rebellion* (New York: Oxford University Press, 2004); Irma Delgado Solórzano, "Crusaders, Martyrs, and Saints: Representations of Christian Militancy in Mexico, 1850–2013" (PhD diss., University of Kansas, 2015); the chapters in Ben Fallaw and Terry Rugeley, eds., *Forced Marches: Soldiers and Military Caciques in Modern Mexico* (Tucson: University of Arizona Press, 2012); Ben Fallaw, *Religion and State Formation in Postrevolutionary Mexico* (Durham, NC: Duke University Press, 2013); Renato González Mello, "Of Intersections and Parallel Lives: José de León Toral and David Alfaro Siqueiros," in *True Stories of Crime in Modern Mexico*, ed. Robert Buffington and Pablo Piccato (Albuquerque: University of New Mexico Press, 2009); Fernando M. González, *Matar y morir por Cristo Rey: Aspectos de la cristiada* (Mexico City: Plaza y Valdés; Universidad Nacional Autónoma de México, Instituto de Investigaciones Sociales, 2001); Jennie Purnell, *Popular Movements and State Formation in Revolutionary Mexico: The Agraristas and Cristeros of Michoacán* (Durham, NC: Duke University Press, 1999); Benjamin T. Smith, *The Roots of Conservatism in Mexico: Catholicism, Society, and Politics in the Mixteca Baja, 1750–1962* (Albuquerque: University of New Mexico Press, 2012); and Robert Weiss, *For Christ and Country: Militant Catholic Youth in Post-Revolutionary Mexico* (Cambridge: Cambridge University Press, 2019). For fiction, see José Revueltas, "Dios en la tierra," in *El apando y otros relatos* (Madrid: Alianza, 1983). For a clear understanding of anticlericalism, see Carlos Martínez Assad, *El laboratorio de la revolución: El Tabasco garridista* (Mexico City: Siglo XXI, 1979). See also Adrian Bantjes, "Idolatry and Iconoclasm in Revolutionary Mexico: The De-Christianization Campaigns, 1929–1940," *Mexican Studies / Estudios Mexicanos* 13, no. 1 (Winter 1997): 87–120; Robert Curley, "Anticlericalism and Public Space in Revolutionary Jalisco," *The Americas* 65, no. 4 (April 2009): 511–33; Matthew Butler, "Sotanas Rojinegras: Catholic Anticlericalism and Mexico's Revolutionary Schism," *The Americas* 65, no. 4 (April 2009): 535–58. For an important overview, see Roberto Blancarte, *Historia de la Iglesia Católica en México* (Mexico City: Colegio Mexiquense and Fondo de Cultura Económica, 1992). For background, I used David Carrasco, *Religions of Mesoamerica* (Long Grove, IL: Waveland, 2014); Antonio Rubial García, *La violencia física y simbólica de los santos en la historia del cristianismo* (Madrid: Trama, 2011); and David Eduardo Tavárez, *Devociones indígenas, disciplina y disidencia en el México colonial* (Oaxaca: Universidad Autónoma Metropolitana, 2012). A wealth of political details can be found in John Watson Foster Dulles, *Yesterday in Mexico: A Chronicle of the*

Revolution, 1919–1936 (Austin: University of Texas Press, 1961). On lynching, see Gema Kloppe-Santamaría, *In the Vortex of Violence: Lynching, Extralegal Justice, and the State in Post-Revolutionary Mexico* (Oakland: University of California Press, 2020). On Tomóchic, see Paul J. Vanderwood, *The Power of God against the Guns of Government* (Stanford, CA: Stanford University Press, 1998); Lilian Illades, *Disidencia y sedición: Región Serrana Chihuahuense Tomóchic, 1891–1892* (Puebla: Universidad de Puebla, 2002); and Heriberto Frías, *Tomóchic: Novela histórica mexicana* (Mazatlán: Valades, 1906).

On right-wing movements, see Luis Alberto Herrán Ávila, "Transnational Anticommunism, the Extreme Right, and the Politics of Enmity in Argentina, Colombia, and Mexico, 1946–1972" (PhD diss., New School for Social Research, 2016); and Claire Brewster and Keith Brewster, "'Patria, Honor y Fuerza': A Study of a Right-Wing Youth Movement in Mexico during the 1930s–1960s," *Journal of Latin American Studies* 46, no. 4 (November 2014): 691–721. For comparison, see Federico Finchelstein, *From Fascism to Populism in History* (Oakland: University of California Press, 2019); Alicia Gojman de Backal, *Camisas, escudos y desfiles militares: Los Dorados y el antisemitismo en México (1934–1940)* (Mexico City: Fondo de Cultura Económica, 2000); and Pablo Yankelevich, "Extranjería y antisemitismo en el México posrevolucionario," *Interdisciplina* 2, no. 4 (2014): 143–59. On Protestantism, see Carlos Monsiváis, *Protestantismo, diversidad, tolerancia* (Mexico City: Comisión Nacional de los Derechos Humanos, 2002).

CRIME AND PISTOLEROS

This is also a growing area of historiography. See, for example, the chapters of Diego Pulido, Víctor Macías, Ricardo Pérez Montfort, and others in Susana Sosenski and Gabriela Pulido, eds., *Hampones, pelados y pecatrices: Sujetos peligrosos de la Ciudad de México (1940–1960)* (Mexico City: Fondo de Cultura Económica, 2020). Essential works also include Paul Gillingham, "'We Don't Have Arms but We Do Have Balls: Fraud, Violence and Popular Agency in Elections,'" in *Dictablanda: Politics, Work, and Culture in Mexico, 1938–1968*, ed. Paul Gillingham and Benjamin Smith (Durham, NC: Duke University Press, 2014); Paul Gillingham, *Unrevolutionary Mexico: The Birth of a Strange Dictatorship* (New Haven, CT: Yale University Press, 2021); and the books of Benjamin Smith: *The Dope: The Real History of the Mexican Drug Trade* (New York: W. W. Norton, 2021) and *Pistoleros and Popular Movements: The Politics of State Formation in Postrevolutionary Oaxaca* (Lincoln: University of Nebraska Press, 2009). On prostitution, see Katherine Elaine Bliss, *Compromised Positions: Prostitution, Public Health, and Gender Politics in Revolutionary Mexico City* (University Park: Pennsylvania State University

Press, 2001), and the titles mentioned in the previous chapter. The works of Elisa Speckman are important: *Crimen y castigo: Legislación penal, interpretaciones de la criminalidad y administración de justicia, Ciudad de México, 1872–1910* (Mexico City: Colegio de México, 2002) and *Horrorosísimos crímenes y ejemplares castigos: Una historia sociocultural del crimen, la justicia y el castigo* (San Luis Potosí and Aguascalientes: Colegio de San Luis and Universidad Autónoma de Aguascalientes, 2018). Additional material can be found in Pablo Piccato, *A History of Infamy: Crime, Truth, and Justice in Mexico* (Oakland: University of California Press, 2017).

On police and charros, see Diane Davis, "Policing and Regime Transition: From Postauthoritarianism to Populism to Neoliberalism," and Marcos Águila and Jeffrey Bortz, "The Rise of Gangsterism and Charrismo: Labor Violence and the Postrevolutionary Mexican State," in *Violence, Coercion, and State-Making in Twentieth-Century Mexico: The Other Half of the Centaur,* ed. Wil G. Pansters (Stanford, CA: Stanford University Press, 2012); also Carlos A. Pérez Ricart, "El papel del Federal Bureau of Narcotics en el diseño de la política de drogas en México (1940–1968)," *Frontera Norte,* no. 31 (January 2019): 1–23. The scandalous and informative book on Durazo is Jorge González González, *Lo negro del Negro Durazo* (Mexico City: Posada, 1983). For a media perspective, see Roberto Blanco Moheno, *Memorias de un reportero* (Mexico City: V Siglos, 1975). For more systematic analyses of the police and corruption, see Diego Pulido Esteva, *La ley de la calle: Policía y sociedad en la Ciudad de México, 1860–1940* (Mexico City: Colegio de México, 2023); Elena Azaola Garrido and Miguel Ángel Ruiz Torres, *Investigadores de papel: Poder y derechos humanos entre la Policía Judicial de la Ciudad de México* (Mexico City: Fontamara, 2009); Stephen R. Niblo, *Mexico in the 1940s: Modernity, Politics, and Corruption* (Wilimington, DE: Scholarly Resources, 1999); Fernando Escalante Gonzalbo, "La corrupción política: Apuntes para un modelo teórico," *Foro Internacional* 30, no. 2 (October 1989): 328–45; Stephen D. Morris, "Corruption, Drug Trafficking, and Violence in Mexico," *Brown Journal of World Affairs* 18, no. 2 (2012): 29–43. For a fascinating account, see Nelson Arteaga Botello and Adrián López Rivera, "Viaje al interior de la policía: El caso de un municipio de México," *Nexos* (April 1, 1998). As in the following chapters, an important work is Sergio Aguayo Quezada, *La charola: Una historia de los servicios de inteligencia en México* (Mexico City: Grijalbo, 2001). Another forensic examination of the crime world is Eduardo Téllez Vargas and José Ramón Garmabella, *¡Reportero de policía! El Güero Téllez: Antología de casos policíacos famosos* (Mexico City: Océano, 1982).

On the early history of drugs, see Isaac Campos, *Home Grown: Marijuana and the Origins of Mexico's War on Drugs* (Chapel Hill: University of North Carolina Press, 2012); Ricardo Pérez Montfort, *Tolerancia y prohibición:*

Aproximaciones a la historia social y cultural de las drogas en México, 1840–1940 (Mexico City: Debate, 2016); Elaine Carey, *Women Drug Traffickers: Mules, Bosses, and Organized Crime* (Albuquerque: University of New Mexico Press, 2014); and Nicole Mottier, "Drug Gangs and Politics in Ciudad Juárez, 1928–1936," *Mexican Studies / Estudios Mexicanos* 25, no. 1 (2009): 19–46. For comparisons, see Salvatore Lupo, *The Two Mafias: A Transatlantic History, 1888–2008* (New York: Palgrave Macmillan, 2015). There are many films on the subject, but none quite like *Distinto amanecer* (dir. Julio Bracho, 1943).

GUERRILLA AND COUNTERINSURGENCY

New generations of historians are transforming what we know about this period. I am referring here to academic studies, testimonies, and other official documents. See Sergio Aguayo Quezada, *La charola* and *1968: Los archivos de la violencia* (Mexico City: Grijalbo, 1998); Alexander Aviña, *Specters of Revolution: Peasant Guerrillas in the Cold War Mexican Countryside* (Oxford: Oxford University Press, 2014); Armando Bartra, *Guerrero bronco: Campesinos, ciudadanos y guerrilleros en la Costa Grande* (Mexico City: Era, 2000); Laura Castellanos and Alejandro Jiménez Martín del Campo, *México armado, 1943–1981* (Mexico City: Era, 2007); Adela Cedillo and Fernando Calderón, eds., *Challenging Authoritarianism in Mexico: Revolutionary Struggles and the Dirty War, 1964–1982* (New York: Routledge, 2012); the works of Verónica Oikión Solano, including *Movimientos armados en México, siglo XX: La guerrilla en la segunda mitad del siglo* (Zamora: Colegio de Michoacán, 2006), and "The Revolutionary Action Movement and the Armed Struggle," in *Challenging Authoritarianism*; Tanalís Padilla, *Rural Resistance in the Land of Zapata: The Jaramillista Movement and the Myth of the Pax Priísta, 1940–1962* (Durham, NC: Duke University Press, 2008); Jaime M. Pensado, *Rebel Mexico: Student Unrest and Authoritarian Political Culture during the Long Sixties* (Stanford, CA: Stanford University Press, 2013), and Jaime M. Pensado and Enrique C. Ochoa, eds., *México beyond 1968: Revolutionaries, Radicals, and Repression during the Global Sixties and Subversive Seventies* (Tucson: University of Arizona Press, 2018); Thomas G. Rath, *Myths of Demilitarization in Postrevolutionary Mexico, 1920–1960* (Chapel Hill: University of North Carolina Press, 2013); and Romain Robinet, "A Revolutionary Group Fighting against a Revolutionary State: The September 23rd Communist League against the PRI-State (1973–1975)," in Cedillo and Calderón, *Challenging Authoritarianism in Mexico*. To understand this period and its connection to the history discussed in the next chapter, see Adela Cedillo's peerless "Intersections between the Dirty War and the War on Drugs in Northwestern Mexico (1969–1985)" (PhD diss., University of Wisconsin–Madison, 2019).

On the events of 1968, a good starting point is Ariel Rodríguez Kuri, *Museo del universo: Los Juegos Olímpicos y el movimiento estudiantil de 1968* (Mexico City: Colegio de México, 2019). On October 2, see Julio Scherer García and Carlos Monsiváis, *Parte de guerra, Tlatelolco 1968: Documentos del General Marcelino García Barragán. Los hechos y la historia* (Mexico City: Nuevo Siglo / Aguilar, 1999). See also the aforementioned thesis by Herrán Ávila, and Kloppe-Santamaría, *In the Vortex of Violence*. On torture, see Gladys McCormick, "The Last Door: Political Prisoners and the Use of Torture in Mexico's Dirty War," *The Americas* 74, no. 1 (February 1, 2017): 57–81. On the complex relationship with Cuba, see Renata Keller, *Mexico's Cold War: Cuba, the United States, and the Legacy of the Mexican Revolution* (New York: Cambridge University Press, 2015).

History and testimonial accounts are contained in Fritz Glockner Corte, *Los años heridos: La historia de la guerrilla en México, 1968–1985* (Mexico City: Planeta Mexicana, 2019); Gustavo A. Hirales Morán, *La Liga Comunista 23 de Septiembre: Orígenes y naufragio* (Mexico City: Cultura Popular, 1977); and Elena Poniatowska, *Fuerte es el silencio* (Mexico City: Era, 1982). On self-criticism, see Carlos Pereyra, *Política y violencia* (Mexico City: Fondo de Cultura Económica, 1974). Separate mention needs to be made of the works of fiction and essays by Carlos Montemayor: *La guerrilla recurrente* (Mexico City: Debate / Random House Mondadori, 2007) and *La violencia de Estado en México: Antes y después de 1968* (Mexico City: Debate, 2010). On women's experiences, see Lucía Rayas, "Hitos de la memoria guerrillera en México," in *Subversiones: Género y memoria social. Ataduras y reflexiones*, ed. Lucía Rayas and Luz Maceira Ochoa (Mexico City: Fondo Nacional para la Cultura y las Artes, Escuela Nacional de Antropología e Historia, and Juan Pablos, 2012). Left-wing histories can be found in Carlos Illades, *La inteligencia rebelde* (Mexico City: Océano, 2012), and Ariel Rodríguez Kuri, *Historia mínima de las izquierdas en México* (Mexico City: Colegio de México, 2020).

Documentary material generated from the truth and reconciliation commission (FEMOSSP) includes José Sotelo Marbán, "El ejército mexicano y la Guerra Sucia en Guerrero," manuscript, December 2002; Fiscalía Especial para Movimientos Sociales y Políticos del Pasado, *Informe histórico a la sociedad mexicana, 2006*, online at "Official Report Released on Mexico's 'Dirty War,'" National Security Archive Electronic Briefing Book No. 209, National Security Archive, accessed May 8, 2025, https://nsarchive2.gwu .edu/NSAEBB/NSAEBB209/index.htm; José Sotelo Marbán, ed., *La verdad negada: Informe histórico sobre la Guerra Sucia del Estado mexicano entre los años 60's a los 80's* (Mexico City: Centro de Investigaciones Históricas de los Movimientos Sociales, 2012).

ORGANIZED CRIME

It is very difficult to separate testimony, propaganda, journalism, and academic research on such recent themes. All these different types of study are in an increasingly productive dialogue. Important reportages include Jesús Blancornelas, *El cártel: Los Arellano Félix, la mafia más poderosa en la historia de América Latina* (Mexico City: Debolsillo, 2004); Ioan Grillo, *El Narco: Inside Mexico's Criminal Insurgency* (New York: Bloomsbury, 2011); Anabel Hernández, *Los señores del narco* (Mexico City: Grijalbo, 2011), and *El traidor: El diario secreto del hijo del Mayo* (Mexico City: Grijalbo, 2020). Diego Enrique Osorno, *El cártel de Sinaloa: Una historia del uso político del narco* (Mexico City: Grijalbo, 2009), and *La guerra de los Zetas: Viaje por la frontera de la necropolítica* (Mexico City: Grijalbo, 2012); Ricardo Ravelo, *Los capos: Las narco-rutas de México* (Mexico City: Debolsillo, 2006), and *Osiel: Vida y tragedia de un capo* (Mexico City: Grijalbo, 2009); Darío Fritz and María Idalia Gómez, *Con la muerte en el bolsillo* (Mexico City: Planeta, 2005); Alejandro Páez Varela and Marcela Turati, *La guerra por Juárez* (Mexico City: Temas de Hoy, 2009); and Marco Lara Klahr, *Días de furia: Memorial de violencia, crimen e intolerancia* (Mexico City: Plaza y Janés, 2001).

See also the syntheses in Smith, *The Dope*; Alexander S. Dawson, *The Peyote Effect: From the Inquisition to the War on Drugs* (Oakland: University of California Press, 2018); Salvador Maldonado Aranda, "Stories of Drug Trafficking in Rural Mexico: Territories, Drugs and Cartels in Michoacán," *European Review of Latin American and Caribbean Studies*, no. 94 (April 2014): 43–66; Carmen Boullosa and Mike Wallace, *A Narco History: How the United States and Mexico Jointly Created the "Mexican Drug War"* (New York: OR, 2015); and Froylán Enciso, "Drogas, narcotráfico," in *Una historia contemporánea de México*, vol. 4 (Mexico City: Océano–Colegio de México, 2009), and "Régimen global de prohibición, actores criminalizados y la cultura del narcotráfico en México durante la década de 1970," *Foro Internacional* 49, no. 3 (July–September, 2009): 595–637. For recent findings, see Romain Le Cour Grandmaison, "Drug Cartels, from Political to Criminal Intermediation: The 'Caballeros Templarios' Mirror Sovereignty in Michoacán, Mexico," in *Cocaine: From Coca Fields to the Streets*, ed. Desmond Arias and Thomas Grisaffi (Durham, NC: Duke University Press, 2021); Adèle Blazquez, "'L'aube s'est levée sur un mort': Anthropologie politique de la violence armée et de la culture du pavot à Badiraguato (Sinaloa, Mexique)" (PhD diss., École des Hautes Études en Sciences Sociales, 2019); and Carlos Resa Nestares, "El valor de las exportaciones mexicanas de drogas ilegales, 1961–2000" (paper, Universidad Autónoma de Madrid, June 2003),

www.academia.edu/22157352/El_valor_de_las_exportaciones_mexicanas
_de_drogas_ilegales_1961–2000. On interactions between drug trafficking
and other businesses, see Patricia Figueroa, "Interacciones entre políticos,
criminales y empresarios: El caso del crimen organizado en Sinaloa" (PhD
diss., Universidad Autónoma de Sinaloa, 2018), and *Ética en tiempos de
guerra y narcotráfico* (Culiacán: Moby Dick, 2017); María Teresa Martínez
Trujillo, "Businessmen and Protection Patterns in Dangerous Contexts: Put-
ting the Case of Guadalajara, Mexico into Perspective" (PhD diss., Sciences
Politiques, 2019). An example of a series of essential studies coordinated
by David Shirk is *2019 Organized Crime and Violence in Mexico*, Justice in
Mexico, April 30, 2019, https://justiceinmexico.org/2019-organizedcrime
-violence-mexico/. On impunity, see the work of Guillermo Zepeda Lecuona,
starting with *Crimen sin castigo: Procuración de justicia penal y ministerio público en México* (Mexico City: Fondo de Cultura Económica–Cidac, 2004).

ON GENDER VIOLENCE

In this area, works are essentially multidisciplinary and have had a direct
impact on public discussion and policy. Texts that productively combine
testimony and analysis include Gloria González-López, *Secretos de familia:
Incesto y violencia sexual en México* (Mexico City: Siglo Veintiuno, 2019);
Rosario Valdez Santiago, "Del silencio privado a las agendas públicas: El
devenir de la lucha contra la violencia doméstica en México," in *Violencia
contra las mujeres en contextos urbanos y rurales*, ed. Marta Torres Falcón
(Mexico City: Colegio de México, 2004); Marta Cecilia Híjar, Rafael Lozano,
Rosario Valdez, and Julia Blanco, "Las lesiones intencionales como causa de
demanda de atención en los servicios de urgencia hospitalaria de la Ciudad
de México," *Salud Mental* 25, no. 1 (2002): 8; and María Aidé Hernández
García and Fabiola Coutiño Osorio, eds., *Cultura de la violencia y feminicidio
en México* (Mexico City: Fontamara–Universidad de Guanajuato, 2016).

Exemplary histories are included in Elisa Speckman Guerra, *"El derecho
a vivir como una mujer amante y amada": Nydia Camargo, su crimen y su
juicio (México, década de 1920)* (Mexico City: Colegio de México, Centro de
Estudios Históricos, 2019); and Víctor Manuel Macías González, "El caso de
una beldad asesina: La construcción narrativa, los concursos de belleza y el
mito nacional posrevolucionario (1921–1931)," *Historia y Grafía*, no. 13 (1999):
113–54. Essential contributions are Martha Santillán Esqueda, *Delincuencia
femenina: Ciudad de México, 1940–1954* (Mexico City: Instituto Nacional
de Ciencias Penales, 2017); Lisette Rivera Reynaldos, "Criminales, crimi-
nalizadas y delatoras: Mujeres involucradas en homicidios pasionales en

Michoacán, 1900–1920," and "Crímenes pasionales y relaciones de género en México, 1880–1910," *Nuevo Mundo / Mundos Nuevos* (2006); and Fabiola Bailón Vásquez, ed., *Prostitución y lenocinio en México, siglos XIX y XX* (Mexico City: Secretaría de Cultura / Fondo de Cultura Económica, 2016). On court procedures in the early 1900s, see Pablo Piccato, *City of Suspects: Crime in Mexico City, 1900–1931* (Durham, NC: Duke University Press, 2001).

On more recent manifestations, see Susana Vargas Cervantes, *The Little Old Lady Killer: The Sensationalized Crimes of Mexico's First Female Serial Killer* (New York: New York University Press, 2019); Julia E. Monárrez Fragoso and César M. Fuentes. "Feminicidio y marginalidad urbana en Ciudad Juárez en la década de los noventa," in *Violencia contra las mujeres en contextos urbanos y rurales*, ed. Marta Torres Falcón (Mexico City: Colegio de México, 2004); Manuel Amador Velázquez and Héctor Domínguez Ruvalcaba, "Violencias y feminicidio en el Estado de México," and Hiroko Asakura and Marta Torres Falcón, "Género y vulnerabilidad extrema: Migración centroamericana y trata de personas," both in *Diálogos interdisciplinarios sobre violencia sexual: Antología*, ed. Patricia Ravelo Blancas and Héctor Domínguez Ruvalcaba (El Paso: University of Texas at El Paso, 2012). Laws and definitions of "femicide" can be found in Marcela Lagarde y de los Ríos, "Por los derechos humanos de las mujeres: La Ley General de Acceso de las Mujeres a Una Vida Libre de Violencia," *Revista Mexicana de Ciencias Políticas y Sociales* 49 (October 9, 2013): 200, and "Del femicidio al feminicidio," *Desde el Jardín de Freud: Revista de Psicoanálisis*, no. 6 (2006): 216–25; Patricia Olamendi, *Feminicidio en México* (Mexico City: Instituto Nacional de las Mujeres, 2016); and Olivia Tena and Jahel López Guerrero, eds., *Mujeres en la policía: Miradas feministas sobre su experiencia y su entorno laboral* (Mexico City: Universidad Nacional Autónoma de México, Centro de Investigaciones Interdisciplinarias en Ciencias y Humanidades, 2017). A wealth of information, including the surveys mentioned in the text, can be found on the website of the Instituto Nacional de Estadística, Geografía e Informática, www.inegi.org.mx.

On masculinities and homosexuality, see Robert McKee Irwin, *Mexican Masculinities* (Minneapolis: University of Minnesota Press, 2003); Robert McKee Irwin, Ed McCaughan, and Michelle Nasser, eds., *The Famous 41: Sexuality and Social Control in Mexico, c. 1901* (Basingstoke, UK: Palgrave Macmillan, 2003); Roberto Garda, "La construcción social de la violencia masculina: Ideas y pistas para apoyar a los hombres que desean dejar su violencia," in *Sucede que me canso de ser hombre . . . : Relatos y reflexiones sobre hombres y masculinidades en México*, ed. Ana Amuchástegui and Ivonne Szasz Pianta (Mexico City: Colegio de México, 2007); Fernando del Collado, *Homofobia: Odio, crimen y justicia, 1995–2005* (Mexico City: Tusquets, 2007);

Carlos Monsiváis, *Salvador Novo: Lo marginal en el centro* (Mexico City: Era, 2001); Víctor Macías González, "Homosexuales," in Sosenski and Pulido, *Hampones, pelados y pecatrices*; Rodrigo Parrini Roses and Alejandro Brito Lemus, *Crímenes de odio por homofobia: Un concepto en construcción* (Mexico City: Letra S, 2012); and Susana Vargas Cervantes, *Mujercitos!* (Barcelona: RM, 2014). On trafficking and the abuse of minors, see Lydia Cacho, *Los demonios del Edén: El poder que protege a la pornografía infantil* (Mexico City: Grijalbo, 2005); and Susana Sosenski, "Robachicos," in Sosenski and Pulido, *Hampones, pelados y pecatrices*.

General reflections can be found in the books by Rita Segato cited in the introduction and in Gloria González-López, "Desde el otro lado: Reflexiones feministas para una sociología de la violencia sexual," in Ravelo Blancas and Domínguez Ruvalcaba, *Diálogos interdisciplinarios sobre violencia sexual*; for a guide to understanding modern-day feminism, see Lastesis, *Antología feminista* (Mexico City: Debate, 2021).

INDEX

memory-building process, 136–37
methamphetamine production, 141.
    See also drug trafficking
Mexican Revolution: battlefield experiences, 11; Battle of Trinidad, 16–17; daily life during, 14–15; Decena Trágica and increasing violence, 12–14; early skirmishes, 10–11; historical interpretations of, 21–22; ideology and propaganda, 21; justice and social protest, 16; Madero, betrayal of, 12–13; photographs of, 14; punitive vs. non-violent approaches, 11; revolutionary divisions, 15–16; stereotyping and racism, 62; technology, use of, 16; terror, use of, 21–22; violent phase after Madero's victory, 12; visual motifs, 14; weapons used in revolutionary cells, 8–9; women's participation, 18–19
Mexico: democracy, shift to, 22; film industry, 98; Golden Triangle, 143, 162; life expectancy pre- and post-Revolution, 21–22; South American nations, relationships with, 135–36; stereotypes concerning, 5, 12
Mexico City: Campo Militar I, 4, 113, 128, 129, 131, 132; police department, 89; post-Revolution monument, 21; prostitution, 92; protests against femicide, 191; during Revolution, 14–15
Meyer, Jean, 54
Michoacán (state), 162–63; agrarian reform, 27; Múgica, 30
militias: chaos and violence, 27; paramilitary organizations, 49, 127–30
Mini-Manual of the Urban Guerrilla (Marighella), 119
Mixteca regions, 40
Moheno, Querido, 62, 180–81
Moheno, Roberto Blanco, 81
Molina, Tereso, 131
Monsiváis, Carlos, 52, 63, 186–87
Montemayor, Carlos, 104, 115, 128–29, 135

Morelos (state): during Mexican Revolution, 12; Plan of San Luis Potosí and land reform, 7–9
Moreno González, Nazario, 163–64
Morfín, María Teresa, 181
Mormons, 63
Movimiento de Acción Revolucionaria (MAR), 119, 121, 122
Movimiento de Liberación Nacional (MLN), 111
Múgica, Francisco J., 27, 55
Múgica, Michoacán, 30
Muni, Paul, 98
Muñoz, Rafael F., 17
Murguía, Francisco, 20

Napoleón Morones, Luis, 106, 128
Naranja, Michoacán, 35
Narcotics Police (Policía de Narcóticos), 92
National League for the Defense of Religious Liberty, 55–56
Nava, Salvador, 79
Nazar Haro, Miguel, 90, 128, 130, 131, 133, 144
Nazism, 64, 66–67
Negrete, Jorge, 84
Nepomuceno Guerra, Juan, 147
Nicaragua: Contra rebels, 144
Nixon, Richard, 142
nota roja press, 71, 98, 99, 101; *Alarma!* magazine, 89, 91, 184, 187; and homophobia, 187; on organized crime, 101

Oaxaca (state): agrarian reform, 28; First Congress of Pistolerismo, 83; homicide rates, 73
Obregón, Álvaro, 15, 54, 89; on agraristas, 31; assassination of, 56, 57; land reform, 26–27
October 2, 1968, massacre, 3, 4, 115, 117–18, 129
Oikión Solano, Verónica, 121
Olmos, Graciela "La Bandida," 83–84, 182
Olympic Games, 116

Vargas Cervantes, Susana, 184, 187, 190–91
Vasconcelos, José, 65, 77
Vázquez, Genaro, 109–12, 126
Veracruz (state): homicide rates, 38; violence, decline in, 1940s, 42
Vikingos (urban gang), 118
Villa, Pancho, 8, 11, 12, 16, 21, 106, 177; as hacendado, 29; racism and violence, 20; and revolutionary violence, 17; violence against women, 18–19
violence: alcohol as factor in, 36–37; arguments for necessity of, 3; assassinations and codes of honor, 154–55; from border towns throughout nation, 140–41; and brutality, 17, 155–56; capitalism and social context, 2, 31, 32, 107, 120; communicative value of, 33–34; counterinsurgency methods, global, 130; definitions and concepts, 1–3; drug trafficking and assassinations, 145–46, 148–50, 165–70; drug trafficking and territories, 152; evolving concepts of in agrarian context, 32–33; feminist critique of, 191–93; gang violence, 100; guerrilla movements, 112–13; homicide, emblematic significance of, 35–36; impact on democratic process, 23; justified by normative systems, 4; legitimacy and legality of pistoleros, 101–2; and male dominance, 69; material nature of, 2; and modernization, 32; and organized crime, 100–101, 138–39; pistoleros and selective use of, 97–98; as resource, 79–80; and revenge, 33; revolutionary, associated with Villa, 17; secrecy contrasted with publicity, 34–35; social context of, 2; state or official violence, 127, 135–36; state or official violence and paramilitary groups, 129–30; student mobilizations, 114–19; symbolic contexts, 2–3, 62, 67–68; twenty-first century, 160–61; weapons used against civilians, 13–14. *See also*

agrarian reform and violence; gender-based violence; religious violence

weapons: Christian justifications for, 68; Cristero rebellion, 53; despistolización campaigns, 82–83; distribution of, post-Revolution, 28; drug-related assassinations, 141; Revolution, and access to, 8–9, 13–14, 22–23; skill with, 167–68; submachine guns, 80, 81; and trade union struggles, 83; from United States, 166
Womack, John, 7
women: abuse and torture of, 132; and Catholic resistance, 51, 56; coronelas, 18; in guerrilla movements, 124; homicide in Ciudad Juárez, 158; mothers' roles in memory-building of disappeared persons, 136–37; role in reducing violence, 43; in teaching profession, 60–61; war, participation in, 18; women's organizations, 60; women's rights, 188–89

xenophobia, 50
Xochicalco massacre, 104

Yaitepec, Oaxaca: homicide rates, 35, 37; women's roles, 43
Yon Sosa, Marco Antonio, 119

Zambada García, Ismael "El Mayo," 138, 148, 149–50, 151, 158, 160
Zambada Niebla, Jesús Vicente "El Vicentillo," 148, 149, 165
Zapata, Emiliano, 7, 23
Zapata, Eufemio, 23
Zapatistas (guerrilla group), 13, 15, 25, 43, 48
Zedillo, Ernesto, 148
Zermeño, Sabino, 97
Zetas (criminal syndicate), 153, 154, 155–56, 158, 159, 163, 167
Zorrilla Pérez, José Antonio, 90
Zuno Arce, Rubén, 144, 146

www.ingramcontent.com/pod-product-compliance
Lightning Source LLC
Chambersburg PA
CBHW020349270326
41926CB00007B/357